THAT THE WORLD
MAY KNOW™

THAT THE WORLD MAY KNOW™

FAITH LESSONS 11–18

Raynard Vander Laan

PUBLISHING

Colorado Springs, Colorado

THAT THE WORLD MAY KNOW ™: Leader's Guide for Faith Lessons 11–18

Copyright © 1996 by Raynard Vander Laan
All rights reserved. International copyright secured.

ISBN: 1-56179-419-8

Published by Focus on the Family, Colorado Springs, CO 80995.
Distributed in the U.S.A. and Canada by Word Books, Dallas, Texas.

Focus on the Family books are available at special quantity discounts when purchased in bulk by corporations, organizations, churches, or groups. Special imprints, messages, and excerpts can be produced to meet your needs. For more information, contact: Sales Dept., Focus on the Family Publishing, 8605 Explorer Dr., Colorado Springs, CO 80920; or phone (719) 531-3400.

All Scripture quotations, unless otherwise indicated, are from the HOLY BIBLE, NEW INTERNATIONAL VERSION ®. NIV ®. Copyright © 1973, 1978, 1984 by International Bible Society. Used by permission of Zondervan Publishing House. All rights reserved.

Editors: Dan Benson and Michele A. Kendall
Black-and-White Maps and Overhead Transparencies 4, 9, 15, and 16: BC Studios
Overhead Transparencies 5, 11, and 14: Leen Ritmeyer
Overhead Transparencies 7, 8, 12, 13, 18, and 19: Charles Shaw
Overhead Transparency 17: Elmer Yazzie
Cover Design: Marvin Harrell
Photograph of Author on Back Cover: Patrick Brock

Printed in the United States of America

96 97 98 99 00 01 02 03/10 9 8 7 6 5 4 3 2 1

CONTENTS

Introduction
"That the World May Know . . ."..1

Lesson 11
In the Shadow of Herod...9

Lesson 12
My Rock and My Fortress...33

Lesson 13
The Time Had Fully Come..55

Lesson 14
No Greater Love 83

Lesson 15
The Rabbi..101

Lesson 16
Language of Culture...127

Lesson 17
Misguided Faith...157

Lesson 18
Living Water..175

Glossary...197

Appendix...201

Overhead-Transparency Masters: 1. The Roman World

2. Topography of Israel: New Testament

3. The Kingdom of Herod the Great

4. New Testament Chronology

5. The Herodion

6. The Judea Wilderness

7. Masada

8. Qumran

9. Religious Movements of Jesus' Time

10. Galilee

11. Chorazin

12. An *Insula*

13. Gamla

14. A Galilean Synagogue

15. The Zealot Movement

16. The Herod Family Tree

17. The Olive Tree

18. Sepphoris Theater

19. Belvoir

OPTIONAL FULL-COLOR OVERHEAD-TRANSPARENCY PACKET

(see page 243 for ordering information)

1. The Roman World
2. Topography of Israel: New Testament
3. The Kingdom of Herod the Great
4. New Testament Chronology
5. The Herodion
6. The Judea Wilderness
7. Masada
8. Qumran
9. Religious Movements of Jesus' Time
10. Galilee
11. Chorazin
12. An *Insula*
13. Gamla
14. A Galilean Synagogue
15. The Zealot Movement
16. The Herod Family Tree
17. The Olive Tree
18. Sepphoris Theater
19. Belvoir
20. The Herodion: A Mountaintop Fortress
21. Inside the Herodion
22. The Herodion's Pool
23. The Herodion: Lower Palace
24. The Wilderness East of Bethlehem
25. The Fortress Masada
26. Cistern of Masada
27. Storehouses of Masada
28. The Opulence of Masada
29. The Essene Water Tunnel
30. An Essene Cistern
31. The Caves of Qumran
32. Qumran: The Main Assembly Hall
33. Building a Typical Galilean Home
34. A Galilean Kitchen
35. A Galilean Family Room
36. Household Implements
37. Synagogue of Gamla

38. Synagogue of Chorazin

39. Synagogue of En Gedi

40. Aerial View of Capernaum

41. Sepphoris: Bird on a Hill

42. The Theater at Caesarea

43. The Theater at Beth Shean

44. Scenes from the Theater

45. Jordan Valley from Belvoir

46. Oasis of En Gedi

47. Scenes from En Gedi

48. A Broken Cistern

Full-Color Maps: ....*Mike Ginsburg Productions*

Overhead Transparencies 4, 9, 15, and 16: ....*BC Studios*

Overhead Transparencies 5, 11, 14, and 40: ....*Leen Ritmeyer*

Overhead Transparencies 7, 8, 12, 13, 18, and 19: ....*Charles Shaw*

Overhead Transparency 17: ....*Elmer Yazzie*

Overhead Transparency 20: ....*JoLee Wennersten*

Overhead Transparencies 21, 22, 26, 27, 28 (upper left, lower right),
29, 31–38, 42, 43, 44 (upper left, lower right), 46, 47 (lower left), and 48: ....*Eyal Bartov*

Overhead Transparencies 23, 24, 25, 28 (upper right),
30, 39, 44 (lower left), 45, and 47 (upper left): ....*Ray Vander Laan*

Overhead Transparencies 28 (lower left), 44 (upper right), and 47 (lower right): ....*Greg Holcombe*

"THAT THE WORLD MAY KNOW . . ."

More than 3,800 years ago, God spoke to His servant Abraham: "Go, walk through the length and breadth of the land, for I am giving it to you" (Genesis 13:17). From the outset, God's choice of a Hebrew nomad to begin His plan of salvation (which is still unfolding) was linked to the selection of a specific land where His redemptive work would take place. The nature of God's covenant relationship with His people demanded a place where their faith could be exercised and displayed to all nations so that the world would know of Yahweh, the true and faithful God. God showed the same care in preparing a land for His chosen people as He did in preparing a people to live in that land. For us to fully understand God's plan and purpose for His people, we must first understand the nature of the place He selected for them.

In the Old Testament, God promised to protect and provide for the Hebrews. He began by giving them Canaan—a beautiful, fertile land where God would shower His blessings upon them. To possess this land, however, the Israelites had to live obediently before God. The Hebrew Scriptures repeatedly link Israel's obedience to God to the nation's continued possession of Canaan, just as they link its disobedience to the punishment of exile (Leviticus 18:24–28). When the Israelites were exiled from the Promised Land (2 Kings 18:11), they did not experience God's blessings. Only when they possessed the land did they know the fullness of God's promises.

By New Testament times, the Jewish people had been removed from their Promised Land by the Babylonians due to Israel's failure to live obediently before God (Jeremiah 25:4–11). The exile lasted 70 years, but its impact upon God's people was astounding. New patterns of worship developed, and scribes and experts in God's law shaped the new commitment to be faithful to Him. The prophets predicted the appearance of a Messiah like King David who would revive the kingdom of the Hebrew people. But the Promised Land was now home to many other groups of people whose religious practices, moral values, and lifestyles conflicted with those of the Jews. Living as God's witnesses took on added difficulty as Greek, Roman, and Samaritan worldviews mingled with that of the Israelites. The Promised Land was divided between kings and governors usually under the authority of one foreign empire or another. But the mission of God's people did not change. They were still to live *so that the world may know that our God is the true God.* And the land continued to provide them opportunity to encounter the world that desperately needed to know this reality.

The land God chose for His people was on the crossroads of the world. A major trade route, the Via Maris, ran through it. God intended for the Israelites to take control of the cities along this route and thereby exert influence on the nations around them. The Promised Land was the arena within which God's people would serve Him faithfully as the world watched. Through their righteous living, the Hebrews would reveal the one true God, Yahweh, to the world. (They failed to accomplish this mission, however, because of their unfaithfulness.)

Western Christianity tends to spiritualize the concept of the Promised Land as it is presented in the Bible. Instead of seeing it as a crossroads from which to influence the world, modern Christians view it as a distant, heavenly city, a glorious "Canaan" toward which we are traveling as we ignore the world around us. We are focused on the destination, not the journey. We have unconsciously separated our walk with God from our responsibility toward the world in which He has placed us. In one sense, our earthly experience is simply preparation for an eternity in the "promised land." Preoccupation with this idea, however, distorts the mission God has set for us. That mission is the same one He gave to the Israelites. We are to live obediently *within* the world so that through us, *it may know that our God is the one true God.*

Living by faith is not a vague, other-worldly experience; rather, it is being faithful to God right now, in the place and time He has put us. This truth is emphasized by God's choice of Canaan, a crossroads of the ancient world, as the Promised Land for the Israelites. God wants His people in the game, not on the bench.

The geography of Canaan shaped the culture of the people living there. Their settlements began near sources of water and food. Climate and raw materials shaped their choice of occupation, dress, weapons, diet, and even artistic expression. As their cities grew, they interacted politically. Trade developed, and trade routes were established.

Biblical writers assumed that their readers were familiar with Near Eastern geography. Today, unfortunately, many Christians do not have even a basic geographical knowledge of the region. This series is designed to help solve that problem. We will be studying the people and events of the Bible in their geographical and historical contexts. Once your students know the *who, what,* and *where* of a Bible story, they will be able to understand the *why.* In deepening their understanding of God's Word, they will be able to strengthen their relationships with Him.

Terminology

The language of the Bible is bound by culture and time. Therefore, understanding the Scriptures involves more than knowing what the words mean. We need to understand those words from the perspective of the people who used them. The people God chose as His instruments—the people to whom He revealed Himself—were Hebrews living in the Near East. These people described their world and themselves in concrete terms. Their language was one of pictures, metaphors, and examples rather than ideas, definitions, and abstractions. Where we might describe God as omniscient or omnipresent (knowing everything and present everywhere), a Hebrew preferred: "The Lord is my Shepherd." Thus, the Bible is filled with concrete images from Hebrew culture: God is our Father and we are His children. God is the Potter and we are the clay. Jesus is the Lamb killed on Passover. Heaven is an oasis in the desert, and hell is the city sewage dump. The Last Judgment will be in the Eastern Gate of the heavenly Jerusalem and will include sheep and goats.

Several terms are used to identify the land God promised to Abraham. The Old Testament refers to it as Canaan or Israel. The New Testament calls it Judea. After the Second Jewish Revolt (A.D. 132–135), it was known as Palestine. Each of these names resulted from historical events taking place in the land at the time they were coined.

Canaan is one of the earliest designations of the Promised Land. The word probably meant "purple red," referring to the dye produced from the shells of murex shellfish along the coast of Phoenicia. In the ancient world, this famous dye was used to color garments worn by royalty. The word for the color eventually was used to refer to the people who produced the dye and purple cloth for trade. Hence, in the Bible, *Canaanite* refers to a "trader" or "merchant" (Zechariah 14:21), as well as to a person from the "land of purple," or Canaan. Originally, the word applied only to the coast of Phoenicia; later, however, it applied to the whole region of Canaan. Theologically, Canaanites were the antithesis of God's people; therefore, the opposition between the Israelite and the Canaanite was total.

The Old Testament designation for the Promised Land derives from the patriarch Jacob, whom God renamed Israel (Genesis 32:28). His descendants were known as the children of Israel. After the Israelites conquered Canaan in the time of Joshua, the name of the people became the designation for the land itself (in the same way it had with the Canaanites). When the nation split following the death of Solomon, the name *Israel* was applied to the northern kingdom and its territory, while the southern land was called Judah. After the fall of the northern kingdom to the Assyrians in 722 B.C., the entire land was again called Israel.

The word *Palestine* comes from the people of the coastal plain, the Philistines. Though *Palestine* was used by the Egyptians long before the Roman period to refer to the land where the Philistines lived—Philistia—it was the Roman emperor Hadrian who popularized the term as part of his campaign to eliminate Jewish influence in the area.

During New Testament times, the Promised Land was called Palestine or Judea. *Judea* (which means "Jewish") technically referred to the land that had been the nation of Judah. Because of the influence the people of Judea had over the rest of the land, the land itself was called Judea. The Romans divided the land into several provinces, including Judea, Samaria, and Galilee (the three main divisions during Jesus' time); Gaulanitis, the Decapolis, and Perea (east of the Jordan River); and Idumaea (Edom) and Nabatea (in the south). These further divisions of Israel only add to the rich historical and cultural background God prepared for the coming of Jesus and the beginning of His church.

Today the names *Israel* and *Palestine* are often used to designate the land God gave to Abraham. Both terms are politically charged. *Palestine* is used by the Arabs living in the central part of the country, while *Israel* is used by the Jews to indicate the State of Israel. In this study, *Israel* is used in the biblical sense. This choice does not indicate a political statement regarding the current struggle in the Middle East, but instead is chosen to best reflect the biblical designation for the land.

Josephus, the Jewish Historian

The most important source of information about life at the time of Jesus comes from a Jewish historian who is known to history as Josephus Flavius. His extensive writings on first-century Israel's history, politics, culture, and religion are invaluable in helping us understand the setting in which God placed His people. Though Josephus's supposedly first-hand accounts, complete with commentary, are written by a man and therefore are subject to the bias any individual would have, archaeology and historical research have shown Josephus to be remarkably accurate in his descriptions of life during New Testament times.

Josephus was born into a wealthy family of priests shortly after Jesus was crucified about A.D. 38. Josephus's Hebrew name was Joseph Ben Mattathias. A brilliant young man, he studied under the leaders of several Jewish movements of his day, including the Pharisees, Sadducees, and Essenes. He was familiar with the Roman world, having spent time in Rome, and was impressed with the glory and might of the empire. He was fluent in Aramaic, Greek, and Hebrew, the major languages of his day.

As the First Jewish Revolt began (A.D. 66), Josephus was placed in charge of the Jewish resistance in Galilee. He surrendered to Vespasian, the Roman general, and boldly predicted that Vespasian would become the next emperor based on Josephus's interpretation of the prophecies of the Old Testament. Since Vespasian was superstitious and Josephus was a priest, Josephus's life was spared. When Vespasian became emperor, Josephus became a personal scribe to the family, even taking their name, Flavius, and receiving Roman citizenship. Josephus spent the rest of his life writing the history of the Jewish people, focusing on the crucial years from 168 B.C. to A.D. 100, the period of the New Testament. Because he was hated by the patriotic Jews for being a traitor, and was suspected by the Romans because of his role in the Jewish revolt, Josephus wrote to justify himself and to present the Jewish people in the best possible light. Given those biases, his major works, *The Jewish War* and *Antiquities of the Jews*, are vital sources for any student of the New Testament.

Josephus did not mention Jesus or the early church (the one passage about Jesus was probably added by Christian writers long after Josephus's death). He did write extensively about the Herod family, including descriptions of John the Baptist's execution, the death of Herod Agrippa, and other characters mentioned in the Bible. Ironically, because they offer extensive background information, Josephus's writings are a key element in understanding Jesus, His message, and His ministry in first-century Israel. Josephus was another part of God's plan that everything should be complete for the coming of His Son.

Introduction to the Study

Because God speaks to us through the Scriptures, studying them is a rewarding experience. The inspired human authors of the Bible, as well as those to whom the words were originally given, were Jews living in the Near East. God's words and actions spoke to them with such power, clarity, and purpose that they wrote them down and carefully preserved them as an authoritative body of literature.

God's use of human servants in revealing Himself resulted in writings that clearly bear the stamp of time and place. The message of the Scriptures is, of course, eternal and unchanging—but the circumstances and conditions of the people of the Bible are unique to their times. Consequently, we most clearly understand God's truth when we know the cultural context within which He spoke and acted and the perception of the people with whom He communicated. This does not mean that God's revelation is unclear if we don't know the cultural context. Rather, by learning how to think and approach life as Abraham, Moses, Ruth, Esther, and Paul did, modern Christians will deepen their appreciation of God's Word. To fully apply the message of the Bible to our lives, we must enter the world of the Hebrews and familiarize ourselves with their culture.

That is the purpose of this curriculum. The events and characters of the Bible will be presented in their original settings. Although the videos offer the latest archaeological research, this series is not intended to be a definitive cultural and geographical study of the lands of the Bible. No original scientific discoveries are revealed here. The purpose of this series is to help students better understand God's revealed mission for their lives by allowing them to hear and see His words in their original context.

This curriculum provides additional cultural background and biblical material for study. Encourage your students to read the appropriate Bible passages and to think through God's challenge for their lives today.

Guidelines for Leading the Sessions

1. Be sure to read through the curriculum and view all the videos before you begin teaching the sessions. To lead this study effectively, you will need to spend several hours preparing for the course. In addition, you will need time to set up your class materials and to decide which activities you will use in each session, depending on the time you have allotted for the course.

2. Develop the answer you want your students to reach for each question, but during class allow them to arrive at their own conclusions before you present yours. This is the essence of the "guided discussion" method. The most effective way to discover the Bible in its setting is for the teacher to be a fellow learner with the class. Cultivate discussion and guide students in their conclusions by becoming adept at asking the kinds of questions that will help them explore different answers. Most important, encourage your students to respect the responses of others.

3. At the beginning of each session, review the key materials. Students need time to absorb and integrate the new information into their understanding of the Scriptures. If you occasionally review important locations on maps, refer to people and events in the biblical chronology, and repeat the main points in previous lessons, students will develop the ability to read the Bible in context. It is also important for you as the teacher to be well versed in the basic cultural background of the Bible. Consider memorizing key details on the maps and in the chronology.

4. To learn more on the cultural and geographical background of the Bible, consult the following resources:

History

Connolly, Peter. *Living in the Time of Jesus of Nazareth.* Tel Aviv: Steimatzky, 1983.

Ward, Kaari. *Jesus and His Times.* New York: Reader's Digest, 1987.

Whiston, William, trans. *The Works of Josephus: Complete and Unabridged.* Peabody, Mass.: Hendrikson Publishers, 1987.

Wood, Leon. Revised by David O'Brien. *A Survey of Israel's History.* Grand Rapids: Zondervan, 1986.

Jewish Roots of Christianity

Stern, David H. *Jewish New Testament Commentary.* Clarksville, Md.: Jewish New Testament Publications, 1992.

Wilson, Marvin R. *Our Father Abraham: Jewish Roots of the Christian Faith.* Grand Rapids: Eerdmans, 1986.

Young, Brad H. *Jesus the Jewish Theologian.* Peabody, Mass.: Hendrickson Publishers, 1995.

Geography

Beitzel, Barry J. *The Moody Atlas of Bible Lands.* Chicago: Moody Press, 1993.

Gardner, Joseph L. *Reader's Digest Atlas of the Bible.* New York: Reader's Digest, 1993.

General Background

Alexander, David, and Pat Alexander, eds. *Eerdmans' Handbook to the Bible.* Grand Rapids: Eerdmans, 1983.

Butler, Trent C., ed. *Holman Bible Dictionary.* Nashville: Holman Bible Publishers, 1991.

Edersheim, Alfred. *The Life and Times of Jesus the Messiah.* Peabody, Mass.: Hendrickson Publishers, 1994.

Archaeological Background

Charlesworth, James H. *Jesus Within Judaism: New Light from Exciting Archaeological Discoveries.* New York: Doubleday, 1988.

Finegan, Jack. *The Archeology of the New Testament: The Life of Jesus and the Beginning of the Early Church.* Princeton: Princeton University Press, 1978.

Mazar, Amihai. *Archaeology of the Land of the Bible: 10,000–586 B.C.E.* New York: Doubleday, 1990.

5. To learn more about the specific backgrounds of the third set of videos, consult the following resources:

Batey, Richard A. *Jesus and the Forgotten City.* Grand Rapids: Baker Book House, 1991.

_____. "Sepphoris: An Urban Portrait of Jesus," *Biblical Archaeology Review* (May/June 1992).

Betz, Otto. "Was John the Baptist an Essene?" *Bible Review* (Dec. 1990).

Broshi, Magen. "The Wealth of Herod the Great," *Jerusalem Perspective* (Mar./Apr. 1992).

Buth, Randall A. "That Small-Fry Herod Antipas, or When a Fox Is Not a Fox," *Jerusalem Perspective* (Sept./Oct. 1993).

Charlesworth, James H. "Reinterpreting John: How the Dead Sea Scrolls Have Revolutionized Our Understanding of the Gospel of John," *Bible Review* (Feb. 1993).

Edersheim, Alfred. *The Life and Times of Jesus the Messiah.* Grand Rapids: Eerdmans, 1985.

_____. *The Temple.* Grand Rapids: Eerdmans, 1985.

Frank, Harry Thomas. "How the Dead Sea Scrolls Were Found," *Biblical Archaeology Review* (Dec. 1975).

Gilbert, Martin. *The Illustrated Atlas of Jewish Civilization.* New York: Macmillan Publishing Company, 1985.

Hareuveni, Nogah. *Desert and Shepherd in Our Biblical Heritage.* Neot Kedumin, Israel: Peli Printing, 1991.

_____. *Nature in Our Biblical Heritage.* Neot Kedumin, Israel: Peli Printing, 1991.

Holum, Kenneth G. *King Herod's Dream: Caesarea on the Sea.* New York: W. W. Norton and Company, 1988.

Killebrew, Ann, and Steven Fine. "Qatzrin: Reconstructing Village Life in Talmudic Times," *Biblical Archaeology Review* (May/June 1991).

LaSor, William Sanford. "Discovering What Jewish Miqva'ot Can Tell Us About Christian Baptism," *Biblical Archaeology Review* (Jan./Feb. 1987).

Laughlin, John C. H. "Capernaum: From Jesus' Time and After," *Biblical Archaeology Review* (Sept./Oct. 1993).

Levine, Baruch A. *Leviticus.* Philadelphia: JPS Torah Commentary, Jewish Publication Society, 1989.

Levy, David M. "Anti-Semitism in the Middle Ages," *Israel, My Glory* (Apr./May 1993).

Milgrom, Jacob. "Of Hems and Tassels," *Biblical Archaeology Review* (May/June 1983).

Netzer, Ehud. "Jewish Rebels Dig Strategic Tunnel System," *Biblical Archaeology Review* (July/Aug. 1988).

_____. "The Last Days and Hours at Masada," *Biblical Archaeology Review* (Nov./Dec. 1991).

_____. "New Mosaic Art from Sepphoris," *Biblical Archaeology Review* (Nov./Dec. 1992).

_____. "Searching for Herod's Tomb," *Biblical Archaeology Review* (May/June 1983).

Pileggi, David. "The Library at Qumran," *Jerusalem Perspective* (Sept./Oct. 1990).

Pope, Marvin A. "Hosanna: What It Really Means," *Bible Review* (Apr. 1988).

Pritz, Ray. "'He Shall Be Called a Nazarene,'" *Jerusalem Perspective* (Nov./Dec. 1991).

Strange, James F., and Hershel Shanks. "Has the House Where Jesus Stayed in Capernaum Been Found?" *Biblical Archaeology Review* (Nov./Dec. 1982).

Syon, Danny. "Gamla: Portrait of a Rebellion," *Biblical Archaeology Review* (Jan./Feb. 1992).

Tsafrir, Yoram. "Glorious Beth Shean," *Biblical Archaeology Review* (July/Aug. 1990).

Uval, Beth. "Streams of Living Water," *Jerusalem Perspective* (Oct./Dec. 1995).

Vander Kam, James C. "The Dead Sea Scrolls and Early Christianity, Part One," *Bible Review* (Dec. 1991).

_____. "The Dead Sea Scrolls and Early Christianity, Part Two," *Bible Review* (Feb. 1992).

_____. *The Dead Sea Scrolls Today.* Grand Rapids: Eerdmans, 1994.

Whiston, William, trans. *The Works of Josephus: Complete and Unabridged.* Peabody, Mass.: Hendrikson Publishers, 1987.

Wilson, Marvin. *Our Father Abraham: The Jewish Roots of the Christian Faith.* Grand Rapids: Eerdmans, 1993.

Yadin, Yigael. *Masada, Herod's Fortress, and the Zealots' Last Stand.* New York: Random House, 1966.

Yeivin, Ze'ev. "Ancient Chorazin," *Biblical Archaeology Review* (Sept./Oct. 1987).

The following articles are from *Jerusalem Perspective,* a bi-monthly publication dedicated to helping people understand Jesus in His Jewish setting. Each issue contains articles written by Jewish or Christian scholars about some aspect of Jesus' life and ministry. It provides excellent background for anyone wanting to know more about Jesus and His times.

"At the Feet of a Rabbi," *Jerusalem Perspective* (Aug. 1988).

"First-Century Discipleship," *Jerusalem Perspective* (Oct. 1988).

"Jesus' Education, Part One," *Jerusalem Perspective* (Nov. 1988).

"Jesus' Education, Part Two," *Jerusalem Perspective* (Dec. 1988).

Safrai, Shmuel. "Master and Disciple," *Jerusalem Perspective* (Nov./Dec. 1990).

"The Traveling Rabbi," *Jerusalem Perspective* (July 1988).

"Was Jesus a Rabbi?" *Jerusalem Perspective* (June 1988).

Young, Brad H. "Understanding Jesus' Parables," *Jerusalem Perspective* (July/Aug. 1989).

6. This curriculum is designed to offer you, the teacher, maximum flexibility in scheduling and pacing the sessions. Depending on how much material you choose to use, each lesson can cover anywhere from one 50-minute session to a series of four, five, or even six 60- or 75-minute sessions. For your convenience, each lesson has been divided into two units. Unit One is an overview to be used if the leader wants to complete a faith lesson in one class period—whether 50 minutes or two hours. It contains key review questions from each element contained in the video without going into a great deal of background or detail. Unit Two is divided into several steps that take the elements in Unit One to greater depth. An example of a lesson layout follows:

A. Unit One: Video Review

    1. Digging Deeper I

B. Unit Two

    1. Step One

        a. Digging Deeper II

        b. Digging Deeper III

    2. Step Two

    3. Step Three

        a. Digging Deeper IV

In preparing your class sessions, be sure to look over the **Digging Deeper** optional sections, as you may find information there that you'll want to present, either as a supplement to the core material or—if time is limited—even in place of some core material. The time needed for the **Digging Deeper** sections will vary greatly depending on the number of students in the class and the amount of detail you wish to discuss. The suggested time allotments range from a minimum to a maximum.

NOTE TO THE TEACHER: *Some discussion sections and topics in Set 3 are repeated from Sets 1 and 2. Although they are relatively few, they do provide important information for the lessons of Set 3. If you have already covered them in the first and second sets, a simple review is probably sufficient. If you have not completed Sets 1 and 2, the sections and topics repeated here are essential background to understanding the material in this set.*

IN THE SHADOW OF HEROD

For the Teacher

The contrast between Jesus and Herod is clear in the Scriptures. Jesus was the promised Messiah, and Herod tried to kill Him because he believed his throne to be threatened. But there is much more to this contrast than meets the eye. To understand this part of the setting of Jesus' life is to be struck by several truths of Christianity. First, God often uses those who appear weak and not always the famous and powerful. Second, believing in Jesus takes great faith because He often asks of us actions and attitudes that do not make sense in our world. Third, several of the prophecies of the Old Testament were fulfilled by Jesus' birth during Herod's time. This lesson helps us ponder all these important truths.

Help your students prepare by reminding them of how God often uses the weak, and that He sometimes asks of us actions that don't make sense to our world. You might ask them to share examples of these truths from biblical as well as modern times.

Your Objectives for This Lesson

At the completion of this section, you will want your students:

To Know/Understand

1. The history of King Herod.
2. The great accomplishments of King Herod.
3. How and why the Herodion was built.
4. The relationship between the Herodion and the birth of Jesus.
5. The history of Bethlehem in God's plan of redemption.
6. The geographic relationship between the wilderness and the fertile hills.
7. The importance of Jacob and Esau in understanding Jesus and Herod.

To Do

1. Identify opportunities to confront the power of the secular world, based on the confidence that God, not Satan, is in control.
2. Identify ways to allow God to use their weakness to demonstrate His strength.
3. Refuse to accept the apparent strength of evil and rely on the ultimate power of God.
4. Seek to recognize God in the weakness and commonness of people around them and not be unduly influenced by the powerful and spectacular.

How to Plan for This Lesson

Because of the volume of material in this lesson, you may need to divide it into several class sessions. To help you determine how to do that, the lesson has been broken into several segments. Note that the time needed may vary considerably depending on the leader, the size of the class, and the interest level of the class.

If you wish to cover the entire lesson in one session, you should complete Unit One, a discussion of major points in the video. It does not go into great depth. You may go into greater depth, or enhance your background knowledge as class leader, by selecting parts or all of the remaining material.

How to Prepare for This Lesson

Materials Needed

Student copies of the maps: "The Roman World"
"Topography of Israel: New Testament"
"The Kingdom of Herod the Great"

Overhead transparencies: "The Roman World"
"Topography of Israel: New Testament"
"The Kingdom of Herod the Great"
"New Testament Chronology"
"The Herodion"

Student copies of the handout: "Herod the Great"

Video: **In the Shadow of Herod**

Overhead projector, screen, VCR

1. Make copies of the maps and handout listed above for your students. (If possible, they should receive and read the handout before the lesson.)

2. Prepare the overhead transparencies listed above. (You'll find them at the back of the book.)

3. Determine which **Steps** and which **Digging Deeper** sections, if any, you wish to use in your class session(s). NOTE: You can use these sections in any order you wish (e.g., you might want to use **Digging Deeper III,** but not **Digging Deeper I** or **Digging Deeper II**).

4. Review the geography of the lands of the Bible from the "Introduction."

5. Prepare your classroom ahead of time, setting up and testing an overhead projector and screen (for the overhead transparencies) and a VCR. If you plan to hand out biblical references for your students to look up and read aloud, prepare 3x5 cards (one reference per card) to distribute before class.

Lesson Plan

UNIT ONE: Video Review

1. Introductory Comments

The contrast between Jesus and Herod is startling in a variety of ways. They are opposites morally, culturally, and certainly in apparent status. Understanding each of them helps us understand that when Matthew said, "Jesus was born in Bethlehem in Judea, during the time of King Herod" (Matthew 2:1), it was more than a historical reference. Jesus and Herod appear together as part of God's plan for the fulfillment of prophecy.

2. Show the Video *In the Shadow of Herod* (*18 minutes*)

3. Map Study: Herod's Kingdom

Display the overhead transparency titled "The Roman World," and ask students to refer to their copies of the map. Identify the following:

> Rome
> Israel
> Egypt
> Jerusalem

Now display the overhead transparency titled "The Kingdom of Herod the Great," and have students refer to their copies of the map. Identify:

> Caesarea
> Jerusalem
> Jericho
> Dead Sea
> Judea Wilderness
> Idumaea
> Herodion

4. Guided Discussion: Herod and Jesus

Have students read aloud the Bible references indicated, then pose the accompanying questions for discussion.

a. Genesis 35:16–19; Ruth 1:22; 1 Samuel 16:1–3. What important Bible characters came from Bethlehem? What was the "reputation" of Bethlehem for the people of Jesus' day?

b. Based on the information presented in the video, what is your impression of Herod? What contrast is presented in Matthew 1:1?

c. Luke 2:8–20. Why was the shepherds' visit such an act of faith? How did it go against all appearances? Think of a similar example in your own experience in which what God asked appeared contrary to all the evidence, but you were asked to respond because you believe Him. Discuss some of these examples with the group.

d. Matthew 2:1–8. What would you have thought if you had been one of the wise men?

e. Genesis 25:21–26; Numbers 24:15–19; Obadiah 8–12. Knowing that Herod was Idumaean (New Testament way to say Edomite or descendent of Esau), why did Herod's greatness and the primitive stable and manger make it appear impossible that Jesus was the Messiah? Why did the shepherds and wise men believe anyway?

f. Think of a situation in your experience in which evil appeared to be stronger than good. Relate this to the group. Is that appearance really true? How should we react to the apparent strength of the devil's power in our world? How should this influence our task of making a difference for God in our own culture?

g. Spend a few moments in prayer together. Ask God to give you the courage to listen to Him even when His words don't make sense when we see what is around us. Ask God to help you act boldly for Him, believing that "he that is in you is greater than he who is in the world." Ask God for the wisdom to distinguish the Herods of our time from the Messiah.

UNIT TWO:
Step One: "The Herodion"

1. Introductory Comments

The Herodion is located in an area rich in biblical history. Jacob, Rachel, Ruth, and David lived or traveled here. Jesus fulfilled Bible prophecy when He was born in Bethlehem, a village sitting in the shadow of the fortress-palace. The presence of the Herodion as a symbol of the great power of King Herod recalled another set of Bible characters, Jacob and Esau, and God's prophecy about their descendants. This section explores the historical setting of Jesus' birth.

2. Map Study: Bethlehem

HINT: *Begin this map study by reviewing the geography of the New Testament world and working down to the area the lesson is dealing with—Bethlehem and the Herodion.*

Using the overhead transparencies titled "The Roman World," "Topography of Israel: New Testament," and "The Kingdom of Herod the Great," help your students find the following regions and locations on their maps:

a. "The Roman World"

> Mediterranean Sea
> Italy
> Rome
> Egypt
> Palestine
> Greece

b. "Topography of Israel: New Testament"

> Dead Sea
> Moab Mountains
> Judea Wilderness
> Shephelah
> coastal plain
> Sea of Galilee

c. "The Kingdom of Herod the Great"

>Caesarea
>Masada
>Jericho
>Jerusalem
>Bethlehem
>Idumaea
>Judea
>Herodion
>Nabatea

3. Review the Overhead Transparency "New Testament Chronology"

Review the overhead transparency titled "New Testament Chronology," highlighting the following dates for your students:

586 B.C.	Babylonian Captivity of Judah
538 B.C.	Return to Israel
332 B.C.	Alexander the Great conquers Palestine
330–198 B.C.	Rule of Hellenistic Ptolemies over Jews
198–167 B.C.	Oppression under Hellenistic Seleucids
167 B.C.	Maccabee revolt
167–63 B.C.	Hasmonaean kingdom
37 B.C.	Herod's reign begins
4 B.C.	Herod's death
c.a. 6 B.C.	Jesus' birth
c.a. A.D. 30	Jesus is crucified
A.D. 70	Roman destruction of Jerusalem during First Jewish Revolt
A.D. 131–135	Bar Kochba Revolt (Second Jewish Revolt)

Note especially the close connection between Herod's death and Jesus' birth.

4. Show the Video *In the Shadow of Herod* (18 minutes)

5. Guided Discussion: Bethlehem's History

Bethlehem was a small village just south of Jerusalem, where the Judea Wilderness meets the Judea Mountains. For this reason, it was the home of farmers, like Boaz, who tilled the fertile valleys and hill-sides of the mountains. It was the home of shepherds, like David, who pastured flocks in the wilderness or on the farmland when no crops were present.

In spite of its small size, this village was the location of some of the most significant events in history, climaxed by the birth of the Messiah. Appreciating its amazing history helps us to understand why Bethlehem was considered so important by the Jewish people and why it was the perfect place for Jesus' birth.

Read the following Scripture passages with your class, share the information provided, then discuss the accompanying questions.

a. Read Genesis 35:1–3,11–20. Jacob had been away from the Promised Land for some time. When he returned, he experienced the presence of God and His promise again. In typical Near Eastern fashion, he set up a stone to mark and remember this significant event. What was the meaning or importance of standing stones? **HINT:** *If you have Set 1, Lessons One through Five, of this series, it might be helpful at this point to review the handout "Standing Stones," in Lesson One.*

b. Read Genesis 30:1,24, 35:16–20. What was Rachel's prayer? Why is it ironic that she died giving birth to Benjamin? What does Jacob do to mark Rachel's burial? Why might this be important to the Jewish people of Jesus' time?

c. Read Jeremiah 31:15–17; Matthew 2:15–18. Note that Jeremiah is using Rachel's tears as a symbol of the tears of Israel as they were taken into captivity. But God will remove their tears (Jeremiah 31:16–17) and restore Israel. Matthew applies this prophecy to the weeping of Bethlehem's mothers for their babies whom Herod's soldiers had killed. How might God have removed the tears of the women of Bethlehem? What is ultimately the only solution to the tears of sorrow all of us have? Note that Bethlehem could be viewed both as the symbol of tears (Rachel, Jacob, Judah being led into captivity) and the removal of tears (God's gift of the Messiah, who will wipe away all tears).

d. Read Ruth 1:1,16–22, 2:1, 3:1–5, 4:1–2,13–22. Note that Naomi left Bethlehem, the Promised Land, with her husband and sons and lost everything. Then God restored her family to her. Have you ever experienced a great loss? Relate an experience where God began to restore to you something that helped you deal with the pain of loss. (NOTE: This does not eliminate the pain of loss, but it does turn one's attention to the blessing of God again, which can enable us to deal better with the pain.)

    Ruth was a daughter of Moab, a nation born of incest (Genesis 19:36–37), whose destruction by Israel was predicted (Numbers 24:17). It was a nation that worshiped pagan gods (1 Kings 11:7), and whose king practiced child sacrifice (2 Kings 3:27). Naomi's gracious act of accepting this woman from a pagan background can be understood in light of Ruth's commitment to Yahweh, God of the Israelites. The most amazing aspect of all is that this Gentile woman was one of the people through whom Jesus' line came. God can use anyone for His purposes, regardless of the sinfulness of his or her past. It simply takes a commitment to Him. Have you known anyone from a sinful past whom God used for His purpose? Have you ever felt that God could not use you because of some failure in your past? How might the story of Ruth help you overcome that feeling?

    From the line of Ruth and Boaz came David and eventually Jesus. God blessed the whole world through them. Bethlehem symbolizes God's gracious act of including the undeserving in His plan to redeem the world. How does this help you to better appreciate the birth of Jesus? (Note that God was at work more than 1,000 years before that birth, that He included undeserving, hurting people in His plan, and that He includes us, through Jesus, for the same reason.)

e. Read 1 Samuel 16:1–13. David is a shepherd, just as God describes Himself as our Shepherd. God's love for His own is often compared to that of a shepherd for his sheep. Note Luke 2:7–8 and John 10:11–15. How does it help you to think of God as our Shepherd?

    David is the youngest of his brothers. Often the one caring for the sheep would be quite young, even a preteen. It is amazing, again, that God would use the youngest and weakest, contrary to the expectations of the culture, to become the king after His own heart. Can you think of an example of God using someone who others felt would not or could not be used, either because of their youth or some other "weakness"?

    Bethlehem links the Messiah to the line and family of David. Jesus would be of the line of David and rule the kingdom of David (Matthew 1:17; Luke 1:32, 2:4). Read Micah 5:2. God was planning the birth of Jesus in Bethlehem already at the time of David, and Micah prophesied that event 700 years before it happened.

OPTIONAL — Digging Deeper I: Jacob's Tears *(20–40 minutes)*

In some Jewish traditions, it is believed that Jacob's bitter sorrow over the death of his beloved Rachel was due to his guilt over causing her death. Though this is quite possible, it cannot be proven. Note the following:

1. Genesis 29:30. Jacob loves Rachel very much.

2. Genesis 30:24. After a long wait, Rachel gives birth to Joseph and prays for another son. (Joseph means "May the Lord add.")

3. Genesis 31:22–30. When Jacob secretly leaves to return to Canaan, Laban accuses him of stealing his idols.

4. Genesis 31:31–32. Jacob condemns to death anyone who has the gods, not realizing that Rachel, pregnant with Benjamin, is sitting on them. One scholar has noted that it is possible Rachel was holding Joseph also, because he was quite small (30:25), and later he was with Rachel as a young child would be (33:2).

5. Genesis 35:1–5. Jacob finds the idols and destroys them at the place where he had met God before. He now must realize that Rachel had the gods and that his strong statement (some would say oath) would now apply to her.

6. Genesis 35:16–20. Rachel dies giving birth to Benjamin. Grieving, Jacob erects a stone (35:20) to mark his sorrow.

7. Genesis 37:3. Jacob loves Joseph, Rachel's son, more than the others. Is it possible he feared that because Joseph had been with Rachel when he made his vow that Joseph would also die?

8. Genesis 42:38. Jacob refuses to part with Benjamin because he is his only beloved son since Joseph disappeared. Is this also because Rachel was pregnant with Benjamin when Jacob condemned the one who had the idols, and he therefore considered Benjamin indirectly involved?

9. Genesis 48:1–7. Jacob adopts Joseph's sons because of Rachel's death. Did he believe he was responsible for that death? Now these two sons replace the sons Rachel could have had if she had lived.

10. Genesis 48:7. One scholar has noted that the phrase "to my sorrow" could be translated "die because of" and is in fact translated that way in Genesis 20:3 and 26:9. This would mean Jacob is saying, "Because of me, Rachel died while I was journeying."[1]

    Whether Jacob believed he was responsible for Rachel's death or not, it is clear that her stealing the idols and Jacob's rash vow created significant tensions. It is possible that Jacob's favoritism toward Joseph and Benjamin, and the grief of his old age, were in part because of the guilt he felt for Rachel's death. It is ironic that the "deceiver" was deceived by his most beloved wife.

- Can you think of an example of a secret sin that later caused great pain for you or for others? Why is it so important to resist sin of every kind and seek forgiveness for any sin that does occur?

- Have you known a person who favored one child over another? Why did this happen, and what was the effect on any other children? Is it similar to Jacob's situation?

OPTIONAL — Digging Deeper II: God Can Use Anyone *(15–20 minutes)*

A. Guided Discussion

There are other people in the Bible whom God chose to use in spite of their pasts. (Ask your students to think of several examples, such as Jacob, David, Paul, etc.) Look up the following passages and summarize what you discover there about the people God used and how He used them. (Students can do this assignment individually or in small groups.)

1. Matthew 1:3 and Genesis 38

2. Matthew 1:5a and Joshua 2

3. Matthew 1:5b and Ruth 1 (Note that verse 16 implies that Naomi's God had not been Ruth's God until then.)

4. Matthew 1:6 and 2 Samuel 11 (Note that the major fault was David's; yet Bathsheba did not protest his sinful actions and was apparently a willing partner.)

B. Questions to Stimulate Discussion

1. From these passages, what can you learn about God's choice of these people to be in Jesus' ancestral line in spite of their sinful pasts? What role did each person's commitment to God play in His choosing to work through him or her?

2. What do you think is the significance of God choosing these women as His servants?

3. What do these passages show us about God's forgiveness? About His ability to use sinful people in His plan?

4. Can you think of a contemporary example of someone who came from a sinful past to a relationship with God and then became His instrument (examples might include Chuck Colson and Nicky Cruz)?

6. Lecture/Discussion: The Shadow of the Herodion

Most visitors to Bethlehem are surprised that just to the east of the city are the ruins of one of the largest fortress-palaces of the ancient world, the Herodion, named after its builder, Herod the Great. While it is evident that Herod fits into the story of Jesus' birth, it is not often recognized that the symbol of his power and splendor could be seen from anywhere in Bethlehem. Some have even suggested that the soldiers who killed Bethlehem's babies came from this fortress.

The video contrasts the two kings of the time: the baby in the manger and one of the most powerful, brilliant kings Israel had ever known. The mark of Herod's power was found throughout the land wherever his magnificent structures stood. But few were more spectacular or more fitting for him than the Herodion. And few could provide a greater contrast with the tiny manger lying a short distance away in Bethlehem. To better appreciate the contrast and its implications for us, spend some time with your students investigating the Herodion.

Use the overhead transparency titled "The Herodion" as the basis for the following information:

The Herodion is one of the most remarkable fortresses of the world. It can be seen from miles away, even as far away as the city of Jerusalem. From a distance, the fortress looks like a gigantic volcanic cone. It includes a lower palace (one of the largest in the world at that time) and an upper fortress-palace. As did many of Herod's creations, it boasted an enormous pool, water cisterns, a garden, and hot and cold baths. Herod chose this location because here he won a decisive battle over the Hasmonaeans, which earned him the Roman nomination to be king of the Jews.

Approximately 30 years before Jesus' birth, Herod built this magnificent fortress to serve as an escape should he ever be endangered in Jerusalem. At Herod's death, it was to be his tomb and monument. Josephus described Herod's glorious funeral procession from the Jericho Palace, where he died, to the Herodion. Herod's golden coffin was studded with precious stones. His army, always an important part of his life, marched with his body. Here, at the edge of the Judean desert, he was buried. His grave has never been found.

On the overhead transparency, point out the following information:

1. The Upper Palace. This cylindrical structure is more than 200 feet in diameter and made of two concentric walls with 40 feet between them. The fortress rose more than 90 feet above bedrock. Earth was taken from inside and piled against the cylinder to nearly half its height, forming a steep rampart and making it nearly impregnable.

   a. An enormous circular tower guarded the upper palace on the east. It was 55 feet in diameter and solid below the top of the wall. It is likely that several levels of apartments were on the upper levels of this tower, providing access to cool breezes as well as the spectacular view all around. Three smaller towers, at the points of the compass, provided additional defense and contained various rooms that were possibly used for guards or guests of the king. From the larger tower, Bethlehem is clearly seen not more than three miles away. Shepherds bring their sheep to the pastures at the foot of the fortress.

   b. Inside the cylinder were several structures: (1) A peristyle garden with columns on three sides and open to the sky. On each end is a niche for statues. This garden probably contained trees, vines, and flowers and provided a quiet retreat for the king. (2) A large hall, called a triclinium, for official receptions and dining. During the Jewish revolts, long after Herod's death, the Zealots made this into a synagogue. The walls were covered with colorful plaster. (3) A complete bathhouse. Water was brought from springs some distance away and stored in cisterns at the base of the fortress. From there, it was carried up to the baths. The floors of the hot, warm, and cold baths were decorated with black and white mosaics. (4) The only entrance was a steep passageway more than 500 feet long that went up on the outside of the mountain for 300 feet and through a tunnel the remaining 200 feet. Josephus says the steps were made of marble.

2. The Lower Palace. At the foot of the mountain (not shown on this transparency), Herod built a complex of buildings more than 400 feet long between the upper palace and a pool. The pool is impressive. It is 10 feet deep, 140 feet long, and 200 feet wide. There is a stairway on one corner to enter the water. Water was brought from over three miles away by aqueduct. In the middle of the pool was an island with a colonnaded circular building (maybe imitating the circular fortress above). Around the pool were colonnaded gardens, a remarkable sight given the wilderness in which the palace was built. Scholars believe the island was a place Herod and his guests could relax and talk in complete privacy. Between the pool and the upper fortress was a huge building complex more than 400 feet long that contained elaborate halls and guest rooms. In front was a terrace more than 1,000 feet long and 75 feet wide. The lower palace was probably the main structure, while the upper portion was more private and secure. The terrace may have functioned as a parade ground between the various buildings of the lower palace and the upper palace stairway. The entire palace complex covered nearly 50 acres, making it one of the largest palace complexes in the ancient world.

The size of the palace, the beauty of its design, and the engineering needed to build it and provide it with water help us gain a sense of the glory and power Herod represented. He was clearly the greatest builder that Israel has ever known. Whether he did it to impress the Romans whose support he needed, or to satisfy his own need for luxury, is not known. What is clear is that he built to establish a reputation for himself. Unbelievably cruel in suppressing his enemies, he clearly tried to bring fame and glory to himself and his country. That is what makes his contrast with Jesus, born in the shadow of the Herodion, so fascinating. The greatest contrast of all may not have been between the fortress-palace and the manger, but between Herod's efforts to honor himself and Jesus' efforts to honor His Father in heaven.

With Herod's impressive construction projects in mind, have your class respond to the following scriptures and questions:

- Read Matthew 2:1; Luke 1:5. Based on your study of the Herodion, what is your impression of Herod? List three or four descriptive terms for him and discuss them with the group.

- Read Luke 2:6–7. Based on this passage alone, give your impression of Jesus. List three or four descriptive terms and discuss them with the group. (You probably know the rest of the New Testament and who Jesus turns out to be. Don't use that information right now. Respond on the basis of the above passage alone.)

- If you had been a bystander that Christmas night, and based on your answers above, who would you have believed was more powerful and worthier of your honor? Why? Could you have believed Jesus was king of heaven and earth and Herod only there to help prepare for His birth? Discuss your reasons with the group.

- How do these passages help you appreciate the shepherds' act of faith in leaving their flocks to go worship the infant Jesus?

- What do you think the wise men thought as they left Herod's Jerusalem palace (nearly as elaborate as the Herodion), walked to Bethlehem with the Herodion visible nearly the whole way, and arrived at the simple house where Jesus was? How would you have reacted?

- Did you realize how prominent Herod's presence was at Jesus birth? Why do you think God brought these two men together in this way? What does it help you to understand about God's work? (Encourage students to think about this. Suggestions include: God often uses the weak instead of the strong; God asks us to believe in Jesus by faith, not on the basis of what appears to us to be true; God wanted the self-glorifying efforts of Herod to make the self-sacrifice of Jesus startlingly clear.)

- Read 2 Corinthians 12:8–10; Philippians 4:13; 1 Corinthians 1:25–29; Romans 8:26. Can you think of some ways in which we as Christians are tempted to trust in our own power, wisdom, and strength instead of God's will? Spend a few moments in prayer, asking God for the courage to trust Him and follow Jesus, regardless of what may appear to be better.

Typically, paintings and crèches portray mangers as wooden boxes. It is much more likely that Jesus' manger bed was a hollowed-out stone. Wood is scarce in the Middle East and stone plentiful. To this day, shepherds use (often ancient) stone mangers like the one shown here to hold food for animals; these mangers are often found near wells for watering flocks. *(Charles Shaw)*

OPTIONAL — Digging Deeper III: A Detailed Look at the Herodion
(15–30 minutes)

(This section requires the use of the optional full-color overhead-transparency packet. For information on ordering it, see p. 243.)

Overhead Transparency 20. The Herodion: A Mountaintop Fortress. Viewed from the north from more than five miles away, the volcano-shaped mountaintop created by Herod dominates the skyline. The powerful appearance of this fortress is even more amazing when you consider that there was a circular palace coming out of the inside of the "cone" and rising more than 45 feet above it. Furthermore, the eastern defensive tower rose an additional 50 feet.

On the lower right of this photograph, the modern-day city of Bethlehem sprawls on the Judean hills. It is clearly shadowed by Herod's magnificent creation. It is ironic that the king represented by the awesome fortress was insignificant in comparison with the King in the manger of Bethlehem barely three miles away.

The forested hills in the foreground give way to the barren wilderness mountains where the Herodion stood. This helps to explain the fact that both the shepherd (such as David and the shepherds of Jesus' birth) and the farmer (such as Boaz and Ruth) were found in Bethlehem. The shepherd normally pastured sheep along the edges of the wilderness, coming to the fertile farmland after the crops were harvested. Exactly where the shepherds were on Christmas is unknown, but it is certain that they could see the Herodion. Did they find it strange to pass such a palace to find a king in a manger? If so, it was God's way of asking them to trust His word rather than how the situation appeared to them. That is always the call of God to the believer: "Accept My truth and serve Me as I ask, even if it doesn't seem the better way."

Ask your students to relate an experience in which they trusted what God said even if another option seemed more logical. Then point out the similarity between their trust and that of the shepherds as they passed the Herodion on their way to Jesus' manger.

OPTIONAL — Digging Deeper IV: More About the Herodion
(20–40 minutes)

(This section requires the use of the optional full-color overhead-transparency packet. For information on ordering it, see p. 243.)

Overhead Transparency 21. Inside the Herodion. This view is from the outer wall of the upper fortress of the Herodion. You can see the astonishing magnitude of this palace. Herod's workers began with a natural hill considerably higher than other hills in the area. They constructed double cylindrical walls nearly 220 feet in diameter, the inside of which can be seen here. The finished cylinder was more than 90 feet high. Between the two walls, seven stories contained apartments, chambers, and storage rooms. The top three stories have been destroyed over time, so you must imagine that the wall the picture was taken from was more than 40 feet higher.

On each of the compass points were defensive towers. Those on the south, north, and west extended outside the cylinder but not inside, so they are not visible in this photo. The massive eastern tower was 55 feet in diameter and more than 120 feet high. The view from the tower was spectacular. Inside the upper stories of this tower were the royal apartments of Herod and his family. Since Herod was buried in the Herodion and his tomb has never been found, some have suggested that he is buried in the base of the tower. Ehud Netzer, the archaeologist responsible for excavating this fortress-palace, believes that is unlikely because Jewish people were usually buried outside the places where they lived. He proposes a site near the lower palace, which has not yet been excavated.

Inside the cylinder were several magnificent structures. On the right side, next to the eastern tower, are the remains of the peristyle garden. Columns stood around the outside with a roof to the wall outside the garden. This left a large area in the center open to the sky for trees, vines, and bushes. On the far end of the peristyle was a semicircular niche where statues were placed. Just above it, on the right, was a doorway that led through a 200-foot tunnel, then down 300 stairs to the colonnaded terrace below. On the lower left are the remains of a large reception hall, called a triclinium, with benches around the outside. Originally, this room had a roof and its walls were covered with colored plaster. The floor was probably a mosaic. During the First Jewish Revolt, well after Herod's death, the reception hall was turned into a synagogue by the religious zealots who defended it against the Romans. Beyond the ramp into the fortress (left behind by the archaeological team and not part of Herod's structure) is the bath complex. It included a vaulted caldarium (hot bath), a small, round tepidarium (warm bath), and a small frigidarium (cold bath). One can imagine Herod enjoying the luxurious warmth of his bath while Jesus was born in a cold stable nearby.

In the distance, in the top center of the photo, looking northeast, is the city of Bethlehem. Today it is a large town of more than 25,000 people. In Jesus' day it was a small town of, at most, a few hundred. The proximity between the massive fortress of Herod and the place where the Messiah was born is a graphic picture of the way the lives of these two Jewish kings were both intertwined and in stark contrast.

Overhead Transparency 22. The Herodion's Pool. The pool of the Herodion was one of the largest in the ancient world. It is 10 feet deep, 140 feet long, and 200 feet wide. Herod typically built as if he could defeat nature. Since the Herodion is located in the desolate Judea Wilderness, Herod chose to bring water from three miles away and create a swimming pool surrounded by a garden, which in turn was enclosed by a colonnade. The island in the middle of the pool also was colonnaded and more than 40 feet in diameter.

The upper fortress stands majestically in the background. Remember, there was a palace more than 40 feet high on top of the existing hill. When he completed the cylindrical palace, Herod had his workers pile dirt against the side of the fortress, covering the lower four stories and creating the cone shape. The present ramp on the side is a modern addition for visitors. The original entrance is on the left side, out of sight.

Between the pool and the upper fortress are the remains of the lower palace, the largest of all the structures. It has not been completely excavated. One of the archaeologists excavating the fortress believes Herod's tomb is located somewhere inside.

OPTIONAL — Digging Deeper V: Still More About the Herodion
(10–20 minutes)

(This section requires the use of the optional full-color overhead-transparency packet. For information on ordering it, see p. 243.)

Overhead Transparency 23. The Herodion: Lower Palace. The lower palace, viewed from the height of the upper fortress, is massive. The pool with its island is most impressive in the wilderness. The remains of the colonnaded garden are clear. On the lower right are the excavations of the lower palace buildings, which were even more extravagant than those of the upper palace. The most striking aspect of this view is Bethlehem in the distance. The city's proximity highlights the contrast the Bible provides in Matthew 2:1: "Jesus was born in Bethlehem in Judea, during the time of King Herod." No greater moral extremes ever existed: Jesus, the Messiah, the sinless One whose life and ministry would be one of sacrifice for others to honor God; and Herod, the king of the Jews, the brutal tyrant whose life was one of cruelty and astonishing building programs, for the honor and glory of himself.

Ask your students to think of other people in history who lived only for their own glory. Then ask them to think of people they know who gave of themselves for others.

Overhead Transparency 24. The Wilderness East of Bethlehem. This photograph is taken from the top of the Herodion looking east toward the wilderness. It is striking how the farms seen in the foreground end where the wilderness begins. Going to the wilderness was a short walk for the people of the Bible. Visitors to Israel are often startled at how small the country is. In the foreground is the Dead Sea, barely 10 miles from Bethlehem. Across the Dead Sea are the mountains of Moab, the country Ruth came from. The fact that Ruth, who moved to Bethlehem with Naomi, could see her homeland on a clear day is quite surprising to the first-time visitor. Ruth probably moved less than 20 miles when she left her gods for Yahweh, God of Israel. Even so, the move was a significant one. Point out to your class how life-changing a commitment to God can be even if life's circumstances change little.

In the immediate foreground is a small village. Although it is not Bethlehem, it is about the size Bethlehem was in Jesus' time. This village helps us imagine what Bethlehem was like. In biblical times, small communities existed around large cities much as suburbs do today. Those communities, including Bethlehem, were known as "daughter cities." Ask your students to read Luke 23:28. Though Jesus is speaking to women, there is also a sense in which He may be referring to the cities surrounding Jerusalem that would be brutally ravaged when the Roman army fulfilled His prophecy in A.D. 70. When a large city was besieged, daughter cities were the first to be destroyed.

As the sun rises at this location, the shadow cast by the Herodion reaches toward Bethlehem. One can almost imagine Herod's shadow looming over the baby Jesus in His manger. Today the Herodion is an interesting ruin, a symbol of Herod's failure, while Jesus' kingdom is eternal and continues to grow. Spend a few moments thanking God that the powerful Herod was stymied by His sovereignty and that Jesus lived to complete His work.

Step Two: "Two Great Kings"
(Matthew 2, Luke 2)

1. Lecture

Have your students read the handout "Herod the Great."

The contrast between Jesus and Herod is much more significant to the writers of the Bible than one might expect. We have established that there is a geographical link. Jesus was born five miles from Herod's main palace in Jerusalem and less than that from his greatest palace at the Herodion. Bible readers have always known that Herod enters the Christmas story as the evil tool of Satan, who would end God's planned redemption by slaughtering the baby boys of Bethlehem.

But there is an even greater link between these two kings, a spiritual connection that clarifies the historical and the geographical. God planned for Herod to be in place so the person and work of Jesus would be seen in exactly the way He wanted. To understand this connection, we must explore the person of Herod more fully in contrast to the person of Jesus.

2. Guided Discussion: Herod or Jesus?

It was difficult for those who heard of Jesus' birth to accept that He was Messiah. He entered our world poor and weak—a baby born in a stable to a young peasant girl. By contrast, Herod was incredibly strong. It was even more difficult to comprehend because of *who* each man was. Read the following passages and discover the dilemma.

a. Genesis 25:21–26. Who would be the dominant person or nation? Contrary to cultural expectations, the older would serve the younger. Esau ultimately would serve Jacob.

b. Genesis 25:30, 36:1. Who were the descendants of Esau? The Edomites, which means "red," were the family line of Esau. They lived in the reddish mountains to the east and south of the Dead Sea.

c. Numbers 24:15–19. What prediction was made about the nation of Israel? About its relationship with Edom? The prophet Balaam, by God's revelation, predicted a star and scepter from Jacob—both cultural symbols of royalty. The result was that Edom would be conquered.

d. Numbers 20:20; 1 Kings 11:15; 2 Kings 8:20; Ezekiel 25:12–14; Obadiah 8–12. What characterized the history of relationships between these two nations? How was it like the relationship between Jacob and Esau? Note that the history of these two nations involved conflict and hatred.

e. Isaiah 34:8–15; Jeremiah 49:7–11; Ezekiel 35:15; Amos 1:11, 9:12; Obadiah (the entire book deals with this relationship). What did God predict would ultimately happen to Edom and Esau's descendants? Note that the complete destruction of Edom would occur in the "day of the Lord," synonymous with the coming of the Messiah.

Conclusion: Stress that though there was constant conflict between the descendants of Esau and Jacob, ultimately Jacob's line would conquer Esau's and be enthroned forever in the person of the Messiah.

f. Point out to the class that (1) Herod was a powerful king who destroyed all opposition and (2) Herod's father was Idumaean (New Testament pronunciation of *Edom,* though referring to a territory greater than Edom), and his mother was a Nabatean (capital at the rose-red city of Petra, the actual territory of Edom). Ask your students to give their description of Herod as the people of the time would have known him. Then ask them to recognize the dilemma that Matthew 2:1 posed for the people of Jesus' time:

- How could such a weak, insignificant baby be God's Messiah when compared with Herod? What do you know that Jesus' original audience didn't know to help you see through the dilemma?

- Could you have bowed to Jesus when Herod seemed so powerful? Why or why not? Why was it such a great act of faith to believe in Jesus?

- The key is to see that the same act of faith applies to us. Today evil seems to grow more powerful all the time. Most people assume that evil is in control. (Note that in Jesus' day, Edom was considered synonymous with the powers of evil.)

- What was Herod's attitude toward potential rivals? Give some examples. In one sense, the slaughter of babies in Bethlehem, a horrendous act, was simply a small event in Herod's bloody reign. Given our culture's view of innocent blood, how might we be similar? Who weeps for our unborn (Matthew 2:18)? What risk did the shepherds take in visiting and worshiping Jesus (Luke 2:16–17)? What similar risks have you taken? Would you take similar risks now? Why or why not?

- The Bible presents Jesus as Lord, seated at God's right hand and having power over evil.

Read Ephesians 1:18–23 (note especially verse 21); Matthew 28:18; John 16:33; 1 John 4:4. Matthew 2:1 asks you to believe that (1) evil is not the dominant force in our world (though it is powerful), (2) Jesus is Lord of heaven and earth, and (3) if you trust Him, you can overcome even the devil himself (James 4:7).

g. Ask the class to discuss the following questions in small groups:

- What or who are the "Herods" of today? (Suggested answers: the power of evil appearing so strong and glorious; anything secular that seems more attractive or more important than following Jesus or that makes following Jesus seem foolish.)

- How is the commitment we are asked to make to Jesus similar to the one people during Jesus' time were asked to make?

- How does our commitment to Jesus as Messiah affect the way we relate to the power of Herod (evil) in our daily lives?

- What would indicate that someone trusted Jesus and rejected Herod during New Testament times?

- What would indicate that someone trusted Jesus today?

- How did the lives of the shepherds change after they acknowledged Jesus? How does the life of a modern-day person change after he or she has acknowledged Jesus?

h. Ask your students if they have been to the "stable" and seen the "manger"—have they acknowledged Jesus as King and rejected "Herod"?

i. Spend time in prayer, asking God to enable each of you to make such a commitment and live accordingly.

Conclusion

The contrast between Herod and Jesus is nowhere clearer than in the contrast between the fortress-palace and the stable. It is important to see this contrast because it gives strength to us as we try to live so that the world may know that Yahweh is God. It reminds us that God uses weakness, lack of status, and even things that appear foolish to show that it is His strength that accomplishes His purpose. If the Messiah had been born in Herod's family, we might be tempted to give some credit to Herod. God uses our weakness so that He, not we, can take the credit. Learn to trust God even when you feel unable to accomplish anything for Him.

The contrast between Jesus and Herod also reminds us that even though evil may be strong, God has the ultimate power and authority. The glorious appearance of Herod as demonstrated by the Herodion was not where the real power resided. The real power was found in a manger. We must remember this fact if we are to have the courage to confront evil in our culture on God's behalf. The secular pagan forces seem so strong. But it is the Lord Jesus Christ, born in a stable, who has "all authority and power." Trust that power and you cannot fail.

Notes

1. Gordon Tucker, "Jacob's Terrible Burden," *Bible Review* (June 1994):21–28.

HEROD THE GREAT

King Herod is known as Herod the Great, with good reason. He was "great" in everything he did, whether it was good or bad. He was able to attain the continual support of the powerful Roman empire by an endless variety of ingenious means. This meant that he ruled with relatively little real opposition over more territory than almost all Jewish kings who had ruled before him.

Yet Herod saw threats in every corner and was cruel in suppressing any resistance, real or imagined, among his Jewish subjects and even within his own family. The slaughter of the babies of Bethlehem, so central to the Bible story, was so small in comparison with his other crimes that it is not even mentioned by Josephus, who left a detailed record of Herod's life, exalting his triumphs and not hiding his failures.

Hated by some of his subjects and loved by others, Herod was one of the greatest visionaries Israel had ever known. Christian travelers to modern-day Israel soon discover that though they may have come to Israel to find the Messiah, there is significantly more physical evidence of Herod than of Jesus. That can be disturbing. Yet there are profound lessons in seeing Herod and Jesus on the same stage of history. Herod may have left the greater physical record, but what he stood for and believed in lies in ruins; whereas the King who was born in a Bethlehem manger lives on and His kingdom has no end.

ALEXANDER THE GREAT AND HELLENISM

More than 300 years before Jesus and Herod, Alexander and his Greek army swept away the remnants of the Persian empire, which had kept the Jews under loose control since the time of Ezra. Alexander's dream was to bring the culture of the Greeks, called Hellenism, to the known world, leaving a legacy that would not soon be forgotten. In almost every way, he succeeded. Hellenism became the philosophy of most of the secular world. Its emphasis on the importance of the human being as the center of reality, its glorification of human accomplishment, its fascination with the human form in the gymnasium and stadium, and its delight in the erotic and bawdy in the theater, made it seductive if not remarkably modern. Hellenism was the antithesis of the God-centered, self-denying religion of the Jews, who took their Bible seriously and refused pagan gods, images, and public nudity and sexuality, focusing instead on a lifetime of obedience. The two worldviews would surely clash, as they have since Satan tempted Adam and Eve to put themselves ahead of the Word of God. The most that can be said is that the spread of the Greek language became the tool used in God's plan to simplify and enhance the spread of the gospel. Thanks to the pagan Hellenists, nearly everyone spoke Greek. But Alexander did not live to see his dream become reality. He died when it had just begun.

His generals divided his empire among themselves. The territory along the eastern shore of the Mediterranean became the Hellenistic kingdoms of

Egypt and Syria. The land of the Jews, located on the trade route between the two, became the prize both kingdoms desired, leaving the Jews in the middle as they had always been. For more than 100 years, the Egyptians controlled Judea, as it was now called, ruled by a dynasty of kings called Ptolemies (after the general who received this part of Alexander's empire). They were benevolent kings who allowed much freedom to the Jews, especially in matters of religion. Apparently, they believed that the attractiveness of Hellenism would serve as its own marketing.

About two centuries before Jesus' birth, the Syrian kingdom, under the rule of the Seleucids (named after another of Alexander's generals), defeated the Ptolemies, and the Jews saw another side to the struggle between Hellenism and biblical faith. Antiochus, a Seleucid king, was determined to forcibly Hellenize his subjects, which for the Jews meant outlawing the Torah (God's Word is always dangerous to those who would make human beings the center of the universe). Antiochus also forbade the Sabbath observance, circumcision, and other important practices in Jewish faith. Revolt was inevitable for a people who believed that obeying God takes priority over all other matters in life.

THE HASMONAEANS AND FREEDOM

The Jewish revolt was led by an old priest from the Hasmonaean family and his five sons. The strongest, Judah, nicknamed Maccabee, led a miraculously successful revolt and gave his people freedom, commemorated in the feast called Hanukkah. After Maccabee's death, his brothers, and then their descendants, ruled as kings over the Jews. The faithful followers of Torah, called Hasidim, prevailed over the humanism of the Greeks.

The Hasidim ruled effectively for more than 100 years. The tiny Judean state grew in size and strength to include Samaria, Galilee, Peraea (east of the Jordan), and even areas east of the Sea of Galilee (today called the Golan Heights). In the region known as the Negev (in the south), the Idumaeans were conquered and forced to convert to the Jewish faith. This was to have a dramatic effect on the Jewish people in the days ahead.

But all was not well for God's people under their own rule. The priestly Hasmonaean family became as fascinated by Hellenism as the Greeks had been. They brought its practices, architecture, and moral values into official status. A gymnasium, a combination school and athletic club for nude athletic events, was built near the holy Temple. And worse, these now-Hellenized priests took for themselves the highest religious office, that of high priest. The country was fragmented. New movements began. The Hasidim, fervent followers of Torah, spawned the Pharisees, who believed that obedience to God was the greatest value; the Zealots, who resisted violently anything that violated their view of Torah; the Sadducees, who were generally Hellenistic and concerned with the Temple practices; and the Essenes, who were so enraged that they separated from the world to wait for the Messiah to come to obliterate the heretics in the Temple. The country had a series of Hasmonaeans trying to make alliances with whatever group seemed to be in power. Assassination became the means of selecting rulers.

Two brothers, Hyrcanus and Aristobulus, rivals for the throne, sought the support of the rapidly growing Roman empire. Hyrcanus built an alliance with the Idumaean ruler, Antipater, and his son Herod. After near civil war, through the support of Julius Caesar (who was grateful for the support of Hyrcanus and Antipater in his war with Pompey), Hyrcanus prevailed and Antipater became procurator of Judea. Antipater's son Herod, barely 20 years old, was made governor of Galilee, and his brother Phasael was given Jerusalem.

THE HEROD DYNASTY BEGINS

Galilee was home to a fiercely independent people known for taking the law into their own hands. In a campaign that set the tone for his reign, Herod showed no mercy in stamping out the opposition. He caught one of the rebel leaders (Ezekias) and many of his supporters and brutally executed all of them, creating a climate for religious rebellion that would still be fierce when Jesus ministered here (note Ezekias's son is mentioned in the Bible, Acts 5:37). For this, Herod was summoned to Jerusalem to be tried by the Jewish religious council, the Sanhedrin. The elders could have sentenced Herod to death, but they were apparently frightened by his growing power. Fearful of a plot against him, Herod fled the country and appealed to his friend Julius Caesar for help. Unfortunately, he lost his patron when Caesar was murdered and Rome fell into turmoil. His father's rivals, sensing that Hyrcanus and Antipater were weakened by this loss of support, rebelled and murdered Herod's father. Hyrcanus, the Hasmonaean on the throne, sought Herod's support against his rival Antigonus (also a Hasmonaean). To convince Herod to support him, Hyrcanus offered him his granddaughter, the beautiful Miriam, as his wife. Herod divorced the wife he had and expelled her and their son from the country.

The Roman power was taken by Mark Antony, who, desperate for support, appointed Hyrcanus ruler of the Jews and continued Herod and Phasael as governors. Herod's paranoid nature led him to fear Antony's lover, Cleopatra, from Egypt on Herod's border. Some of his huge fortresses probably provided Herod the security of an escape route should Antony give in to Cleopatra's wish for Herod's territory.

Meanwhile, Hyrcanus's rival Antigonus invaded Jerusalem with a Parthian army (the land to the east of Palestine from India to Mesopotamia). Hyrcanus was arrested and had his ears cut off so he could never be high priest again (Leviticus 21:16–23). Phasael, knowing he would be tortured, committed suicide, reportedly by bashing his head against his cell wall. Herod, as he always seemed to do, escaped and went to Rome with a huge sum of money to beg for Antony's support. Antony saw Herod as a defense against the Parthian threat and a fiercely loyal king whose brutal tactics could keep the peace in Judea.

With renewed Roman support, Herod sailed home. He landed at Acre in the north and proceeded to Galilee. He burned Sepphoris and broke the resistance of the rebels near the Sea of Galilee. The remaining rebels and their families hid in caves in the cliffs along Mount Arbel, overlooking the sea. Herod was so determined to destroy any opposition that he commanded his troops to make platforms to be let down with ropes to the openings of the caves, and there they lit fires. Refugees who came out for air were pulled out with long poles with hooks on them and dropped down the sheer cliff. One old man killed his seven children and his wife before leaping to his death. Herod's reign began in blood.

Antony now gave Herod two additional legions who marched south and laid siege to Jerusalem. For weeks the Jews held out until the city wall was breached. Many retreated to the Temple, a walled enclosure, and held out longer. Herod recognized the importance of the Temple to the Jewish people and begged the Romans to spare it, but it was too late. The Temple and upper city were breached. The slaughter was beyond description. Women were raped and slaughtered, children brutally killed, soldiers tortured and chopped to pieces. The Hasmonaean dynasty ended; in 37 B.C. Herod took his throne.

Now he would have to keep it. The battle for Jerusalem made it impossible to ever win the support of many of the God-fearing Jewish people he would rule. Herod would need the power of Rome, the support of the Temple authorities, and the favor of the Hellenistic Jews of the land to stay in power. Any threat would be ruthlessly destroyed, as parents in Bethlehem were to discover (Matthew 2:16).

HEROD'S REIGN OF TERROR

Herod now embarked on a campaign to make his throne secure and assure his place as the greatest of kings. To accomplish the former, he executed 45 of the 70 Sanhedrin members who had resisted him. Their property enriched his family's fortune considerably. He promised the Pharisees that they could have their religious freedom if they would stay out of the political matters of the nation. They regularly denounced him as a foreigner (Deuteronomy 17:15) but commanded their followers to obey his rule.

Pressured by the Jews in Jerusalem, Herod appointed one of the Hasmonaean family (his beloved Miriam's brother) high priest. Though only 17, Aristobulus soon became popular because of his link to the Hasmonaean family line. Herod soon became frightened of a potential rival, so he invited Aristobulus to the palace in Jericho. After filling him with much imported wine, Herod suggested a swim in the palace pool. Herod's friends, apparently by his plan, drowned the unfortunate young priest and claimed that it was an accident. Though the family reported the matter, Rome did nothing because of their need for Herod's skills to keep the peace in his part of the world. Herod also executed his brother-in-law for a supposed affair with Miriam, with whom he was passionately in love.

The civil war continued in Rome. Herod's master, Antony, committed suicide with his Egyptian lover. Octavian, soon to be Caesar Augustus, became the ruler of the Roman world. Herod, fearing a plot, executed his old friend Hyrcanus, who had given him his start. Then he journeyed to Rome to plead with Augustus, leaving orders that his beloved Miriam should be killed if he was executed, as Herod could not bear the thought of her marrying another.

Herod returned to his throne with even greater support from Rome. However, his mother convinced him that Miriam had been unfaithful, so he had Miriam executed. Miriam's mother plotted revenge, so Herod had her killed as well. Hundreds of friends and family members, along with supporters of these last of the Hasmonaeans, were slaughtered on the slightest of accusations.

Herod had two sons from Miriam whom he favored greatly—Alexander and Aristobulus. He sent them to Rome to get the best Hellenistic education available. Apparently, they were being prepared to be Herod's successors. Herod's sister began to plot against them and spread vicious rumors about their desires to take Herod's throne before he died. Herod recalled his divorced wife, Doris, and their son, Antipater, whom he had exiled years earlier, and presented Antipater as his successor.

Even by Herod's cruel standards, his life descended into madness. He took nine wives, apparently hoping he would find happiness and an heir he could trust. Each marriage added to the plotting and hatred found in his palace. Over the next years, countless members of his family and court were tortured. Under the pain of being torn apart, they accused guilty and innocent alike. Finally, after years of accusation, Herod's two sons were accused for the last time. Their accusers were tortured and beaten to death in a public display, along with more than 200 soldiers who expressed support for the brothers. Then Alexander and Aristobulus were strangled and buried with honor—marking the end of Herod's love for Miriam.

Antipater appeared to be the chosen heir to Herod's throne. But a new wave of intrigue swept the palaces Herod had built. He appointed a series of high priests and then quickly deposed them because he feared their popularity. He weakened the office to "chief priest." Accusations and torture continued as a regular part of life. Antipater was imprisoned and appeared doomed. Herod determined to give his throne to another son, Antipas.

Then Herod became ill. Some believe he had a sexually transmitted disease; others believe it was a disease of the digestive system. Josephus's description is unclear. Herod was in great pain with gangrene, rotting of his sexual organs, and convulsions. Sensing his weakness, two important Pharisees, disregarding their nonpolitical status, encouraged their students to chop down the hated Roman eagle Herod had placed over the Temple gate years before, because it violated the commandment against graven images (Exodus 20:4). Forty students were captured. The teachers who instigated the plot and the students who had actually cut the eagle down were burned alive; the others were executed more humanely.

To compound matters, the Pharisees spread the belief that Herod was king of the Jews only by Roman decree and that he was not of the house of David. Therefore, he and his family were unfit for the throne. Messianic "prophets" predicted a bizarre list of upcoming events that would occur as the kingdom was taken from Herod and given to God's anointed. This stirred even more paranoia in Herod, and many more lost their lives as a result.

Into this web of hatred and suspicion, "Magi from the east came . . . and asked, 'Where is the one who has been born king of the Jews?' . . . When King Herod heard this he was disturbed" (Matthew 2:1–3). His deception of the wise men and his subsequent order to kill the infant boys of Bethlehem were only small additions to the bloody list of Herod's accomplishments.

THE MASTER BUILDER

There was another side to Herod. His visionary building programs, his ingenious development of trade with the rest of the world, and his advancement of the interests of his nation are legendary. Many of his building projects were designed to strengthen the loyalty of his subjects, a goal he never achieved. Most seem to have been built to strengthen his relationship with Rome and to establish himself as the greatest king the Jews had ever had. Herod built on a magnificent and grandiose scale. His building projects included:

Jerusalem: The Temple was rebuilt in a splendid setting unsurpassed in the ancient world. Some of the limestone blocks of the supporting platform weigh more than 500 tons. The Temple, made of marble and gold, was taller than a 15-story building. On the western hill of the city, Herod built a spectacular palace complex that contained reception halls, royal apartments, a fortress for his personal guard, fountains, gardens, and baths. The Antonia, a huge fortress as luxurious as Herod's own palace, defended the city. Some scholars believe it was the site of Jesus' trial. A Greek theater and hippodrome provided the Hellenistic emphasis Herod appreciated. Streets were paved, sewers were built, and water carriers were constructed to make Jerusalem one of the great cities of the world.

Masada: Part of a line of fortresses that included the Alexandrion, the Herodion, and Machaerus, Masada was one of the wonders of the ancient world. Perched atop a plateau in the Judea Wilderness with a spectacular view of the Dead Sea nearly 2,000 feet below, it was a luxurious fortress-palace combining all the essential elements of a Herod project. A three-tiered palace hung precariously from one end of the plateau, almost defying gravity. The western portion contained hot and cold baths, mosaic floors, and plastered walls. Masada also boasted swimming pools, barracks for soldiers, huge storehouses with supplies for years of siege, and cisterns holding millions of gallons of water.

The Herodion: This mountain fortress overlooked the town of Bethlehem. Standing on a high hill, the upper fortress was round and more than 200 feet in diameter. Originally, it was seven stories high with an eastern tower that stood more than 40 feet higher. Packed dirt covered the first four stories, giving the upper fortress a cone shape. Inside were a peristyle garden, reception hall, Roman baths, and countless apartments. The lower palace included an enormous pool, a colonnaded garden, a 600-foot-long terrace, and a building more than 400 feet long. The Herodion was the third largest palace in the ancient world.

Jericho: This palace was built on both sides of a deep wadi (dry streambed) with a bridge across the bed. One wing contained a huge, marble-floored hall where Herod received guests. Next to it were peristyle gardens, dining halls, and a complete Roman bath. Across the wadi, Herod built another monumental building, with baths, a swimming pool, and gardens.

Caesarea: Herod needed contact with the Roman world for its military support and its market for the spice trade and other goods his people controlled. Thus he built Caesarea, on the Mediterranean coast, into one of the most spectacular seaports of the ancient world. Founded in 22 B.C., the city housed a large theater, an amphitheater, a hippodrome, and a massive temple to Augustus. Caesarea was almost completely covered with imported marble. It had an elaborate sewer system designed to be cleansed by the sea.

The glory of Caesarea was its man-made harbor spanning more than 40 acres. An enormous lighthouse stood near the narrow entrance, able to be seen from great distances at sea. This harbor welcomed the Roman legions, the marble and granite for Herod's projects, and the Hellenistic culture so dear to him. From it, ships carried spices, olive oil, grain, and most important, the gospel to the far reaches of the world.

The visitor cannot help being impressed with Herod's vision and ingenuity. However, all that remain are spectacular ruins, because Herod lived for Herod. By contrast, another builder, a humble carpenter born in Bethlehem, used a different material than did Herod (Matthew 16:18; 1 Peter 2:4–8). Jesus' buildings continue to grow because He built for the glory of God. Like David (1 Samuel 17:46), Elijah (1 Kings 18:36), and Hezekiah (Isaiah 37:20), He lived so that the world may know that Yahweh, the God of Israel, is truly God. His construction projects will last forever because He built for the glory of God the Father.

THE DEATH OF THE KING

Herod went to Jericho to die in agony, hated even by his family. Truly mad and fearing that no one would mourn his death, he commanded his troops to arrest important people from across the land, lock them in the hippodrome, and execute them after he died—if people would not mourn him, they would at least mourn. At the last moment, Herod ordered the execution of his son Antipater and changed his will, dividing his kingdom between three other sons: Archelaus, Philip, and Antipas. Finally, the bloody, brilliant reign of this king of the Jews came to an end. Although the King of the world was born during his reign, Herod never knew Him.

Why was Herod never accepted by his own people? Was it his cruelty? That is possible. Was it his commitment to the pagan values of

Hellenism? That is probable. But there is another important factor to understand. Herod was a Gentile, an Idumaean (called Edomite in the Old Testament). And God's Word made clear that no Gentile could ever be king over His people (Deuteronomy 17:15). Regardless of Herod's power or greatness, his reign violated God's rules. Consequently, God-fearing people could not accept him.

In addition, God's Word frequently predicted that the descendants of twin brothers Jacob and Esau would be in conflict. Ultimately, a ruler would emerge from Jacob who would overpower Esau and be God's Messiah (Genesis 25:23; Numbers 24:17–19; Obadiah 17–18; Amos 9:12). The Messiah must be from Jacob (Israel) and must rule over Esau (Edom or Idumaea). To the follower of God's Word, Herod could not be Messiah or God's king.

But could Jesus be Messiah? How could He be Messiah if He (Jacob's descendant) was in a manger while Herod (Esau's descendant) sat in power in a fortress? This dilemma helps us understand why it was so difficult for people to accept Jesus as Messiah, for every appearance said otherwise. Esau was in control. Rabbis referred to Herod's city of Caesarea as the "daughter of Edom" (probably a reference both to Herod's Idumaean origins and to Rome's symbolic identification as Edom, the nation rejected by God). How could Jesus be the star of Jacob if Herod was in power? Second, this dilemma helps us understand the tremendous faith the Christmas story demanded of the Jewish people and of us today. They were (and we are) asked to accept by faith the fact that, contrary to appearance, it was not Herod who was in control but the boy in the stable. If someone had (or has) the faith to believe in Jesus as Messiah, he or she has recognized God's reality.

Today it may sometimes appear as if Jesus is not at the right hand of God, Lord of heaven and earth (Ephesians 1:18–22). Look around you and it may seem as if the evil descendants of Herod (the followers of the devil) are the dominant power. In times like these, just as in Jesus' day, God asks us to commit to and live by the reality that Jesus is Lord. Be encouraged. Evil may appear strong, but God is in control. Herod appeared all-powerful, but God was in the manger.

MY ROCK AND MY FORTRESS

For the Teacher

This lesson presents two biblical truths. First, we must see God, not our own efforts, as our protection and strength. And second, God sent Jesus to be Messiah. But He was different from the self-proclaimed messiahs of His time. Jesus was humble and kind, and He was a sacrifice. Many rejected Him because He did not fit their concept of the Messiah. Those who longed for a military messiah ultimately won out; Masada was the result of their efforts. This lesson will help your students understand how important it is to listen to Jesus' description of the true Messiah— the Messiah He in fact was. We cannot conform Him to our own version of a messiah, as this lesson demonstrates.

Your Objectives for This Lesson

At the completion of this section, you will want your students:

To Know/Understand

1. The fortress was David's picture of God's work in his life.
2. David used wilderness images to describe God.
3. How and why Herod built Masada.
4. The contrast between David and Herod.
5. Why the battle for Masada occurred.
6. The contrast between the kingdom Jesus represented and the kingdom the Jewish Zealots longed for.

To Do

1. To commit to finding their fortress in God and not in their own strength.
2. To recognize Jesus as the Messiah.
3. To commit to living by Jesus' way and not some other.
4. To decide that their love of Jesus will be the basis for their working for freedom.
5. To select one way to preserve the freedom God has provided.

How to Plan for This Lesson

Because of the volume of material in this lesson, you may need to divide it into several class sessions. To help you determine how to do that, the lesson has been broken into several segments. Note that the time needed may vary considerably, depending on the leader, the size of the class, and the interest level of the class.

If you wish to cover the entire lesson in one session, you should complete Unit One, a discussion of major points in the video. It does not go into great depth. You

may go into greater depth, or enhance your background knowledge as class leader, by selecting parts or all of the remaining material.

How to Prepare for This Lesson

Materials Needed

Student copies of the maps:	"The Roman World" "The Kingdom of Herod the Great" "The Judea Wilderness"
Overhead transparencies:	"The Roman World" "The Kingdom of Herod the Great" "The Judea Wilderness" "Masada" "New Testament Chronology"

Student copies of the handout: "The Jewish Revolts"

Video: **My Rock and My Fortress**

Overhead projector, screen, VCR

1. Make copies of the maps and handout listed above for your students. (If possible, they should receive and read the handout before the lesson.)

2. Prepare the overhead transparencies listed above. (You'll find them at the back of the book.)

3. Determine which **Steps** and which **Digging Deeper** sections, if any, you wish to use in your class session(s). NOTE: You can use these sections in any order (e.g., you might want to use **Digging Deeper III,** but not **Digging Deeper I** or **Digging Deeper II**).

4. Review the geography of the lands of the Bible from the "Introduction."

5. Prepare your classroom ahead of time, setting up and testing an overhead projector and screen and a VCR. If you plan to hand out biblical references for your students to look up and read aloud, prepare 3x5 cards (one reference per card) to distribute before class.

Lesson Plan

UNIT ONE: Video Review

1. Introductory Comments

The story of Masada is one of the great dramas of the ancient world. Masada was a magnificent fortress-palace created by one of the greatest builders the Middle East has ever known. Its history includes the siege of the fortress by the Roman army against a few Jewish freedom fighters who were willing to die for their beliefs. Masada has become a symbol for Jewish freedom in the nation of Israel today.

Besides the drama and the passion for freedom to which people in any democracy relate, there are lessons for Christians to learn. The mountain symbolizes the power of God and the protection and security He provides. The battle of Masada helps us understand the longing for the Messiah among the Jewish people in Jesus' time; it also shows us why He wept because some missed the peace He offered and chose the course that led to Masada instead. Learning these lessons helps to make Masada a symbol of devotion—not only to freedom but to God's Messiah as well.

2. Map Study: The Judea Wilderness

While displaying the overhead transparency titled "The Roman World," help your students locate the following on their maps:

> Rome
> Judea
> Egypt

Display the overhead transparency titled "The Kingdom of Herod the Great," and help your students locate the following on their maps:

> Caesarea
> Jerusalem
> Sea of Galilee
> Jericho
> En Gedi
> Qumran
> Masada

Display the overhead transparency titled "The Judea Wilderness," and help your students locate the following on their maps:

> Dead Sea
> Judea Wilderness
> Jerusalem
> Jericho
> En Gedi
> Masada

3. Show the Video *My Rock and My Fortress* (21 minutes)

4. Guided Discussion: The Fortress

a.   David hid from Saul in this wilderness. While he was there, he wrote psalms using the imagery of the wilderness to describe God's answers to prayer. Have your students read the following passages and respond to the suggested questions:

1. Read 1 Samuel 23:14,24. (The Desert of Ziph is west of En Gedi; the Desert of Maon is west of Masada.) Why did David run for his life? Why do you think he came to the wilderness?

2. Psalms 18 and 63 and 2 Samuel 22 were written during David's wilderness days. Read each passage below. What is the image David used in his description? What does this image tell you about God? Did you recognize it from the video images of the wilderness?

   - Psalm 18:1–2
   - Psalm 18:31–33
   - Psalm 18:46
   - Psalm 63:1

b. David used the term *fortress* to describe God. The Hebrew for *fortress* translates into English as "masada." We do not know if David used this location or another as his fortress picture. He was in the general area and it is a great location for a fortress. But it doesn't matter because Masada is a fortress and as such is a picture David used to describe God.

   Read the passages listed below. Based on the image of a fortress, what is God like according to David?

   - 2 Samuel 22:1–7
   - Psalm 31:1–5,9–13
   - Psalm 91:1–16

c. Read Matthew 2:1–18. King Herod built the fortress Masada for his own security and to satisfy his need for opulence. David trusted God to be his "fortress." What does your study of Masada add to this passage? What were the key differences between David and Herod? In what ways can we be more like David and less like Herod?

d. Masada was the final battle of the Jewish revolt. The revolt occurred because of the Jewish people's passionate desire for freedom and the oppression they experienced at the hands of the Romans. The people's response to Jesus was in part explained by their desire for a political messiah to drive out their pagan masters and restore them as God's free people.

   - Read John 6:15. Why would people want this?

   - Read John 18:36. Why did Jesus need to say this?

   - Read Matthew 8:4, 9:30. What could be one reason Jesus commanded this?

   - Read Luke 19:37–42. Why did Jesus cry? What were some people looking for? What did Jesus predict would happen because of their choice of "peace"?

   - Why did the Romans want to destroy the Jews of Masada so totally?

   - Can you explain the choice the Zealots made? Was it the right one?

   - In what way was Masada's fall the result of the people's desire for a political messiah? What is ultimately the only source of peace?

   - How can you work passionately for freedom in your own country and yet be committed first to Jesus' kingdom? Is there any conflict between the two?

UNIT TWO
Step One: "The Fortress"

1. Introductory Comments

The wilderness where King Herod constructed his fortress named Masada is the location of many significant Bible events. For the Israelites, any wilderness was a significant location because this is where God formed them as a people, led them to freedom, gave them the Torah and the Tabernacle, and taught them faith. To be in the wilderness was to return to these roots and to find new strength from God.

The particular wilderness where Masada is located is called the Judea Wilderness. Here David hid from Saul, the Essenes prepared for the imminent arrival of the Messiah, John the Baptist "prepared the way of the Lord," and Jesus endured temptation for 40 days and nights. Recalling David's time in this desert holds important lessons for us in learning to trust God and depend on Him, particularly in times of trouble.

2. Map Study: The Judea Wilderness

HINT: *Begin this map study session by reviewing the geography of the overall region and working down to the area the lesson is dealing with—Israel's wilderness.*

Display the overhead transparency titled "The Roman World," and point out the following areas. Then have your students locate them on their maps.

> Mediterranean Sea
> Italy
> Rome
> Egypt
> Judea
> Jerusalem
> Caesarea

Display the overhead transparency titled "The Kingdom of Herod the Great," and point out the following areas. Then have your students locate them on their maps.

> Galilee
> Gaulanitis
> Gamla
> Sea of Galilee
> Caesarea
> Samaria
> Judea
> Idumaea
> Nabatea
> Jerusalem
> Masada
> Dead Sea
> Judea Wilderness

Display the overhead transparency titled "The Judea Wilderness," and point out the following areas. Then have your students locate them on their maps.

Dead Sea
Jordan River
Judea Wilderness
Jerusalem
Bethlehem (Note its location on the edge of the wilderness.)
Jericho
Qumran
En Gedi
Masada

3. Show the Video *My Rock and My Fortress* (*21 minutes*)

4. Guided Discussion: David's Wilderness Experience

David was one of the great heroes of the Old Testament Israelites. It was through his line that the Messiah would come and his throne the Messiah would hold (Luke 1:32). David also became one whose relationship with God was to be emulated. In fact, Samuel the prophet said of David, "The LORD has sought out a man after his own heart" (1 Samuel 13:14). David's faith in God, his willingness to submit to His will, and his sorrow when he sinned have become the model for today's believers. While a study of David's life would be instructive, it is beyond the scope of this study. However, one lesson David learned and taught occurred in the same wilderness where this study is set. It provides an excellent example of why David is a worthy role model for modern-day Christians.

Have a class member read the suggested passages listed, then pause after each one to have students respond to the related questions.

a. 1 Samuel 15:10–11. Why did God reject Saul as king? Compare this verse with the reason God selected David (1 Samuel 13:13–14). What can we learn from these two passages as we try to be the people God has called us to be?

b. 1 Samuel 17:48–49. David became a hero. What was his motivation (1 Samuel 17:46–47)? What is God's lesson through David for us?

c. 1 Samuel 18:6–8. As David became famous, Saul grew jealous. Why do you suppose Saul was jealous of David instead of proud of him? What was it in the spiritual makeup of David and Saul that made their responses predictable?

d. 1 Samuel 18:10–11, 19:9–10. Saul hated David and would spend the rest of his life trying to kill him. What do you think David's state of mind would have been during that time? (Read Psalm 62:4–6, which is believed to have been written during this time.) Following God always brings opposition (John 15:20). It did for David and it will for any devout follower of Jesus. What kind of opposition have you experienced?

e. 1 Samuel 23:14,25. David hid from Saul in the wilderness. Note that the Desert of Ziph is the part of the wilderness of Judea west of En Gedi, and the Desert of Maon is the part of the Judea Wilderness west of Masada. This wilderness is barren and rugged. Arid and with little water, it is crisscrossed with wadis that can flood at a moment's notice and sweep away the unsuspecting traveler. Steep mountains are separated by narrow, deep canyons. David was hiding in a lonely, stark area.

   Have a class member read the following passages while the others close their eyes and envision the desert imagery. These psalms are believed to have been written while David was hiding in this desert.

- Psalm 18:16—flooded wadis
- Psalm 18:33—the deer that climb the heights
- Psalm 18:42—the fine desert dust
- Psalm 62:2—extremely rocky
- Psalm 63:1—little fresh water
- Psalm 63:7—birds of prey with outstretched wings, the need for shade to avoid the heat

Ask: What can you hear in these words of the barrenness of David's experience? Can you relate to the group a time when your own life felt as empty and hopeless as David's in the wilderness?

f. 1 Samuel 26:1–25. God delivered David. Exhilarated with God's deliverance, he described what God had done by using the language of the wilderness.

Have a student read the following passages as the others listen:

- Psalm 18:2—rock common in the desert, God provided fortresses and strongholds
- Psalm 18:10—again, the wings of the wind
- Psalm 18:33—preserved from physical danger of climbing
- Psalm 18:46—strength of a rock gives David security
- Psalm 63:7—shadow and shade

For each passage above, have students relate an example from their own experience that parallels David's. (For example: Can you think of a time when God was a "rock" to you? When He satisfied your thirst? Provided "shade" to you during a "hot" time?)

5. Guided Discussion: The Fortress

The archaeological excavations on the plateau Masada reveal little from Old Testament times. The Hasmonaeans (around 100 B.C.) left few remains. Most of the ruins date from the time of Herod and the subsequent use of his palace and fortress by the Zealots of the First Jewish Revolt. Masada can, however, provide insight into a concept used frequently in the Old Testament to describe God: "God is my fortress." David makes frequent use of this image, including the time he hid from Saul in the wilderness where the plateau Masada is located. To better understand this image in light of the fortress Masada, consider the questions below.

a. Was David at the plateau Masada?

- 1 Samuel 23:15,24. David was in the Desert of Ziph (the Judea Wilderness west of En Gedi) and the Desert of Maon (the Judea Wilderness west of Masada). He hid from Saul near the plateau Masada.

- 1 Samuel 23:14,19. David hid in strongholds in these areas. The Hebrew word translated as "stronghold" comes from the same root as *masada*. One of these strongholds could have been Masada, though the Bible does not specify. We do not know if David visited the plateau of Masada. We know that he was in the area and described God as his "masada" or "fortress."

- 2 Samuel 22:2; Psalm 18:2. David, writing of his time in this wilderness, described God as his *metsudah*, the Hebrew for "fortress." This word is the same as the English *masada*. The word, however, can mean any fortress.

b. Can we learn about God from Masada? Since God is described by David (and others) as a fortress and Masada is an imposing example of a fortress, it gives us a picture of God as the Hebrew writers understood Him. For each passage, note the context (what was happening to the writer) and what God provided as David's "fortress."

Passage	Context	Provision
2 Samuel 22:1–7	oppressed by enemies	rescue, shelter, refuge
Psalm 18:1–6	oppressed by enemies	rescue, shelter, refuge
Psalm 31:1–5,9–13	grief, slander, weakness	deliverance, refuge
Psalm 71:1–4,9	enemies, weakness	rescue, strong shelter
Psalm 91:1–16	danger, terror, trouble	protection, shelter
Psalm 144:1–4	conflict, war, death	strength, protection

c. What can we learn from the image portrayed by Masada?

Display the overhead transparency titled "Masada," and ask your students to describe ways in which the fortress Masada is like God in their lives.

OPTIONAL — Digging Deeper I: The Lord Is My Rock
(15–30 minutes)

Israel is a rocky land. The wilderness is especially rocky, making travel difficult. This geographical condition, combined with the Hebrews' practice of describing spiritual reality in concrete images of the world in which they lived, resulted in the frequent use of the concept of "rock" to describe the character of their God. Summarize the following highlights for your class:

1. David found safety in the "rock" in the desert (2 Samuel 22:1–3).

2. The rock image is often used to describe:

   - God—Deuteronomy 32:4,15,18,30–31 (note the desert context); Isaiah 44:8; Genesis 49:24 (notice how the writers indicate there is no other rock)

   - God's unfailing strength—Psalm 18:1–2,31; 31:1–3; 42:9; 62:7; 71:3; 94:22

   - God's deliverance—Psalm 19:14; 62:2; 78:35; 89:26; 95:1; Deuteronomy 32:15 (water from the rock probably helped them understand that it was Yahweh who provided)

   - Symbol for Jesus combining all three (God, strength, deliverance)—1 Corinthians 10:1–4

The perception of God as a rock probably came from the desert terrain where the Israelites learned faith and trust before they entered the Promised Land. David connected the image of rock with Israel's Rock (2 Samuel 23:3), making it a synonym for God. His desert experience of finding shelter, shade, and a hiding place among the rocks led to the frequent use of this concept in the psalms he wrote. God as "rock" became a permanent image in the language of His people. The hymn "Rock of Ages" carries on that desert picture of God ministering to us just as He ministered to David.

- Have your students think of specific times when God has been a rock for them and share their experiences with the class.

- Read Isaiah 32:2. As God is rock (strength, provision, protection, deliverance), we must be as rock for others. This beautiful passage combines the image of life in a desert (wind, floods, heat) with the shelter, water, and shade the rock provides.

- Ask your students to think of an example in which someone else was a rock for them.

Prayer: Divide the class into small groups for prayer. Before they pray, have them share some specific ways in which they might use God's strength to become a rock for others. Then have them pray for one another, asking God for His strength and love as they seek to provide encouragement, shelter, or strength for a friend.

6. Guided Discussion: Herod's Fortress-Palace

Have your students read the handout "Herod the Great" from Lesson Eleven.

Display the overhead transparency titled "New Testament Chronology," highlighting the following dates for your students:

198–167 B.C.	Oppression under Hellenistic Seleucids
167 B.C.	Maccabee revolt
167–63 B.C.	Hasmonaean kingdom
37 B.C.	Herod's reign begins
c.a. 6 B.C.	Jesus' birth
4 B.C.	Herod's death
c.a. A.D. 30	Jesus' death
A.D. 66–73	First Jewish Revolt
A.D. 70	Jerusalem and the Temple are destroyed
A.D. 73	Masada falls

Lecture: Although he died shortly after Jesus' birth, Herod, the Idumaean king appointed by the Romans over the Jews, had a significant impact on the people of Israel throughout Jesus' lifetime. Herod's legacy included sharp division among the Jews regarding the Roman occupation, an undercurrent of violence that occasionally erupted into open conflict, and great longing for the Messiah, who was expected at any moment. But none of these could compare with the significance of the buildings Herod constructed. The Temple in Jerusalem remained the glorious center of the Jewish faith throughout the New Testament. Jesus, the disciples, Mary, and Paul all worshiped in its magnificent courts. Herod's seaport at Caesarea was the site of Peter's first witness to the Gentiles and became the seaport from which he and other early missionaries left to bring the gospel to the world outside Palestine.

Herod's magnificent buildings also provide insight into the character of this brilliant king whose cruel policies were infamous. Of all Herod's constructions, none provide greater insight into his life, and into the Jewish people's struggle for peace, than his fortress-palace of Masada.

Display the overhead transparency titled "Masada" and relate the following to your students:

1. The Mountain. Masada is a huge rock plateau located on the shore of the Dead Sea. The top of the plateau, more than 21 acres in size, is nearly 1,300 feet above the sea. Narrow on the north and south ends, it stands majestically above the barren Judea Wilderness, which surrounds it. The only ascents were a path on the east called the Snake Path (because it twisted endlessly across the face of the mountain) and a path on the west where the height of the mountain above the valley floor is much less.

   On the top of this mountain, Herod built a magnificent fortress named Masada. Not satisfied with the plateau's natural defenses, Herod surrounded the summit with a wall and 30 defensive towers. On the east and west, strong gates were constructed where the paths entered the fortress. Inside the wall were extensive structures providing the level of luxury and safety Herod desired.

2. The Northern Palace. This remarkable building is known as the "hanging palace." It was built into the northern end of the mountain with the upper level on top of the mountain and the

lower two levels into the cliff face. The upper terrace contained living quarters in Herod's typical lavish fashion. Its floors were mosaics, its walls frescoed, and a semicircular balcony provided spectacular views of the Dead Sea and the wilderness below. The middle terrace was round with two concentric rows of columns, creating a beautiful balcony for relaxation. The lower terrace was surrounded by low walls and columns with a roof between, providing an open court inside a colonnade. The walls were frescoed to look like marble. On the east side there was a small bathroom with mosaic floors.

3. The Western Palace. This was Herod's main living quarters on Masada. This building was more than 37,000 square feet and contained the royal apartments and a large reception hall with magnificently decorated mosaic pavement. There were also bathrooms and a cold water pool, all paved with mosaic floors. Nearby were servants' quarters, workshops, a huge kitchen, and three richly decorated palaces—probably for the families of Herod's wives, who did not get along.

4. Roman Bathhouse. This was one of the largest bathing complexes of its time. The largest room was a caldarium (hot bath) with a heating room beneath it. The tepidarium (warm bath) and frigidarium (cold bath) were adjacent. All were elegantly decorated with frescoes and mosaic floors.

5. Cisterns. One of the most amazing details of Masada is its water system. The fortress is located in the dry Judea Wilderness with the closest source of fresh water some miles away. But the mountain is located between two wadis that flood when it rains in the mountains to the west even though it may not be raining in the wilderness. Herod created a system to divert some of the flood water through open channels along the base of the mountain into 12 cisterns cut into the side. The volume held in these cisterns was more than 1,500,000 cubic feet. On top of the mountain, several large cisterns were dug and filled by carrying the water from below. This amount of water in the middle of the barren wilderness provided a nearly endless supply of drinking water and plenty for the baths and swimming pools. These installations highlight both Herod's obsessive fear for safety and his craving for opulence and luxury.

6. Storehouses. On the western side of the fortress-palace was an enormous row of storehouses for food, weapons, and whatever else Herod's need for security and luxury demanded. In some of these storehouses, rows of amphorae (large pottery jars) were used as containers. The amount of storage space again highlights Herod's obsessions: safety and luxury.

Have your students form small groups to discuss the following questions. Then have one member of each group sum up their answers for the class:

- If the fortress Masada were our only record, how would you describe its builder, Herod?

- Read Psalm 18:2. David trusted God to be his masada (or "fortress"). Herod built an incredible fortress for security. How are David and Herod different? Which man are you most like? That is, where do you find your security—in things you provide (like income, insurance, burglar alarms, weapons, hard work), or in God? Discuss your thoughts with the others. Remember, there is nothing wrong with seeking to provide security and stability for yourself and others. The issue is what you ultimately depend upon—your own efforts, as Herod did, or on God, as David did.

- How can a Christian find a balance between using common sense to provide for security and trusting completely in God? How can we communicate this to our children?

- Read Matthew 6:25–34. Was Jesus discouraging hard work, one's best efforts, an ambitious career? How can you do these things and still obey His words? How are Jesus and Herod (as exemplified by Masada) different?

- Read Matthew 2:1–18. How does your study of Masada help you to understand this passage?
- Read Matthew 11:1–11. Compare Herod's tastes with Jesus' description of John (note especially verse 8). Ironically, John taught in the same wilderness where the plateau Masada is located, though some miles north, and Herod's son Antipas executed John. How can we enjoy luxury without becoming obsessed like Herod? How can we teach our children the proper values concerning possessions?

OPTIONAL — Digging Deeper II: Masada (20–45 minutes)

(This section requires the use of the optional full-color overhead-transparency packet. For information on ordering it, see p. 243.)

Overhead Transparency 25. The Fortress Masada. The plateau Masada is located in the remote Judean desert. Because this desert was bordered by the more fertile mountain ridge of the land of Israel, Masada was close to more hospitable areas. The attraction of the location for Herod was that he could quickly leave Jerusalem for the safety of his impregnable fortress (1) if the Jewish people revolted, or (2) if his Roman master, Antony, were to give his kingdom to Herod's enemy to the south, Cleopatra. Masada was also located near the southern areas of Nabatea and Idumaea, the countries of Herod's origin. Therefore, Masada's primary function was to provide Herod with an emergency escape. In spite of the luxury and the cost of the fortress-palace's construction, there is no evidence that Herod spent much time here.

Notice the main entrance from the east. This trail, winding across the face of the mountain, was called the Snake Path. It is a testimony to Herod's vigor that he created a fortress in such a remote location so difficult for him (and therefore others as well) to reach. At the top (near the modern staircase) was a heavily guarded gate that provided a final barrier to anyone wishing to enter Masada.

The barren wilderness around underscores the ingenuity of Herod's workmen, who were able to provide adequate water to the fortress from the infrequent floods that swept through the wadis on either side of the mountain. The wadi on the left can be clearly seen. The wadi on the right emerges from behind Masada.

The three-tiered Northern Palace can be seen on the right side of the mountain. Great retaining walls held up the lowest level, a testimony to the genius of Herod's engineers and their vision for creating structures that defy nature. The chalk-colored soil in the foreground was at one time beneath the Dead Sea, which has since receded to about a mile away.

Overhead Transparency 26. Cistern of Masada. This photograph highlights the huge size of the cisterns Herod built to provide water during times of siege and to fill his luxurious swimming pools and supply his bathing complexes. The amount of water needed was staggering. There were several swimming pools on top of the desert mountain, where little rain fell. The main bath complex was one of the largest in Israel, and there were several smaller, private ones for Herod in each of his palaces. Since the floods in the wadi below were unreliable, Herod needed water sufficient for his family and staff. One scholar has estimated that if all the cisterns were full, there would be enough water to sustain thousands of people for 10 years. The contrast between the surrounding desert and the abundance of water inside the fortress would have impressed anyone who visited this place. They probably marveled at the vision and ingenuity of Herod, a result he passionately desired.

The water flowed into cisterns cut into the base of the mountain on the western side. It was then carried to the top of the mountain and emptied into cisterns like this one, which held more than 1 million gallons. The cistern was probably originally a quarry that provided stone for the buildings on Masada. It has been noted that Herod frequently defied nature in his attempt to build a legacy for himself. Providing the amount of water needed on Masada was part of that legacy.

Note for your students that visitors to Israel are still amazed at the great vision Herod displayed in his building programs. Point out several important truths:

- God evaluates people differently than we do. Despite all of Herod's great achievements, the Bible records only Herod's execution of the babies of Bethlehem (Matthew 2:16). God saw Herod's heart. We must learn to view life as God does or the glitter of the secular world can distract us from Him.

- Jesus and Herod were both builders. Herod's buildings are now in ruins. Jesus continues to build His structure, the church (1 Peter 2:4–5). It is important to remember that only those things built for God truly last.

- You can try to defy nature, but you cannot defy God. Herod was so close to Jesus and eternal life. He could have met the Messiah! But his own self-centeredness blinded him to who Jesus was. Do we miss Jesus because we focus on our own interests more than we should?

Overhead Transparency 27. Storehouses of Masada. This photograph shows the remains of the 15 storehouses on the eastern side of Masada. The one on the left is as it was found by archaeologists; the others have been reconstructed. In the background above the storehouses, you can see the Dead Sea, which is partly dried up at this spot due to extensive mining of the minerals in the water. The mountains of Moab can be seen beyond. The plastered wall in the foreground is part of Herod's Western Palace. Originally, the floors as well as the walls of the storerooms were plastered. Oil, wine, flour, and other provisions were stored in separate rooms in special jars. The rooms themselves were more than 60 feet long and 12 feet wide.

Overhead Transparency 28. The Opulence of Masada. These four photographs display the remains of the luxury Herod included in all of his palaces. The upper left shows the remains of the caldarium (hot bath) of the public bathhouse. The floor of this room, now gone, was originally placed on the more than 200 columns seen here. The floor itself was probably a mosaic. The walls were faced with vertical rows of clay pipes through which hot air flowed from under the floor up and into the room. The hot air included steam from the water in the pipes. The caldarium functioned much like a sauna.

The upper right picture shows the mosaic floor of the private bathhouse in the Western Palace. The multicolored geometric designs are typical of Herod's construction. Some scholars think he chose not to use figures of animals, people, or gods out of respect for his subjects, who believed that these would violate their commandment against making images. Made of many tiny stones (called *tessarae*) of differing mineral types, mosaic became a significant skill of the Jewish people during and after Herod's time. The structures in the upper corners were built over the mosaic by the Jewish rebels during the First Jewish Revolt. Since these rebels were fighting for life itself, they were not concerned about preserving Herod's luxury.

The photograph on the lower left displays a column style used by Herod on Masada. The columns were made of sandstone pieces that were plastered to look like fluted columns. When new, they probably looked like polished limestone or even marble. In the same palace, the stone panels are painted to look like marble. Even when Herod could not afford the greatest luxury, he attempted to create that impression.

The photograph on the lower right shows fresco panels from one of the lesser palaces on

Masada. The stone wall was plastered and then painted in deep, rich colors. Much of the plaster has fallen off, but enough remains for us to envision the beauty of entire rooms decorated in this manner. This style of decoration was popular with wealthy people during Jesus' time and after.

The ruins of Herod's constructions on Masada underscore his devotion to himself. Providing for his own safety, satisfying his need for the finest luxuries, and establishing a name for himself were his obsessions. His presence provides an important dimension of the setting in which God placed Jesus. Could anyone believe Jesus was Messiah, Son of the Most High, when He appeared so ordinary compared with Herod?

Step Two: "The Fall of Masada"

1. Preparation

Have students read the student handout titled "The Jewish Revolts." Encourage them to read all the Bible passages mentioned in the handout.

2. Introductory Comments

The battle for Masada and the death of the Zealots is gripping drama. But it can be better understood in the context of the larger struggle of which Masada was the climax. Though it has no direct bearing on the ministry of Jesus and His teaching, the struggle does help to clarify aspects of His message and His actions. The following passages deal with Jesus' interaction with the political hopes and dreams of the people of His day. Many of His teachings have additional and possibly more crucial application to other events—even events of the Last Days. The following material does not in any way deny or belittle those applications; it simply looks at them in the context of the cultural setting in order to gain additional understanding of Jesus' words.

3. Guided Discussion

Have your students read the following scriptural accounts. Then pose the questions or relate the information following each reference:

a. People's responses to Jesus:

- John 6:15; Acts 1:6. Why would the people make this request?

- John 18:36. Why did Jesus need to say this?

- Matthew 4:8–10. What did Satan tempt Jesus to pattern His kingdom after? Why would this have been attractive to first-century Jews?

- Luke 19:37–42; Matthew 21:9–10; John 12:12–16. Palm branches were a patriotic symbol, and "Hosanna" was a chant used in Maccabee celebrations asking for God's deliverance. The disciples did not understand this when it happened, and obviously the crowd didn't either (John 12:16). Their response led Jesus to weep and predict what would happen to them because they sought military-political salvation.

- Matthew 26:50–54. Considering the political climate, why do you think Peter was tempted to fight? What was Jesus' response? How did it contradict popular beliefs?

b. Read the following and notice Jesus' commands to the people:

- Matthew 8:4, 9:30, 12:16; Luke 8:56; Mark 1:44, 3:12, 5:43, 7:36. Based on the political climate of the time, what is one reason Jesus gave such commands to His Jewish audience?

- Mark 5:18–19. Why would Jesus give such a different command to a Gentile? (Possibly because the political expectations of a messiah were not part of the Gentile world?)

c. Read the following and notice Jesus' connection to the Zealots (those who started the Jewish revolt):

- Matthew 10:4; Mark 3:18; Luke 6:15; Acts 1:13. Why would Jesus call a Zealot "disciple"? What would have been the Zealots' expectation of Jesus?

d. Read Matthew 24:1–2; Mark 13:1–2; Luke 21:5–6. When did Jesus' prediction come true?

e. Read Luke 19:41–44. Keeping in mind that part of Jesus' weeping was due to the unbelief of the Pharisees (verse 39), notice that Jesus also weeps for people who are chanting "Hosanna" (meaning "Yahweh, save us"). Even His disciples did not understand that He was a peaceful Savior (John 12:16). Would you have recognized Jesus as Messiah among all the other claimants? Why or why not? What could have been a barrier to believing?

f. Based on the video and "The Jewish Revolts" handout, discuss the following:

- What brought the Zealots to Masada?

- Why were the Romans so determined to destroy them?

- Why do you think the Zealots destroyed themselves to avoid being captured by the Romans?

- How does such passionate desire for freedom help you understand the people's reaction to Jesus?

- Was their solution right? Why or why not?

- Do you think Jesus' weeping may in part have been due to His sorrow over what would happen at Masada?

- What, ultimately, is the only solution to world problems? To the human desire for freedom?

- How can we be patriotic citizens defending freedom and still be good citizens of Jesus' peaceful kingdom?

g. Prayer: Spend some time together in conversation with God. (1) Ask Him to help you put His kingdom first in your life. (2) Ask Him to help you understand and appreciate your Jewish roots, lost in part because of the Jewish revolt. (3) Pray for the Jewish people that they may find the peace, and the True Peace, that has so often eluded them.

OPTIONAL — Digging Deeper III: The Fall of Jerusalem (10–20 minutes)

Matthew 24 (see also Mark 13; Luke 21:5–36) has normally been interpreted as applying to end-time events. Without questioning that application, there is also a sense in which the passage was partially fulfilled in the fall of Jerusalem. Based on what they have learned from the video and the student handout, have your students investigate this passage.

- Verses 1–2. The disciples admire Herod's Temple. Jesus describes how the Temple will be destroyed. This occurred in A.D. 70.

- Verses 3–51. Read these verses and look for items that could have at least a partial or preliminary fulfillment in this same destruction. (Example: verse 11. During the siege of Jerusalem, several proclaimed themselves to be messiahs speaking on God's behalf.) There are several. See if students can find them.

- What events could not have been fulfilled in the Roman destruction?
- How does the fall of Jerusalem during the revolt give us a foretaste of events at the end of time?

Conclusion

The deep longing by God's people for the Messiah was part of His preparation for the coming of His Son. As Jesus revealed Himself to be the Messiah, many believed Him. For others, this longing was translated into a passionate desire for political freedom from the Romans. Many false messiahs appeared, each catering to this misguided search for the kingdom of God. It is crucial that we listen carefully to what and whom Jesus claimed to be. We must not be guilty of trying to make Him something else, thus missing the peace and salvation He offers. The fortress of Masada, a picture of the strength and security of God our Fortress, must also be a poignant reminder of what can happen to those who misunderstand the gospel of Jesus.

THE JEWISH REVOLTS

Lesson Twelve
Handout #1

Jewish people of Jesus' day had a passionate desire for freedom from the domination of the pagan Romans and the oppressive Herod dynasty that had ruled them for many years. Revolt seethed continuously, mostly underground, for more than 100 years—from the time Herod became king (37 B.C.) until the Romans destroyed Jerusalem and the Temple (A.D. 70).

It is helpful to realize that this underlying struggle is the backdrop for Jesus' ministry, and why so many hoped He would be a conquering king. This helps us understand why the adulation of the crowds during the triumphal entry reduced Jesus to tears, and probably why many rejected His message.

THE RISING STORM

Ever since the Romans arrived on the scene in 64 B.C., the Jewish people were divided over how to respond to the rule of their often-corrupt governors or the Herod family who served them. The religious community, particularly the Pharisees, believed the Jewish people were to be God's instruments on earth, from whom the Messiah would come to institute that glorious age when Israel would be a great and free nation. Many others, especially the secular community and apparently some of the Sadducees, noted the present reality of the rule of Rome and determined that cooperation was the best policy. The contrast between the situation at hand and the messianic hopes was heightened by the tyrannical rule of Rome and the paganism of its religious and Hellenistic culture. This difference produced increasing fragmentation of the people, and several movements developed in response.

The *Zealots,* an ultra-nationalistic group, proclaimed revolution to be God's solution (Acts 5:37). The *Essenes* withdrew, waiting anxiously for the Messiah to lead a violent overthrow of the Romans and their Jewish supporters. The *Sadducees* apparently practiced a form of cooperation since it was Rome who kept them securely in their position over the Temple and therefore over the people (John 11:49–50). The *Herodians* appeared satisfied with the Herod dynasty (Matthew 22:16). The *Pharisees,* condemning Rome's pagan excesses, were removed from politics and viewed the foreign oppressors as God's hand punishing His people for their unfaithfulness to the Torah. The country was in turmoil, each faction longing in a different way for the freedom they desired. To this climate of confusion, hatred, and division, many so-called messiahs came, each preaching his own brand of salvation (Acts 21:38). Jesus presented His unique message of redemption. Some followed His lead, but many did not. During feast days, especially Passover, tensions reached fever pitch and the Romans increased their military presence to prevent open revolt. The climate existed, however, for revolution to begin.

Herod Agrippa I, grandson of Herod the Great, died in A.D. 44 (Acts 12:19–23). The Romans appointed a series of governors called procurators, each apparently more corrupt and cruel than the previous ruler. Groups of rebel *sicarii* (assassins) were everywhere, killing Romans and the Jews who cooperated with them. Jonathan the high priest was assassinated. During this time, Paul was arrested (Acts 21:27–37) and accused of being one of the rebels (Acts 21:38). Popular support for the Zealots grew. The priesthood became more dependent on the Romans for security and support, and in so doing, they grew increasingly corrupt. This drove the common people toward the radical approach of the Zealots.

Felix (Acts 24) was replaced by Festus (Acts 25) as governor. Both were brutal but ineffective in their attempts to quell the rising revolt. Festus died after a short time. The high priest, Ananus, took this opportunity to murder his opponents, including many in the Christian community and James, brother of Jesus. Ananus was deposed and replaced with a man named Jesus, and then another priest named Jesus. These two were in such opposition that their followers fought in the streets.

The Roman administration was in disorder, and the Zealots and *sicarii* flourished. Florus, another governor, attempted to stop the violence by flogging and crucifying hundreds of people. The time was ripe. The desperate hope of a messiah who would bring freedom from political oppression was ready to bear fruit.

THE REVOLT BEGINS

While Christians and Jews were thrown to the wild animals by the emperor Nero in Rome, violence flared in Judea. In Caesarea, a conflict between Jews and Gentiles over activities next to the synagogue had been brewing for some time. In A.D. 66, on the Sabbath day, a Gentile offered a "pagan" sacrifice next to the entrance to the synagogue. There was an outcry from the citizens of Caesarea. The authorities in Jerusalem decided to end all foreign sacrifices, including the one for Caesar himself, in the Temple. Florus the governor, who lived in Caesarea, came to Jerusalem with troops, entered the Temple treasury, and took a large amount of gold. When people gathered to protest, Florus unleashed his legionnaires on innocent civilians of the city. Hundreds of women were raped, whipped, and crucified. More than 3,500 people were killed, including women and children.

The reaction was outrage. Mobs swarmed the streets, driving the outnumbered soldiers out of the city. The people stormed the Antonia (the Roman fort) and burned the archives, destroying records of debts. The revolt spread. The Zealots surprised the Roman garrison and occupied the fortress of Masada. From this fortress, huge supplies of weapons were distributed. Though there were voices urging calm, even the nonpolitical Pharisees joined the Zealot movement in droves.[1]

The violence mounted within the rebel movement. Zealot leader Menahem was assassinated by another Zealot leader, Eleazar, who then ordered the slaughter of the Roman prisoners remaining in the city. There was no turning back.

A BLOODY REBELLION

The Gentiles in Caesarea, hearing of the violence against fellow Romans in Jerusalem, rose against the Jews of that town. Within a day, 20,000 Jews were killed. This slaughter of men, women, and children, young and old, was repeated in many places in the country and throughout the empire, including Syria and Egypt. Fifty thousand were killed in Alexandria alone. The land ran with blood.

Gallus, the governor of Syria, advanced on Jerusalem with the twelfth legion. But he was ambushed by Zealots in the mountain pass of Beth Horon and his force destroyed. The Romans had lost their advantage, and the Jews gained their national freedom (albeit temporarily) and the weapons of an imperial legion. Nero acted quickly. He ordered his leading general, Vespasian, to end the Jewish problem once and for all.

Vespasian began his campaign in A.D. 67 in Galilee, where a young priest, Joseph, was in command. His army numbered more than 50,000 men. Vespasian took Sepphoris, Jotapata (where Joseph surrendered to the general and became the Roman scribe Josephus), and several other towns with brutal force. He also destroyed Gamla, where the Zealot movement began, putting 10,000 people to the sword. Most of the towns of the region were left as smoking ruins. Many men were executed, often crucified, and the women and children were sold into slavery. A few were saved for the games in the arena. Galilee was again Roman.

Vespasian then conquered the coast, including Joppa, and the lands to the east of Judea. He took Jericho, which guarded the eastern approach to Jerusalem, and Emmaus, which guarded the western. Jerusalem was now isolated.

In A.D. 68, the campaign halted due to the suicide of Nero. As Josephus had predicted (a prediction that apparently spared his life), Vespasian became emperor. He left his son Titus to complete the campaign against Jerusalem.

The situation in Jerusalem was horrible. Several factions of Zealots converged on the city, having been defeated elsewhere. They blamed each other for their defeats. One group controlled the Temple Mount and appointed their own priest. When the Sadducee priests resisted, they were slaughtered along with 8,500 of their supporters. The sewers of the city ran with Jewish blood. Simon Bar Giora, another self-proclaimed messiah, entered the city and fought the Zealots. Confusion and terror reigned. Jerusalem was divided into three sections, each fighting the other as the Romans tightened the noose. Apparently, the Christian community, possibly remembering Jesus' words (Matthew 24:15–16), fled to the mountain regions east of the country, beginning the long separation of Jew and Christian that would bear horrible consequences later.

In the spring of A.D. 70, Titus arrived outside Jerusalem. His army now numbered 80,000 or more. Titus breached the third wall near the end of May and slaughtered the people of that part of the city. Five days later, the second wall fell. Half of the city belonged to the Romans. In July the Romans built a siege wall around the city to prevent escape and to starve the citizenry.

Unbelievably, the killing between Jewish factions continued. People killed each other over scraps of food. Anyone suspected of contemplating surrender was killed. Because some Jews had swallowed gold coins before trying to escape, their fellow citizens began to disembowel those they caught, looking for money. In one night, 2,000 were ripped open. No one bothered to bury the dead. Many who did surrender were crucified just outside the walls so the hapless defenders could watch their agony. Josephus records that the Roman soldiers nailed people in various positions for their own amusement until they couldn't find enough crosses for the victims.

The famine took its toll as well. Josephus reports that 600,000 bodies were thrown out of the city. This may be an exaggeration, but gives a sense of the carnage.

THE END OF THE REVOLT

The Antonia fortress fell in mid-July. On August 6, the sacrifices ceased in the Temple. The Temple itself was burned and destroyed on the ninth of the Jewish month of Ab (the end of August), the same day it had been destroyed by the Babylonians more than 600 years before. It has never been rebuilt.

On August 30, the lower city fell, and in September the upper. Titus ordered all buildings leveled, except for three towers in Herod's palace, which were left as evidence of his former strength. All the citizens of the city were executed, sold into slavery, or saved for the games in the arena. The slaughter was beyond description. Infants were thrown to their deaths from the top of the city walls, and people were burned alive; the alleys of the city were choked with corpses. Eleven thousand prisoners died of starvation waiting for their execution. Josephus records that more than 1 million perished and nearly 100,000 were sold into slavery. The Jews' holy city was gone and their Temple destroyed.

A few Zealots took refuge at Herod's fortress of Masada. Here they hoped to outlast the Romans. One can only imagine the state of mind of these people, some of whom had seen Jerusalem fall. Titus left their fate in the hands of Silva, the new governor. The tenth legion laid siege to Masada in A.D. 72. A wall was built by Jewish slaves around the base of the enormous mountain plateau, six feet high and more than two miles in length. But there was little chance of starving out the defenders because Herod's extensive storehouses were still filled with food and weapons and his cisterns with water. The Zealots apparently felt safe here.

Over the next seven months, the Romans built a siege ramp against the western side of the mountain. When the ramp was finished, a battering ram was winched to the top, and Roman soldiers smashed a hole in the fortress wall. The Zealots fortified their wall with timbers, but these were set on fire. That night the Zealots met. Their leader, Eleazar from Gamla, argued forcefully that suicide was the only honorable action. They had seen what the Romans would do to them, their wives, and their children. They had lived their lives for freedom and the opportunity to serve God alone. Now they must remove all possibility of serving anyone else.

Every man killed his family. Ten men were chosen to kill the Jewish soldiers; one killed the other nine and then committed suicide. In so doing, the Zealots stole the final victory from the Romans. But the revolt was ended. Two old women and five children survived to share the story with the world.

POSTSCRIPT

The Romans eventually built a temple to Jupiter on the Temple Mount. Emperor Hadrian (A.D. 117–138) desired to remake Jerusalem as a Roman city named Aelia Capitolina. The few Jews who remained held to their desire for freedom and their hopes of a conquering messiah. When Simon Bar Kochba, a descendant of David and apparently a charismatic leader, began a new resistance, the religious community declared him Messiah. Open rebellion (the Second Jewish Revolt) began in A.D. 131, and the Jews rallied around his leadership.

The Romans were surprised and initially defeated, but their follow-up was swift and devastating. The Roman commander Julius Severus, and even Hadrian himself, responded with overwhelming force. Nearly a thousand villages were destroyed, and Bar Kochba was killed. In A.D. 135, the Second Jewish Revolt ended. Any Jews who had not fled the land were killed or enslaved. Jerusalem became Hadrian's Roman city, the Jewish religion was outlawed, and Judea became Palestine. The Jews were a people without a land.

Out of this disaster came two new religious movements: Christianity and rabbinic Judaism. The revolt drove Christianity to the ends of the earth, and it soon became a largely Gentile faith. Only today are its Jewish roots being recognized. Rabbinic Judaism became the Orthodox faith of the Jewish people of today, the descendants of the Pharisees. The Sadducees, the Essenes, and the Zealots are no more.

JESUS AND THE REVOLTS

The First and Second Jewish Revolts were a disaster for God's people. The agony suffered over two millennia can be traced to those events. Jesus was crucified (by the same Romans) nearly 40 years before the first revolt. Understanding the climate that led to the revolt and His anticipation of that event make His teaching clearer.

Often people saw in Jesus a Davidic king, a military conqueror who would rescue them from the Romans (John 6:15; Acts 1:6). But His kingdom was not the kingdom of the Zealot or the sword (Matthew 26:51–52), though He had a Zealot disciple (Matthew 10:4). Jesus frequently commanded those He taught or healed not to tell anyone, possibly because they would misunderstand, given the political climate of the day (Mark 1:44, 7:36, 3:12, 5:43; Matthew 8:4, 9:30, 12:16; Luke 8:56). When we remember how many messiahs proclaimed their message during this time, we can understand the uniqueness of Christ's message and the reticence of His audience.

Clearly, Jesus predicted the destruction that would result from the revolt (Matthew 24:1–2). It led Him to weep on one occasion as He described exactly what would happen (Luke 19:41–44). It seems that Jesus was saddened because His fellow Jews looked for military solutions to their problems rather than spiritual ones—to a political messiah rather than the Lamb of God. He warned His followers not to take part in that method of bringing in God's kingdom. The coming destruction was not

God's judgment as much as it was the natural result of human beings seeking salvation through their own political and military might. Jesus' method was the opposite of such an approach.

While we cannot fully understand God's reasons for shaping history the way He has, we must be able to weep with Jesus because the destruction wrought by the two Jewish revolts resulted from people seeking God in the wrong places and ways. We must be devoted to Jesus the Messiah's message, for He truly is God's hope of peace (Luke 2:14).

NOTES

1. Judah of Gamla apparently revolted against a census ordered by Quirinius, governor of Syria, and was executed by Herod Antipas (who also executed John the Baptist). Judah probably founded the Zealot party, though not the movement. His sons Jacob and Simon were executed by the Romans for resistance, and his son (possibly grandson) Menahem was a leader in the First Jewish Revolt.

THE TIME HAD FULLY COME

For the Teacher

Christianity has tended to see Jesus' role in history as a startling phenomenon completely unique to the people of His day. But the discovery of the Dead Sea Scrolls and studies of archaeology and the Judaic writings of Jesus' time are beginning to help us understand what Paul meant when he wrote, "When the time had fully come, God sent his Son" (Galatians 4:4).

Clearly, Jesus' message was in many ways different from others', and His sacrificial death was unique. But God placed Jesus in a carefully prepared setting—the first-century Jewish culture. Jesus, God's Son, was a Jewish boy who spoke Hebrew and learned in a synagogue. He became a Jewish man and later a Jewish rabbi, using the same teaching techniques, and in some cases the same parables, as His peers. He selected *talmidim* (students) as did other rabbis. He celebrated the Jewish feasts of Passover, Shavuot (Pentecost), and Hanukkah. He taught other Jews, Greeks, and Romans. He ate the diet of a Galilean, learned the building trade, and knew the countryside well enough to use it as the basis for His teaching.

It becomes increasingly clear that the setting of Jesus' life and death was determined by God and therefore was significant to the ministry of His Son. Understanding the culture in which Jesus lived helps us see and understand His message in all its vibrancy.

God chose the time and place, and therefore the culture, for Jesus. Our New Testament studies, Sets 3 and 4, will concentrate on understanding Jesus' message in its setting. And we begin with a group whose theology and practice have great similarities to that of Jesus (and some significant differences as well).

The main point of Lesson Thirteen is to challenge your students to try to see Jesus in first-century Palestine. You can help them understand how God's careful planning makes that setting important. There are lessons they can learn from the people of Jesus' day as well as from the message He brought to those people. As your students observe God's careful preparation for the earthly life of His Son, they will be able to see and trust God's plan in their own lives.

Your Objectives for This Lesson

At the completion of this section, you will want your students:

To Know/Understand

1. The geographic setting of the Essene settlement of Qumran.

2. The importance of the wilderness for the coming of the Messiah.

3. The nature of the Dead Sea Scrolls and their importance for our Christian faith.

4. The beliefs and worldview of the Essenes.

5. The similarities of the Essenes to John the Baptist, Jesus, and the early church.

6. How carefully God prepared for Jesus' birth and its confirmation of God's planning for our lives.

7. That the battle between good and evil continues in our time.

8. The wilderness as an appropriate place for Jesus' temptation.

To Do

1. Commit to being a son or daughter of light in our world.

2. Identify wilderness experiences and commit to living by trust in God's Word.

3. Become more faithful in the study of God's Word in appreciation of His protection of it over the centuries.

How to Plan for This Lesson

Because of the volume of material in this lesson, you may need to divide it into several class sessions. To help you determine how to do that, the lesson has been broken into several segments. Note that the time needed may vary considerably depending on the leader, the size of the class, and the interest level of the class.

If you wish to cover the entire lesson in one session, you should complete Unit One, a discussion of major points in the video. It does not go into great depth. You may go into greater depth, or enhance your background knowledge as class leader, by selecting parts or all of the remaining material.

How to Prepare for This Lesson

Materials Needed

Student copies of the maps:	"The Roman World"
	"Topography of Israel: New Testament"
Overhead transparencies:	"The Roman World"
	"Topography of Israel: New Testament"
	"New Testament Chronology"
	"Qumran"
	"Religious Movements of Jesus' Time"
Student copies of the handouts:	"Not on Bread Alone"
	"The Dead Sea Scrolls"
	"The Sons of Light"

*Video: **The Time Had Fully Come***

Overhead projector, screen, VCR

1. Make copies of the maps and handouts listed above for your students. (If possible, they should receive and read the handouts before the lesson.)

2. Prepare the overhead transparencies listed above. (You'll find them at the back of the book.)

3. Determine which **Steps** and which optional **Digging Deeper** sections, if any, you wish to use in your class session(s). NOTE: You can use these sections in any order you wish (e.g., you might want to use **Digging Deeper III,** but not **Digging Deeper I** or **Digging Deeper II**).

4. Review the geography of the lands of the Bible from the "Introduction."

5. Prepare your classroom ahead of time, setting up and testing an overhead projector and screen and a VCR. If you plan to hand out biblical references for your students to look up and read aloud, prepare 3x5 cards (one reference per card) to distribute before class.

Lesson Plan

UNIT ONE: Video Review

1. Introductory Comments

"But when the time had fully come, God sent his Son, . . . to redeem . . ." (Galatians 4:4–5). Paul used these words to describe God's careful preparation from Noah to Abraham to David and now to Jesus. Included in His preparation are individuals, nations, cultures, and, we discover in this lesson, religious movements among the Jewish people.

The presence of the Essenes, as revealed in the Dead Sea Scrolls, helped prepare the Jewish people for Jesus' message. By understanding this religious subculture, we can better understand why Jesus said and did the things the Gospels record. We can better recognize what God wants us to do and be because of the Messiah. And we can praise God for His careful preparation of the setting for Jesus' ministry.

2. Show the Video *The Time Had Fully Come* (18 minutes)

3. Guided Discussion: When the Time Had Fully Come

a. Read Matthew 3:1–3. Using the overhead transparency titled "Topography of Israel: New Testament," have students locate:

> Dead Sea
> Judea Wilderness
> Qumran
> Mediterranean Sea
> Jerusalem
> Sea of Galilee

b. Read Psalm 78:9–16; 95:6–10. The desert is the place where God created faith in His people. When they grew hungry, He fed them. When they complained of thirst, He gave them water from the rock. By nurturing and disciplining His people, God taught them to depend solely on Him. The Old Testament people understood that the wilderness is the place where people learn to trust God. Isaiah predicted (40:1–3) that the Messiah would come from the wilderness where a way had been prepared.

> Ask your students the following questions:

- Why do you think the Essenes went out to the wilderness?

- Why did John the Baptist go to the wilderness (Matthew 3:1–3)?

- Why was Jesus tempted in the desert (Matthew 4:1)?

- What is your wilderness—in what ways have you been tested? As you look back on these experiences, how do you think they prepared you to live for God?

c. The Essene movement began as a reaction against Hellenism, the secular worldview that was sweeping the world. This worldview glorified the human being as the ultimate value in the world. It emphasized physical pleasure and sensual practices in its art, nude athletic contests, and public baths. Hellenism's theaters were unacceptable to the Essenes because of the erotic themes celebrating the exploits of pagan gods and heroes. Many religious Jews abandoned their biblical worldview for the attractive lifestyle of Hellenism.

Ask your students:

- What modern-day values or practices do you think might be similar to Hellenism? In what ways are they similar?

- The Essenes resisted Hellenism by separating and living in the desert. Is that the right approach? Why or why not?

- Have students read Matthew 28:19–20. What is the right approach to secular worldviews, values, and practices? Think of some examples of how Jesus dealt with the pagan people and practices He encountered.

d. The Essenes had several practices similar to those of the early Christians. Some of their ideas appear identical to those in the Bible. Read Acts 2:44–45. The Essenes held their possessions in common. Why did the early Christians share their possessions? Should we do the same? Why or why not?

e. The Essenes practiced a "ceremonial meal" that prefigured a great messianic banquet that they believed would occur soon. So they blessed bread and wine in anticipation of that banquet. Read Matthew 26:26–29 and ask: What similarities do you see with the Lord's Supper? How might this add to our understanding of our celebration of the Lord's "meal"?

f. The Essenes used many words and phrases common to the New Testament and not elsewhere. Note the following examples:

1.	sons of light	John 12:36
2.	light and darkness	Matthew 6:22–23; John 1:5, 3:19
3.	Belial	2 Corinthians 6:14–15
4.	poor in spirit	Matthew 5:3
5.	Melchizedek	Hebrews 7:1–3
6.	Son of God (Son of the Most High)	Luke 1:35
7.	Way of the Lord	Isaiah 40:3; Matthew 3:3

- How would the Essenes' use of these terms (and many others) have affected Jesus' audience?

- How did this help prepare people for Jesus' coming?

g. The Essenes were one influence on the world of Jesus' time. Jesus was not an Essene and had some significant differences with them. However, understanding this movement can help us better understand the New Testament. Read Galatians 4:4–5. Ask your students:

- How were the Essenes part of God's careful plan for the coming of the Messiah?

- What effect did their presence have on the people who listened to Jesus' message?

h. God worked in all circumstances so that Jesus' coming occurred when every factor was the way God desired. Read Romans 8:28 and ask: Is this passage saying the same thing about all of us who follow Jesus?

i. Ask students to discuss, either in small groups or with the whole class, an experience in which God worked out all circumstances (before, during, and after) for His (and their) good.

j. Spend a few moments in prayer. Together, thank God for preparing so carefully for Jesus' life. Thank Him for showing the same care and concern for you.

UNIT TWO
Step One: "Prepare in the Wilderness"

1. Introductory Comments

The wilderness had an intense effect on the people of the Bible, including those of the New Testament. It was the place where God had formed them into His own people, taught them how to serve Him, and shaped their faith. It was the place to which some of their own ancestors, such as Elijah and David, fled to find God in their times of stress and trouble.

The wilderness was located close to where the Israelites lived. The Negev wilderness was located in the southern part of the country barely 40 miles from Jerusalem, their holy city. The Judea Wilderness was much closer, just to the east of Jerusalem and within sight of anyone who lived in the mountains in the center of the country. The reality of the wilderness was unavoidable to the people of the land simply because of its proximity.

It is important to understand the significance of the wilderness in the minds of the Jewish people. Because the prophets predicted that the Messiah would appear from the wilderness to bring redemption and freedom, people looked to the wilderness for their salvation. God fulfilled prophecy and announced His Son as the true Messiah by placing the beginning of Jesus' ministry in "the wilderness."

2. Map Study: Wilderness of Judea

HINT: *Begin this map study session by reviewing the geography of the overall region and working down to the area the lesson is dealing with—the Judea Wilderness.*

Have your students refer to their copies of "The Roman World" as you display the overhead transparency of this map. Point out the following locations and have students locate them on their maps:

> Roman Empire
> Egypt
> Nile River
> Mediterranean Sea
> Arabian Desert
> Israel (note its location between the desert and the sea)

Now have students refer to their copies of "Topography of Israel: New Testament" as you display the overhead transparency of this map. Point out the following areas and have your students locate them on their maps:

> coastal plain
> Negev
> Jerusalem
> Jericho
> central mountain range
> Great Rift Valley
> Judea Wilderness
> Qumran
> En Gedi

3. Show the Video *The Time Had Fully Come* (18 minutes)

4. Read the Handout "Not on Bread Alone"

Students should review the Bible passages listed in this handout.

5. Guided Discussion: The Wilderness Experience

In the wilderness, God formed Israel into His people. It was here that they learned to trust God to provide for them, and it was here that God disciplined them and shaped their faith. In later times of trouble, the prophets called for the Israelites to return to the faith of their infancy in the desert (Jeremiah 2:1–8, 9:2, 31:31–32; Psalm 81:1–10; Hosea 2:14–15).

Have your students (individually or in small groups) read the following passages and state the geographical setting of each passage and the significant contribution each person or event made to the formation of God's people:

- Genesis 12:1–9
- Genesis 21:1–7 (note also Genesis 20:1)
- Exodus 3:1–15
- Exodus 20:1–17 (note also Exodus 19:1–2)
- Deuteronomy 2:7 (Moses speaking to the people of Israel)
- 1 Samuel 23:14, 24:1, 25:1, 26:2–4

Notice that Israel's forefathers (Abraham, the father of the Israelite nation; Moses, the lawgiver; and David, the founder of the kingdom of Israel) all prepared for the missions God gave them by spending time in the desert (Genesis 12:9; Exodus 3:1; 1 Samuel 24:1).

Later biblical writers understood the desert as the place where God created faith in His people. When they grew hungry, God fed them manna from the sky and quail from the sea. When they complained of thirst, He gave them water from the rock. When their fear of the unknown overwhelmed them and they began to curse Moses for leading them out of Egypt, God sent a plague of poisonous snakes as punishment for their unfaithfulness. By nurturing and disciplining His people, God was teaching them to depend solely upon Him. And though the Israelites continued to rebel, God remained faithful. God made His covenant with the Israelites in the wilderness, and their experience there transformed them from a band of people into a powerful nation. Believers must constantly relearn these wilderness lessons.

Ask your students to look up the following passages and note the link between the people of that day and their past wilderness experience.

- Psalm 78:9–16
- Psalm 78:17–32
- Psalm 95:6–11
- Jeremiah 2:1–2
- Deuteronomy 8:1–5, 10–18

The prophets also taught that God's redemption and restoration of His people after their captivity in Babylon would come by way of another "wilderness experience." Ask your students to look up the following passages and note the place of the wilderness in the coming age of the Messiah.

a. Hosea 2:14–23. God's restoration of His people will be a cleansing in the desert similar to His establishment of Israel in the beginning.

b. Isaiah 40:1–5. The restoration of God's people would include passing through the wilderness even as it had with Israel the first time.

c. Matthew 3:1–3. John the Baptist fulfilled Isaiah 40:3 in part because his ministry occurred in the wilderness.

d. The Dead Sea Scrolls quote the same Isaiah passage to support the fact that John and Jesus ministered in the same Judea Wilderness (Manual of Discipline 8:13–15).

Ask your students to summarize the lessons Israel learned in the wilderness. Point out that the wilderness was never meant to be the Israelites' permanent home; rather, it was a place of learning to trust the faithfulness of God and it was the way to the Promised Land. The desert was for them a "conversion" experience, after which they were called to live in obedience to God in His chosen land.

The same principle applies to modern-day Christians because it is through wilderness experiences that we learn obedience (1 Corinthians 10: 6). Jesus' ministry began with His baptism by John and His subsequent temptation in the wilderness (Matthew 4:1–11).

OPTIONAL — Digging Deeper I: Tempted in the Desert
(30–70 minutes)

A key event in the life and ministry of Jesus is His temptation by Satan in the wilderness. This story, important enough to be included in three Gospels, has been an encouragement to followers of Jesus Christ for centuries as they struggle with temptations of their own.

Given the importance of the wilderness to Jesus' culture, and the connection of the 40-day temptation to His baptism by John, the intense struggle Jesus faced may be more foundational to His message than has been emphasized. The wilderness in which Jesus was tempted is the same as the community of the Essenes at Qumran.

A. Scripture and Discussion

Read the following passages aloud and note the facts for your students:

- Genesis 1:2; Matthew 3:16; Genesis 3:1–7; Matthew 4:1–11

  1. God drew a new creation, including people, out of watery chaos. These people were immediately tempted to disobey God and so were separated from Him.

  2. Jesus came up out of the water of the Jordan River to begin His work of "creating" a new community. Immediately, He was tempted, but He resisted by indicating He would live by God's commands alone.

  3. Discuss:

     a. Why do you think Jesus was able to resist Satan, while Adam and Eve fell into sin?

     b. Read Romans 5:15,17–18. What is the importance of Jesus' resistance to Satan when compared with Adam's? (Just as Adam's sin made us unrighteous, so Jesus' victory over temptation enables us to be righteous before God.)

     c. Why did Jesus have to be tempted? (As the first Adam represented his descendants before God, Jesus represented His "spiritual descendants" before God. He was tempted for us.)

- Exodus 32:1–6; Numbers 21:5–7; Numbers 25:1–3

  1. The Israelites were tempted when they came through the desert.

  2. Their experiences were for our example (1 Corinthians 10:1–11).

3. Discuss:

    a. What can be learned from Israel's wilderness temptations?

    b. What was Jesus saying to His Jewish audience by being tempted in the wilderness as the Israelites had been? (He was the new "Israel.")

- Leviticus 16:10,22,26; Isaiah 13:21–22, 34:13–14; Revelation 18:2

  1. The scapegoat, sent out each year on the Day of Atonement (Yom Kippur), symbolically carried the sins of the people into the wilderness.

  2. The desert is a place of wild animals, including goats. This term is connected with demons (goat idols) in Leviticus 17:7 and 2 Chronicles 11:15. Isaiah 13:19–22 predicts the fall of the city of Babylon, which would become the dwelling place of wild animals, including goats. Revelation 18:2 indicates that desolate Babylon is the home of demons and evil spirits. The Israelites viewed the desert as the place of temptation and the dwelling place of evil spirits.

  3. Discuss:

    a. Where is the "wilderness" for you? That is, where do you tend to come into contact with temptation in a significant way? (Note that one can never escape the presence of Satan completely; however, as in Jesus' case, the enemy often has greater influence in certain places than others in our lives.)

    b. Should we avoid such places? Is there a time to confront evil situations directly? How does one decide when to avoid the presence of evil and when to confront it?

- Matthew 4:1–11; Mark 1:12–13; Luke 4:1–13

  1. Jesus was tempted in the wilderness.

  2. He faced the devil himself.

  3. He resisted the devil by completely submitting Himself to the Word of God. Note that with each response, Jesus quoted passages that were written during the time the Israelites were in the wilderness.

  4. Discuss:

    a. How can we learn from Jesus' example about how to resist temptation?

    b. Does a follower of Jesus ever face the devil alone? Explain your answer.

    c. How is every temptation, in a sense, the devil's attempt to lure us to follow our own ideas rather than trust the words of God?

B. Conclusion

The wilderness temptation of Jesus is a foundational event in His life on earth.

- It is the beginning of His new creation: the church.
- It is on behalf of those who follow Him.
- It confronts the power of the devil directly, providing an encouraging example (Hebrews 2:18; 1 Corinthians 10:13).
- It establishes the method of resisting temptation: knowing and trusting God's Word.

Step Two:
"Qumran and the Essene Community"

1. Lecture: The Dead Sea Scrolls

The Dead Sea Scrolls are among the most significant archaeological finds of modern times. Discovered accidentally by a shepherd boy searching for a stray goat, these ancient documents have profoundly affected our understanding of biblical texts and provided striking insight into the cultural setting of Jesus' life, the early church, and the history of Judaism.

The recent discovery of these writings has not only affirmed our faith in the accuracy of the Scriptures, but it has also provided fresh insight into our understanding and application of the Bible's message. God sent His Son after centuries of preparation. He established His people Israel, the line of David, the Temple system, and the Promised Land—providing the theological context for the life and work of Jesus.

Clearly, part of God's preparation for the birth of the Messiah included the presence of a community of people whose beliefs would be similar to many of the teachings and practices of Jesus and the early church. Thus, Jesus' message would fall on fertile soil prepared over more than a century by people waiting expectantly for the Messiah to appear. The Greek empire ensured that there was a universal language in which the message of redemption could be communicated to the whole world. Roman peace and a system of roads offered optimum conditions for the spread of the gospel. This same God apparently prepared by establishing a community of people whose beliefs would enhance the popular acceptance of Jesus' message and provide vivid insights into its truth nearly 2,000 years later.

The writings known as the Dead Sea Scrolls were found in the Judea Wilderness near the ruins of a settlement known as Qumran and appear to echo the beliefs of a group known as the Essenes. However, it is important to note that significant scholarly debate continues as to whether the scrolls were written or used at Qumran, whether they were the product of the Essenes, and whether the Essenes actually lived at Qumran. The best evidence to date indicates the Dead Sea Scrolls are the product of the Essenes and were written or collected at the Qumran settlement. This writer considers this to be the best understanding presently, and the following studies are based on that perspective. The actual contents of the scrolls, and the similarity of the writers' beliefs and practices to early Christianity, are subject to significantly less debate.

2. Review the Overhead Transparency "New Testament Chronology"

Using the overhead transparency titled "New Testament Chronology," highlight the following dates for your students:

586 B.C.	Babylonian Captivity of Judah
538 B.C.	Return to Israel
332 B.C.	Alexander the Great conquers Palestine
330–198 B.C.	Rule of Hellenistic Ptolemies over Jews
198–167 B.C.	Oppression under Hellenistic Seleucids
167 B.C.	Maccabee revolt

167–63 B.C.	Hasmonaean kingdom
37 B.C.	Herod's reign begins
4 B.C.	Herod's death
c.a. 6 B.C.	Jesus' birth
c.a. A.D. 30	Jesus is crucified
A.D. 70	Roman destruction of Jerusalem during First Jewish Revolt

3. Guided Discussion: The Settlement of Qumran

The remains of the settlement at Qumran have been extensively excavated by archaeologists over the last 50 years. The finds provide significant information for understanding the people who lived and worked there. Using the overhead transparency titled "Qumran," point out the following to your students:

(**HINT:** *The Qumran transparency is also found in the optional full-color overhead-transparency packet. Additional information provided in this Guided Discussion requires this packet as well.*)

Archaeological Data:

- The earliest settlement on this site dates to the Israelite period shortly before the Babylonian Captivity (c.a. 600 B.C.). It was probably destroyed at that time.

- It was resettled during the time of the Hasmonaean king Hyrcanus around 140 B.C. During that time, it developed into the form shown in the transparency.

- This settlement was severely damaged by an earthquake believed to have occurred in 31 B.C. and was deserted for some time.

- Qumran was resettled around the time of Jesus' birth (c.a. 6 B.C.) and was an active community until approximately A.D. 68, when it was destroyed by the Roman army under the command of Vespasian.

Important Structures:

1. Aqueduct and Reservoir System. Water was important to the Essenes partly because their community was located in the wilderness and partly due to the significance of living water and a type of immersion (baptism) in their theology. Their water was runoff from rainfall in the Judea Wilderness to the west. The water ran through an elaborate system of tunnels and aqueducts till it reached the foot of the cliff, where it followed an aqueduct along the plateau and entered the community as shown here. The water was stored in a series of reservoirs. The entire system was coated with plaster. At least two installations were probably used for ritual bathing. New members were cleansed with water in a type of baptism. Unlike Christian baptism, this bathing occurred regularly.

    The Essenes believed that water used as a symbol of purification must be "living" or moving water, so they prepared a system in which rainwater ran on its own to the ritual bath. It could not be drawn by hand. This meant the Essenes had to trap rainwater, dig tunnels through solid rock, and prepare a system of channels along the cliffs so the water could run into the reservoirs and baths in the community. This commitment to doing what they believed God wanted is exemplary. One wonders if today's followers of Jesus would expend similar effort to do what He has required of us. (It may be that John the Baptist used the Jordan River because it was "living" water.)

2. Defense Tower. Since this was essentially a religious community, scholars debate the importance of such a large tower. It probably functioned as protection against bandits or other less "military" threats. Though the Essenes are described as separatists who lived a peaceful, almost monastic existence, they believed in the imminent arrival of the Messiah and that a great battle

would ensue between the sons of light (the Essenes) and the sons of darkness (followers of evil). This image of light and darkness is a common theme in the New Testament, written almost a century later (John 3:16–21, 12:35).

3. Scriptorium. Archaeologists believe that this room is where the Dead Sea Scrolls were written. The ruins revealed tables and benches similar to those used by scribes, as well as inkpots and basins in which the Essenes could ritualistically wash their hands before and after writing God's sacred name. Among the scrolls, scholars have identified all the books of the Old Testament except Esther (some say Nehemiah as well).

4. Main Assembly Hall and Refectory. The Essenes practiced a communal meal in anticipation of the great banquet of the messianic age. Archaeologists believe this room was the location of that ceremonial meal. In one corner, a small water channel entered where the floor sloped slightly down toward the opposite end of the room. This may have allowed the room to be washed in preparation for the sacred meal. Nearby was a kitchen with five fireplaces. Adjacent was a smaller room that contained the remains of more than 1,000 pottery jars, dishes, plates, and cups. Scholars have found many similarities between the Essenes' ceremonial meal and the Last Supper recorded in the Gospels (Matthew 26:26–29).

   It should be noted that the members of the community did not live in the buildings archaeologists have uncovered. They probably lived in caves nearby or pitched tents around the settlement. The buildings were for their communal meals and religious studies.

5. Potters' Workshop. In this area, archaeologists have found a basin for preparing clay, a base for a potter's wheel, and two kilns. It is likely that the clay jars in which the Dead Sea Scrolls were hidden were made here. These jars helped preserve the scrolls for nearly 2,000 years.

6. Possible *Mikveh* (Ritual Bath; pl. *Mikvoth*). It is clear from their writings that the Essenes practiced ritual cleansing. The presence of *mikvoth* from other places (e.g., the Temple Mount, Masada) have led some scholars to identify some of the water installations (especially those with steps the entire width of the pool) as ritual baths. It is likely that this practice of the Jewish people provides the background for the baptism practiced by John as well as Christian baptism.

7. Cemetery. To the east of the community was the main cemetery, containing more than 1,000 grave sites. The graves were carefully arranged in typical Essene fashion: in orderly rows, with each grave marked by a small mound of stones. Individuals were buried with their heads facing south. While ancient writers, including Josephus, indicate that there were no women among the Essenes, several graves contained the bodies of women. Scholars have suggested that these were family members of the Qumran community.

Optional: More About the Aqueduct and Reservoir System

Overhead Transparency 29. The Essene Water Tunnel. The Essenes created catch basins just west of their community where the runoff from rain in the Judea Wilderness cascaded over the cliff. They dug more than 100 feet of tunnel through solid rock to bring the water to the foot of the cliff; from there it ran in plastered channels more than 1,000 feet to the settlement on the plateau below. The effort to dig through this solid rock is an indication of the level of commitment of the Essenes.

Overhead Transparency 30. An Essene Cistern. In the Qumran community, the Essenes created several cisterns that, as shown here, were plastered and had steps to allow them access to the water. At least two of these cisterns are believed to be *mikvoth*, ceremonial or ritual baths used for actual cleansing. Impurity resulted from a variety of conditions, some of which are listed in Numbers 5:1–4 (e.g., touching a dead body, having a skin disease or issue of body fluid). More important, these baths indicated the spiritual cleansing that resulted from repentance and forgiveness (Matthew 3:6,11).

The Essenes apparently believed that any breaking of God's law required cleansing, which the *mikvoth* symbolized. While there are several Jewish practices that provide a foundation for baptism, the Essene *mikveh* practice certainly contributed to our understanding of the meaning of the ritual cleansing.

Optional: More About the Caves of Qumran

Overhead Transparency 31. The Caves of Qumran. At least 11 caves containing scroll material have been found in the area of Qumran. The caves shown here are the closest to the community and are labeled Caves 4 and 5, in the order they were found. These caves probably contained the "library" of the community. The scrolls found here were not stored in jars, indicating a possible hasty exit by the Qumran community; they were also fragmented, possibly from the caves being plundered through the centuries. Scholars believe the fragments represent several hundred manuscripts. The extremely dry climate of the region helped preserve the documents until they were found nearly 50 years ago.

Optional: More About the Main Assembly Hall

Overhead Transparency 32. Qumran: The Main Assembly Hall. With the Dead Sea to the east of Qumran in the background, we can see the size of the assembly hall. On the right is the kitchen where the food was prepared. The size of the room and its prominence highlight the importance of this sacred meal to the community.

OPTIONAL — Digging Deeper II: The Dead Sea Scrolls
(10–20 minutes)

Have your students review the handout titled "The Dead Sea Scrolls." Divide the class into small groups to discuss the following questions; then have each group report their findings to the full class.

1. What circumstances surrounding the discovery of the Dead Sea Scrolls might indicate God's involvement in this remarkable event?

2. What is contained in the scrolls? What would you consider the most significant to you personally? Why?

3. Which Old Testament books were most important to the Qumran community? What does this tell you about that community? Which books of the Old Testament are the most significant in your life? Why? What conclusions can you draw about your own religious faith based on which books are most significant for you?

4. How does the fact that God so carefully protected His Word affirm your faith?

5. Spend a few moments in group prayer, thanking God for His Word and for His careful protection of the Scriptures over the centuries.

4. Guided Discussion: The Essenes

Have your students read the handout titled "The Sons of Light."

a. *Lecture*

Christians have often assumed that the Judaism Jesus interacted with was of one opinion. In fact, the Jewish community of that time held a wide variety of differing practices and beliefs. A helpful analogy to the religion of Jesus' day might be the variety of denominations and churches in present-day Christianity. One group, not mentioned by name in the New Testament, was the Essenes. Described in several ancient sources, this group probably numbered more than 4,000, lived a strict—almost ascetic—existence, held strong opposition to the Temple authorities in Jerusalem, and had many significant similarities to John the Baptist, Jesus, and the early Christian church. It is important to remember that most of their writings and practices predate Jesus by many years—sometimes by more than a century.

b. *Comparison*

Using the overhead transparency titled "Religious Movements of Jesus' Time," briefly compare the Essenes, Sadducees, and Pharisees.

c. *Personal Application*

Divide students into small groups to discuss the following:

1. What caused the Essene movement to begin? What is Hellenism? Think of at least three modern-day cultural values or practices that are similar to these movements.

2. How did the Essenes resist the pagan ideas and practices of their day? Is that the right approach for a Christian today? Why or why not? If not, what should be our approach to pagan beliefs or practices in our culture? Think of an example in which Jesus took a different approach to unbelief or pagan people than separating from them.

3. Read John 12:35–36, 3:16–21. The Essenes believed there is a great struggle in our world between the sons of light (God's followers) and the sons of darkness (Satan's followers). Do you believe a similar struggle exists? Where do you see the struggle in your experience? How have you been a son or daughter of light?

4. Read Acts 2:44–45. The Essenes shared their possessions with members of the group. How were the early Christians similar? Why do you think the Essenes shared their property? (No one really knows.) Why did the early Christians have possessions in common? What does the passage in Acts teach you for your life today? Is it possible that the model of the Essenes influenced the early believers?

5. Read Matthew 26:26–29. The Essenes celebrated a regular meal that was to prefigure a great banquet to occur when the Messiah arrived. What are the similarities to your celebration of the Lord's Supper (Communion or Eucharist)?

6. Read Acts 2:14–21. The Essenes interpreted the Scriptures differently from the other religious movements of that time. They interpreted the Old Testament as being fulfilled in the events of their day. Is Peter's method similar? Why would his method of Bible interpretation have been familiar to that of his audience? Should we use this method today (i.e., see Bible passages fulfilled by specific people or events of our time)? Why or why not?

7. Read Luke 1:32–33. The Essenes referred to the expected Messiah as the Son of God and the Son of the Most High whose kingdom is eternal. Does it surprise you that the terms for Messiah were used by the Essenes years before Jesus was born? How would the Essenes' use of these titles help prepare the way for Jesus?

8. There are some key differences between the Essenes and the early Christians. These include:

Essenes	*New Testament Teaching*
Strict Sabbath observance	Matthew 12:1–13
Living separately from the world	Matthew 28:19–20
Two Messiahs, a priest and a king	Hebrews 7:15–17, 8:1–2; Luke 1:32

Note that both the New Testament and the Essenes trace the priesthood of the Messiah to Melchizedek and not Aaron.

9. How did God use the Essenes as part of the preparation for Jesus? What does this tell you about God? What does this teach about the importance of seeing Jesus in the Jewish context in which God placed Him in first-century Palestine?

OPTIONAL — Digging Deeper III: Was John the Baptist an Essene?
(20–50 minutes)

Is it possible that John the Baptist was an Essene? Did he live at Qumran? Did he see the Dead Sea Scrolls? Write any of them? These questions have gripped scholars as the remarkable similarities between John's teaching and practices and those of the Essene culture have been revealed by the scrolls.

On a blank overhead transparency or a sheet of newsprint, note the following comparisons for your class:

John	*Essenes*
1. Family of priests (Luke 1:5)	1. Many were priests who disagreed with the Temple authorities
2. Lived in the wilderness (Luke 1:80)	2. Settlement of Qumran was in the Judea Wilderness
3. Mission was to "prepare the way for the LORD" (Isaiah 40:1–5)	3. Lived in the wilderness to prepare the way for the Lord
4. Baptized as a sign of repentance and inner cleansing (Mark 1:4)	4. Practiced ritual cleansing as a sign of the cleansing of the soul
5. Proclaimed that the one to come would baptize with fire (Mark 1:7–8)	5. God would pour out His Spirit like water to cleanse perverse hearts
6. Was not accepted (Matthew 21:32)	6. Complained that they were not heeded
7. Did not participate in the normal lifestyle of his people (Mark 1:6)	7. Lived an ascetic existence, preparing their own food
8. His disciples fasted and recited prayers (Mark 2:18; Luke 11:1)	8. Fasted and had specific prayers
9. Had conflict with the Jerusalem authorities (Matthew 3:9)	9. Looked to create a new Temple and religious practices

Although it is possible that John was an Essene, the most that can be said conclusively is that his message and practice were familiar to his audience. It is amazing that God prepared a theological context in such a way that John's mission to prepare for the Messiah was one that his audience recognized. However, there are several factors that make it impossible to definitively place John at Qumran. He is never called an Essene, he was not a member of a community, and he proclaimed his message in a public way and did not remain sheltered in a monastic setting.

OPTIONAL — Digging Deeper IV: God's Preparation *(15–35 minutes)*

So far we have focused on the theology of the Jewish culture as God's preparation for Jesus' coming. But there are other significant events, movements, and people that God arranged to make the time of Jesus' birth perfect for the beginning of the church.

Ask four students to look up and read each passage below. Then note the comments that accompany each scripture to illustrate some of the other preparations God made for His Son.

Galatians 4:4–5	God prepared the time *fully.*
Acts 6:1, 9:20–21	Because of the conquests of Alexander the Great, 350 years before Christ the known world was conversant in one language, a significant help for the early spread of the gospel.
Luke 2:1	The Roman Empire now controlled the world. Its contributions to God's preparation included:

World peace. This made the spread of the gospel across nations possible.

Roads. The Romans built roads everywhere for their legions and for trade. The missionaries traveled these roads.

Execution practice. The Bible predicted that Jesus would be pierced at His execution (Psalm 22:16–17). Crucifixion, the method the Romans used, fulfilled this.

There are other subjects we will study in the future that enhanced Jesus' ministry by helping His audience understand His teaching within the context of their culture. We could include the Pharisees, the Sadducees, marriage customs, the teaching style of the rabbis, and so many more. Understanding them makes Jesus' life and ministry clearer and more relevant—for the people of His day as well as for us. Take a few moments to discuss the following:

1. What does God's careful planning tell you about His character?

2. Have you ever experienced His careful planning in your life? Relate an example to the group if you can think of one.

3. How might God's planning for Jesus' coming, and His careful planning in the lives of people today, be an encouragement to you?

Conclusion

It is important to understand the Essenes, Qumran, and the Dead Sea Scrolls as part of God's plan for the coming of the Messiah. God apparently planned so carefully and so far ahead that the Essenes were in place at the right time. Understanding their culture makes the message of Jesus Christ clearer and more relevant to modern-day Christians.

Understanding God's plan also underscores the fact that His planning continues in our lives today. Though we may not always recognize or understand His plan, He is always in the process of using our circumstances, our accomplishments, and even our failures to accomplish His will in us. Knowing this truth helps give us courage to face the tough times and the desire to be part of His purpose.

NOT ON BREAD ALONE

Handout #1

Israel is mostly rugged desert. The variety of Hebrew words for *desert* or *wilderness* indicates the significant role the landscape played in biblical history and imagery. For the Hebrews, the desert was far more formative than the sea, probably because of their desert roots (which caused them to fear the ocean) and because there were few seaports along the Mediterranean coast.

Most of the year, the desert is an uncultivated area receiving just enough rainfall during the winter months to sustain the nomadic shepherds who live there. The deserts of the Bible are more rock than sand and are often quite mountainous. The two most significant wilderness areas in Israel are the Judea Wilderness in the east and the Negev in the south.

THE JUDEA WILDERNESS

The Judea Mountains form the middle section of the central mountain range of Israel. On the eastern side of this ridge, descending into the Great Rift Valley more than 1,300 feet below sea level, is the solitary, rocky wasteland of Judah. Because of the change in altitude, little rain falls here. The land is split by deep wadis formed by centuries of rain runoff in the mountains, and even shepherds find it difficult to live here. This wilderness borders the fertile mountain ridge for more than 50 miles, so the line between farmland and wilderness is a clear one. Throughout biblical times, shepherds lived on the fringes of the desert, and farmers worked the soil of the mountains. Villages like Bethlehem were able to sustain both shepherds (David) and farmers (Boaz and Ruth).

THE NEGEV

The Negev lies south of the Hebron Mountains, which form the southern section of Israel's central mountain range. This arid land (*Negev* means "dry") has few natural water sources and receives less than eight inches of rainfall in the north and less than half that amount in the south. Except for a few settlements that employ advanced methods to catch rain runoff, the Negev is nonarable, hospitable only to nomads.

The northern region of the Negev, from the Hebron Mountains to the Zin Wilderness, is good sheep country. Its rolling hills surround large, broad valleys—such as the Valley of Beersheba, where Abraham settled.

The central region of the Negev is rugged, with deep canyons in the Zin Wilderness. The climate and terrain are inhospitable, even to nomads, for most of the year. At least one scholar has suggested that the "valley of the shadow of death" (Psalm 23) may refer to the canyons of the central Negev.

The southern portion of the Negev is called the Wilderness of Paran in the Bible and is the most barren area of all.

WANDERING IN THE WILDERNESS

It was in the Negev and the Sinai Wilderness to the south and west that the children of Israel wandered after God miraculously delivered them from Egypt. They received the Torah on Mount Sinai and built the tabernacle at the base of the mountain. When they reached the northern edge of the Negev, the Israelites sent spies into Canaan to discover the nature of their new home. Upon hearing the spies' reports of giants and huge fortified cities, the Israelites grew afraid and refused to enter the Promised Land. Because they were disobedient and lacked faith, God commanded His people to remain in the wilderness, where they wandered for 40 years, a year for each day the spies had been gone. The Bible records the place as "the vast and dreadful desert" (Deuteronomy 8:15).

In the wilderness, God taught His people faith and trust, preparing them to live obediently in the Promised Land *so that the world might know that He was God.* He sent them water from rock, manna from heaven, and quail from the sea. Their feet did not swell (a remarkable blessing to anyone who has hiked in the Negev) and their clothes did not wear out (Deuteronomy 8:4).

In the wilderness, God disciplined His people for their lack of faith, their disobedience, and their complaining. Moses recorded that God humbled them so they would learn to depend on Him for everything, because "man does not live on bread alone but on every word that comes from the mouth of the LORD" (Deuteronomy 8:3–5).

LESSONS OF THE WILDERNESS

The Jewish people's 40-year journey in the wilderness made a significant impact on them. The psalmist reminded the Hebrews of God's faithful love in the wilderness (Psalms 105:38–45 and 107:4–9) and warned them against repeating their earlier sins (Psalms 81:11–16 and 78:14–40). The prophets recalled to the people's minds the lessons learned there (Jeremiah 2:6 and 7:22–25; Micah 6:3–5), and the writers of the New Testament compared the experience to the lives of believers (Hebrews 3:16–19; 1 Corinthians 10:1–13). In Judea, when Jesus, as the new "Adam," faced the tempter on our behalf, He used the lessons of the wilderness to defeat him: "Man does not live on bread alone" (Matthew 4:4; see also Deuteronomy 8:3) and "Do not put the LORD your God to the test" (Matthew 4:7; see also Deuteronomy 6:16).

WILDERNESS AS REFUGE

Because the wilderness was so close to settled areas, it became a refuge for those who sought solitude or safety from authorities. Here David hid from Saul's anger (1 Samuel 26), John the Baptist isolated himself from the religious practices of the day (Matthew 3), and Jesus faced the devil (Matthew 4). Here the Essenes labored over their scrolls and early Christians built monasteries, some of which still function today.

The wilderness was also associated with the coming of the Messiah. Isaiah 40:3–4 says, "In the desert prepare the way for the LORD; make straight in the wilderness a highway for our God. Every valley shall be raised up, every mountain and hill made low." When Jesus entered Jerusalem on Palm Sunday, He came from the wilderness, which might have added to the crowd's fervor.

CONCLUSION

The wilderness image is a rich one in the Bible. It refers to our lives here on earth as we prepare for our "promised land" in heaven. It portrays those difficult times in our lives when we learn to trust the faithful provision of our God. The wilderness also offers a picture of God's disciplining us for our sinful lives. And it reminds us of the Messiah's eventual return.

In the wilderness, we learn that we cannot live on bread alone.

THE DEAD SEA SCROLLS

A "CHANCE" DISCOVERY

It was 1947. The day was like so many others for the three shepherds of the Bedouin family who had settled near the northern end of the Dead Sea. They watched their goats graze at the foot of barren cliffs near an old ruin thought by many to be a Roman fort. Some of the goats climbed along the cliff face, looking for the small tufts of grass that grow among the rocks.

One of the shepherds climbed after the animals that were getting too far away from the flock. A small opening caught his eye. It was barely large enough for a man to squeeze through, but it was definitely the opening to a cave. He threw a stone into the opening and heard the sound of pottery breaking inside. After an excited discussion of possible treasure, the shepherds decided to return as soon as they could, as it was getting late and the goats had to be taken back home.

When Mohammed edh Dhib returned, he was able to squeeze into the opening. The floor of the cave was covered with broken pottery. Ten jars were still intact, some with their bowl-shaped lids still in place. All but two jars were empty. These two contained a large scroll and two smaller ones. Mohammed showed these to the others. Disappointed in their "treasure," the shepherds had no way of knowing the incredible discovery they had just made.

Scholars determined that the three scrolls were the book of Isaiah, the Manual of Discipline (describing Qumran community rules), and a commentary on the book of Habakkuk. The Dead Sea Scrolls have been called the greatest archaeological discovery of modern times. Though discovered accidentally, they have dramatically enhanced our understanding of the world of the New Testament, the teachings of John the Baptist and our Lord Jesus, and the early church. They have also provided remarkable confirmation of the truth of the Bible. It all causes us to wonder whether their discovery was truly by chance or whether the same God who had inspired some of the books contained in the scrolls also preserved them for the future of the people who carry His name.

THE WORLD LEARNS OF THE SCROLLS

Mohammed left the scrolls hanging in a bag from his tent pole for several months. Eventually, he found a buyer, an antiquities dealer in Bethlehem named Kando. The dealer found the cave and located additional scrolls. He brought the three original scrolls to Jerusalem's Syrian Orthodox Monastery of St. Mark's, hoping to discover their worth, and sold them to a metropolitan dealer named Samuel for less than $100.

As church officials began to consult scholars to determine the nature of the ancient Hebrew texts, word of the discovery began to spread. Professor E. L. Sukenik of the Hebrew University purchased the additional scrolls held by Kando, recognizing their antiquity and their immense value for understanding the period during which they were written. Sukenik was unable to purchase the others from Samuel, who by then had brought them to the United States.

On June 1, 1954, Samuel placed an ad in the *Wall Street Journal* to sell the scrolls. Dr. Sukenik's son, Yigael Yadin, happened to be in the United States at the time. He saw the ad and, through a middleman, purchased the original find for $250,000 and presented them to the State of Israel. The scrolls are then in the Israel Museum in Jerusalem.

MORE DISCOVERIES MADE

The Bedouin from Mohammed edh Dhib's tribe soon located more caves near Qumran containing additional scrolls. In one cave (called Cave 4), they found thousands of scroll fragments. Soon an official archaeological investigation was launched in the original cave as well as in the additional caves and nearby ruins that had been discovered. The archaeologists found evidence convincing them that there was a definite relationship between the ruins and the scrolls found in the caves. Especially convincing was the discovery of pottery within the ruins similar to the jars found in the caves themselves.

THE SCROLLS

The most common material of the scrolls was parchment, which is made from animal skins. Several sheets were sewn together to make a scroll. Since parchment is much more durable than papyrus (made from the leaves of the papyrus reed), these scrolls are in much better condition than the few surviving papyrus fragments.

Most of the discovered scrolls were small fragments that had to be carefully pieced together. In many cases, only a few fragments exist from an entire scroll. For this reason, the process of deciphering the scrolls has been painstakingly slow, resulting in most of the scrolls being unavailable to the public until just a few years ago, more than 40 years after their discovery by the Bedouin shepherds.

The scrolls contain three main types of literature: (1) copies of all the Old Testament books except Esther; (2) Jewish writings known also from other sources such as the apocryphal book of Jubilees; and (3) specific writings from the community such as commentaries interpreting the Old Testament, liturgical writings such as hymns, and specific rules for community conduct. More than 600 separate scrolls are represented, though most are mainly fragments.

The most well known include: (1) the Isaiah Scroll, which is nearly intact; (2) the Copper Scroll, which describes 64 locations where the treasures of the Temple were hidden (scholars are divided as to whether the scroll literally describes the hiding places of the Temple valuables—none of which have been found—or whether the scroll is a figurative account with another meaning); (3) the Habakkuk Commentary, in which the prophesies of God's judgment are applied to the Romans and those who resisted the Essenes' beliefs; and (4) the Manual of Discipline, an important description of the rules of the Essene community.

The Psalms represent the largest number of scrolls (36), with the next two being Deuteronomy (29) and Isaiah (21). Exodus has 17 scrolls, Genesis 15, Leviticus 13, and the book of Numbers eight. These counts probably indicate which writings were the most important to the community and had the widest usage. The fact that nearly all the writings are religious, and that the legal books and the Psalms are the most common, affirms the strong commitment of the community to following God's path.

SCROLLS IMPORTANT FOR CHRISTIANS TODAY

The Dead Sea Scrolls represent the most spectacular discovery of modern times, and the impact of these writings on the Jewish and Christian communities continues to be significant. At least two aspects of the scrolls provide great value for today's believers.

First, they offer a window into the theological and cultural setting of the life of Jesus and the early church. While the perspective contained in the writings belongs to one, small community, there are remarkable similarities to (and some significant differences from) the teachings of Jesus, Paul, and the early Christians. Understanding the theological context of the life of Jesus and the early church helps us to understand the meaning of their teachings and affirms the careful planning God used to make sure that the context of the New Testament was perfect for the ministry of Jesus to occur and the gospel to spread. God put the Romans in place (providing peaceful conditions and a system of roads) and caused the Greek empire of Alexander the Great to make that language universal (providing optimum conditions for the spread of the gospel). Most significant, God shaped the theological context so that the teaching of Jesus would be understood both by its similarity with existing belief and by its uniqueness. It is in this context that the scrolls provide great enlightenment. The scrolls include a significant number of terms common to the New Testament. Examples include "the many" to describe the group; "the works of the law" (translated "observing the law" in Romans 3:20,28; Galatians 3:2,5,10); "sons of light" (John 12:36); "light and darkness" (Matthew 6:22–23; John 1:5, 3:19); "Belial" to describe the evil one (2 Corinthians 6:14–15); "poor in spirit" (Matthew 5:3); Melchizedek, an important figure for the Qumran community (Hebrews 7:1–3); and possibly the most remarkable: "Son of the Most High" and "Son of God" (Luke 1:35, referring to Jesus, while the person referred to in the scrolls is yet unknown).

The scrolls describe practices similar to those of early Christianity, including common property (Acts 2:44–45); a sacred meal prefiguring a great messianic banquet (Matthew 26:26–29); a ceremonial cleansing (baptism?) (John 3:23); and a commitment to be in the wilderness to "prepare the way for the LORD" (Isaiah 40:3; Luke 3:3–6). There are common eschatological views between the New Testament and Qumran, including a belief that they were living in the last days (Acts 2:17; Hebrews 1:2); a view of Messiah who would be both king and priest (the Essenes apparently believed in two Messiahs, while the New Testament sees Jesus as king and priest in Hebrews 7:14–17 and Luke 1:32); and a view that the world is engaged in a great ethical struggle between the followers of light and darkness (2 Corinthians 6:14–18). The scroll writers used an interpretation method similar to the New Testament by interpreting Old Testament passages as fulfilled specifically in their present situation and no other (Acts 2:14–21). All of these similarities affirm God's careful plan to have a language and practice present in the world of Jesus so His audience could perceive His message.

The second great contribution of the scrolls is their affirmation of the reliability of the Bible. Until the Dead Sea discoveries, the oldest copies of the Hebrew Bible dated to approximately A.D. 1000. Were there errors? Had mistakes crept in over centuries of copying by hand? Had God's Word stood the test of time? The Dead Sea Scrolls take us back beyond 100 B.C., more than 1,000 years before the existing manuscripts. Scholars were amazed to find little difference—most involved spelling changes. The Bible has not changed since the time of Jesus. While a follower of God trusts the truth of His words by faith, without evidence, the scrolls affirm that our faith in the Bible is fully supported by scholarly evidence. Truly, "All scripture is God-breathed and is useful for teaching, rebuking, correcting and training in righteousness" (2 Timothy 3:16). And certainly Jesus was born ". . . when the time had *fully* come" (Galatians 4:4, emphasis added).

THE SONS OF LIGHT

In Jesus' time, there were four major religious groups (or "philosophies," as Josephus, the Jewish historian of the time, called them). They were the Zealots, the Sadducees, the Pharisees, and the Essenes. It is impossible to place every person in one group or another, and each group probably contained a number of subgroups. While each group provided a key part of the framework within which God placed the ministry of Jesus, in Lesson Thirteen we are focusing on one group, the Essenes.

ESSENE ORIGIN

The Essenes were a fascinating part of Jesus' world. The New Testament never mentions them, but its pages contain remarkable similarities with the movement that Josephus believed to be as important as the Pharisees. In 332 B.C., Alexander the Great's armies swept through Palestine. His successors continued his campaign to bring Greek culture to every part of the known world. The Hellenistic worldview glorified the human being through culture, philosophy, athletics, and religion. The devout Jews of Palestine were deeply troubled by its subversion of their biblical worldview. To the nonreligious, this philosophy was seductive, and soon most of the Jewish people were deeply involved in secular Hellenism.

Initially, Alexander's successors, the Ptolemy family from Egypt, controlled Palestine, allowing the Jewish people significant religious freedom. During this time, the Old Testament was translated into Greek, a version known as the Septuagint. Later, the Seleucids, the Greek dynasty in Syria, brought Palestine into their empire. Ambitious empire builders, the Hellenistic Syrians brought a more aggressive approach to the spread of Greek culture, defiling the Temple in Jerusalem with pig's blood and dedicating it to the Greek god Zeus. The Torah was banned, as were observing the Sabbath and circumcision. To violate these bans meant death.

Faithful Jews, led by the Hasmonaean family (known to history as the Maccabees) revolted. By God's blessing, Judah Maccabee and his brothers were victorious and drove out the pagans, reestablishing Jewish independence for the first time in nearly 500 years. The Temple was cleansed and rededicated, and the worship of Yahweh resumed. The Maccabees' great victory became the focus of the Feast of Dedication, known today as Hanukkah (John 10:22).

But soon the descendants of the Jewish heroes, known as the Hasmonaeans, became as Hellenistic as the Greeks had been. They openly flaunted the despised pagan practices and fought bitterly with those who followed the Torah. When Jonathan the Hasmonaean took the office of high priest, it was the final straw. Not only was Jonathan Hellenistic in his lifestyle, he also was not of the line of Zadok, Solomon's high priest, a requirement supported by the religious community.

The Hasidim, a pious group of Jewish believers, had been the main supporters of the Maccabee revolt. They now became the major opponents of the descendants of Judah and his family. Out of the Hasidim (a word meaning "pious ones") came two movements: the Pharisees and the Essenes. Scholars believe that the appointment of Jonathan as high priest was the moment when the Essenes decided the Temple was now defiled and the true worship of God had ended. They declared the religious establishment invalid and established a religious movement dedicated to the restoration of the true worship of God.

While there were apparently Essene communities scattered throughout Galilee and Judea and in Jerusalem itself, the majority of this separatist movement lived in the community of Qumran, near the Dead Sea. Here, in obedience to the prophet Isaiah, they went to the desert to "prepare the way for the LORD" (Isaiah 40:1–5). Though small in number (ancient sources indicate 4,000), they exerted significant influence on the religious community of their day. Their influence continues on our own world through their writings, the Dead Sea Scrolls.

GOD'S ARMY

The Essenes took their devotion to God seriously. Living in the barren Judea Wilderness, they were ascetic, probably celibate, and dedicated to waiting for the imminent "day of the Lord." They believed themselves to be the sons of light preparing for a great battle with the sons of darkness (John 12:35–36). The sons of light would be victorious, and the sons of darkness, ensnared by the power of evil, would be destroyed.

The mission of the faithful community of Essenes was to prepare the way (Matthew 3:3). They felt they must be ready to take their place in God's army by keeping their hearts and minds pure and their practices obedient. Their lifestyle reflected this commitment. The Essene community was carefully organized. They lived in small, self-sufficient communities having all property in common (Acts 2:44–45). They practiced ritual washing, similar to the baptism practices of John, to purify themselves of any sin that might disqualify them from being part of God's work. They wore white as a symbol of their purity. They grew their own food and were forbidden to eat food prepared by others. They spent significant time in study and in careful copying of their sacred texts. It is these scrolls, probably hidden when the Romans destroyed Jerusalem in the First Jewish Revolt, that are known as the Dead Sea Scrolls.

The Essenes were stricter than the Pharisees in observing the Sabbath. They ate a sacred meal as an anticipation of the victory banquet of the Messiah, who would soon arrive (Matthew 26:26–29). They practiced obedience to God and justice to people. Their lives were guided by a principle taken from the Old Testament prophet Habakkuk: "The righteous (just) shall live by his faith" (Habakkuk 2:4). Those who failed were cut off from the community (2 John 9–10).

The Essenes were committed to opposing the corrupt and wicked religious establishment of the Temple in Jerusalem (Matthew 21:12–13);

resisting the interpretations the Pharisees had elevated above the Torah (Matthew 15:1–3); and avoiding marriage because the coming battle would create hardship on raising a family (Matthew 19:11–12). Josephus described them as those who love God and who love their fellow man (Mark 12:30–31).

The end came for the Essenes when the Romans destroyed Qumran in approximately A.D. 68. It is likely the Essenes joined in the revolt, thinking it to be the final cosmic battle. This is probably when they placed their sacred scrolls in jars and hid them in caves nearby, to become a gift from God to our generation. Some Essenes apparently escaped to Masada and died there after burying their scrolls near the synagogue. Though this community disappeared from history, its legacy is only now being realized.

THE ESSENES AND THE CHRISTIAN FAITH

A few scholars have suggested that the Essene community included the early Christians. This claim is not supported by evidence to date. It is probable that some of them became Christians in the early years, since many of the Essenes were priests and were concerned about the existing Temple authorities. One scholar has suggested they may be the converts referred to in Acts 6:7. Many scholars have noted the similarity between Essene theology and practices and those of John the Baptist. It is possible he had contact with, or was a member of, the Essene community (he too came from a priestly family but apparently left the priestly practice). None of these possibilities can be clearly demonstrated. What is clear is the similarity of many Essene beliefs and practices to those of the New Testament. Clearly, God provided a context in which the message of Jesus would be understood (even by those who rejected it). It is amazing to see God's careful planning for the arrival of His Son.

Jesus was the Messiah the Essenes longed for. Did they recognize Him? That we cannot yet answer. Can they help us recognize Him and understand His message better? That answer is a resounding yes! Praise God for preparing for Jesus by creating the Essenes!

NO GREATER LOVE

For the Teacher

The next several lessons investigate the teaching ministry of Jesus in the context in which He lived and worked. This lesson is based in Chorazin, where we will see Jesus in the setting of religious Jews. Lesson Fifteen, set in Gamla, shows us how the Zealots and Pharisees heard and interpreted what Jesus had to say. In Lesson Sixteen, we will watch Jesus teach in the context of the Herodians and secular communities at Herod's magnificent capital city of Sepphoris. Lesson Twenty, in Set 4 of this series, follows Jesus across the Sea of Galilee to the pagan Decapolis and the beautiful mountain city of Susita.

As we study the ministry of Jesus, encourage your students to develop mental pictures of the places He lived and taught. The more they understand the cultural background of those who listened to the Master, the more they will discover new meanings and applications of Jesus' message. They'll grow in awareness that Jesus was God's Messiah, His Son, but fully human as a first-century Jewish rabbi. His life and lessons will come alive as they learn to view them in their cultural settings. As you study together, ask your students to consider how the *setting*, as seen in the video and the overhead transparencies, adds to their understanding of the Bible text. The more vivid and real their encounter with Jesus is, the more they will be gripped by His message and His person.

Your Objectives for This Lesson

At the completion of this section, you will want your students:

To Know/Understand

1. Where Jesus conducted most of His miracles and teaching ministry.
2. Who the various types of people were who lived in that area.
3. The importance of the Sermon on the Mount.
4. How the Sermon on the Mount would be received differently by the various people among whom He worked.
5. The location of the cities in which Jesus ministered.
6. What a household (*insula*) is and how it relates to Jesus' teaching.
7. The customs of Jewish marriage and the teachings Jesus based on them.
8. The difference between a student and a disciple.
9. How Jesus was a typical rabbi.

To Do

1. Accept Jesus' challenge to adopt a "kingdom lifestyle" by accepting His "yoke."
2. Prepare themselves to be Jesus' brides.
3. Recognize the great responsibility they have for having met Jesus, and determine how to be more obedient.

4. Make a commitment to be disciples *(talmidim)* and not simply students of Jesus.

5. Accept Jesus as Rabbi.

6. Become more active as members of God's household.

How to Plan for This Lesson

Because of the volume of material in this lesson, you may need to divide it into several class sessions. To help you determine how to do that, the lesson has been broken into several segments. Note that the time needed may vary considerably depending on the leader, the size of the class, and the interest level of the class.

If you wish to cover the entire lesson in one session, you should complete Unit One, a discussion of major points in the video. It does not go into great depth. You may go into greater depth, or enhance your background knowledge as class leader, by selecting parts or all of the remaining material.

How to Prepare for This Lesson

Materials Needed

Student copies of the maps:	"The Roman World"
	"Galilee"
Overhead transparencies:	"The Roman World"
	"Galilee"
	"Chorazin"
	"An *Insula*"
	"Religious Movements of Jesus' Time"

Video: **No Greater Love**

Overhead projector, screen, VCR

1. Make copies of the maps listed above for your students.

2. Prepare the overhead transparencies listed above. (You'll find them at the back of the book.)

3. Determine which **Steps** and which optional **Digging Deeper** sections, if any, you wish to use in your class session(s). NOTE: You can use these sections in any order (e.g., you might want to use **Digging Deeper III,** but not **Digging Deeper I** or **Digging Deeper II**).

4. Review the geography of the lands of the Bible from the "Introduction."

5. Prepare your classroom ahead of time, setting up and testing an overhead projector and screen and a VCR. If you plan to hand out biblical references for your students to look up and read aloud, prepare 3x5 cards (one reference per card) to distribute before class.

Lesson Plan

UNIT ONE: Video Review

1. Introductory Comments

Jesus lived and worked primarily in a small area around the Sea of Galilee. He proclaimed God's love and spoke of the kingdom of heaven that was now unfolding to these common people. Not everyone responded positively to His words and miracles. Some interpreted them differently from what He intended. Others rejected His work entirely. But many believed, embracing and experiencing the personal exhilaration of the new kingdom. Ask students to pay careful attention to the message Jesus brought in the location where this lesson is set. It will be exciting all over again as they hear Jesus' words through the eyes and ears of that first audience.

2. Map Study: Galilee

Display the overhead transparency titled "The Roman World," and point out the following areas as your students locate them on their maps:

> Rome
> Judea
> Egypt
> Persia

Display the overhead transparency titled "Galilee," and point out the following areas as your students locate them on their maps:

> Sea of Galilee
> Nazareth
> Capernaum
> Gamla
> Decapolis
> Tiberias
> Chorazin
> Bethsaida

3. Show the Video *No Greater Love* (*22 minutes*)

4. Guided Discussion: The Kingdom of Heaven

a. Display the overhead transparency titled "Galilee," and have students refer to their "Galilee" maps. Point out where each group (Herodians, Orthodox Jews, pagans, Zealots) lived.

b. No one knows for sure the exact location of the Sermon on the Mount. It was close to Capernaum and near the Sea of Galilee. The hillside where the video *No Greater Love* was filmed is probably close to the right location and certainly provides a picture of what the place must have looked like.

   • Scholars view the Sermon on the Mount as a collection of Jesus' teachings that provided His audience with an understanding of the lifestyle of the kingdom of heaven He came to introduce.

- Read Matthew 4:17. Ask: What was the basic theme of Jesus' message?

- Read Matthew 5–7. Ask class members to choose a favorite verse and share it with the class, along with their reason for selecting it. Explain that these passages were designed to help Jesus' audience understand the kingdom and distinguish it from that of the Zealots and the Pharisees.

c. The Hebrew word behind the concept of "disciple" is *talmid*. Popular rabbis in Jesus' time would select students called *talmidim* (plural) who would follow them around, learning their interpretations of obedience to God's law (Torah).

- Jesus was a rabbi (Luke 7:40, 12:13, 19:39).

- The system of obedience to Torah each rabbi taught was called the "yoke of Torah." Read Matthew 11:28–30. Ask: How would Jesus' audience have reacted? Would the use of the "yoke" picture have surprised them? What was unique about Jesus' yoke (His way of obedience to God)?

- Read Matthew 10:1–4. Jesus chose disciples in much the same way that other rabbis did.

- Read Matthew 17:24 and 20:29. Jesus' disciples learned from Him as they followed Him around, as did the disciples of other rabbis.

- A *talmid* was much more than a student. A *talmid* wanted more than to know what his teacher knew; he wanted to become like his teacher. Have students look up these references: Matthew 10:24–25; Luke 6:40; John 8:31, 13:13–15. After each passage is read aloud, pose this question to your class: What is a *talmid*, or disciple, of Jesus?

d. The people of Chorazin were criticized by Jesus because they saw His miracles and heard His teaching but did not respond.

- Read Matthew 11:20–24. Ask: Who would be like Chorazin today? What is the great responsibility of those who know about Jesus? What is God's reaction to those who repeatedly hear and do not respond?

e. Display the overhead transparencies titled "Chorazin" and "An *Insula*" as background for this section. The city of Chorazin contained several family complexes, or *insulae* (Hebrew for "households"; sing. *insula*), around the synagogue. Jesus often uses marriage to illustrate His love for His people. Read Ephesians 5:22–33, and focus your students' attention on the Savior's relationship to His church. Ask: How does the institution of marriage illustrate Jesus' love for you?

- A bridegroom's family agreed to pay a high price to the bride's family for their loss of a daughter. After the price was settled, the couple drank a glass of wine to indicate the commitment of their lives to each other.

- Read 1 Corinthians 6:19–20. Ask: What was the price Jesus paid for you?

- Read Luke 22:20. Ask: How does Jesus symbolize the commitment of Himself to you? How doe He symbolize your commitment to Him?

- The bridegroom returned to his father's *insula* and prepared a place for the bride. No one knew when the wedding would occur.

- Read John 14:1–3. Ask: Where is Jesus now? What does it mean to you that He is our spiritual Bridegroom?

- The bride-to-be remained at home, preparing herself to be a wife and mother. One day, unexpectedly, the bridegroom and his friends arrived at her village. They announced the beginning of the wedding with singing, dancing, and shouting. The wedding party returned to the prepared chamber and the wedding was consummated. A celebration of several days followed.

- Read 1 Thessalonians 4:16–17. Ask: How will our Bridegroom announce His arrival?
- Read 1 Corinthians 6:19–20. Ask: What should be our motive for godly living now?
- Read Matthew 25:1–13. Ask: Why must we always be ready for Jesus' return?

5. Conclusion

Jesus, our Bridegroom, loves us so much that He paid the price for us by giving His own life. Now He is preparing the perfect place for us in His father's household. Revelation 19:7–9 promises that He will return to begin an eternal wedding celebration.

Wrap up this session by having the class discuss this question: Because Jesus wants to be our spiritual "husband," how should we live if we are spiritually "engaged" to Him?

Then pray together, thanking God for His remarkable love through Jesus. Ask Him for the strength and diligence to live expectantly, as did the bride-to-be preparing for her wedding.

UNIT TWO
Step One: "Jesus' Method: The Sermon on the Mount"

1. Introductory Comments

Jesus came to declare that the kingdom of God had arrived. The context of that proclamation was a nation of people who longed for that kingdom but had different ideas of what it should be and what they should do to be part of it. We often overlook the fact that Jesus' audience had discussed for centuries the very topics He came to teach and had varying opinions on what God intended.

Jesus' message, while proclaiming a well-known theme, was unique. His definition of the kingdom was quite different from what people expected or longed for. What He commanded His followers to do to join that kingdom was distinctive. What He proposed to do as God's sacrifice to bring in the kingdom was nearly unheard of. If we understand how Jesus' method of kingdom living came across to the others of His world, we can better focus on how important it is to understand and obey His call to obedience. After all, a *talmid* strives not only to know what the rabbi knows, but to become *like* him. Seeing Jesus as He was, and understanding His similarities to the people of His world as well as His uniqueness, helps us in our mission to become like Christ (Luke 6:40).

In this lesson, your students will see Jesus as a rabbi of first-century Galilee with a unique plan for the coming of the kingdom of God. To be part of that kingdom, we must enter as Jesus commands and live by the kingdom lifestyle He proclaimed. Your students will see and hear Jesus present that message through the cultural images of His people and His land.

2. Map Study: Galilee

Display the overhead transparency titled "The Roman World." Point out the following areas as your students locate them on their maps:

Rome
Mediterranean Sea
Egypt

Judea
Caesarea

Display the overhead transparency titled "Galilee." Point out the following areas and have your students locate them on their maps:

Nazareth
Capernaum
Galilee
Sea of Galilee
Bethsaida, Chorazin, Capernaum (sometimes called the Gospel Triangle because most of Jesus' miracles were performed here; see Matthew 11:20)
Traditional Mount of Beatitudes
Mount Arbel
Decapolis
Gamla
Via Maris

3. Show the Video *No Greater Love* (22 minutes)

4. The handouts "The Zealots: No One But God," in Lesson Fifteen, and "Pharisees or Sadducees?" in Lesson Sixteen, would provide helpful background information at this point.

5. Guided Discussion: Religious Movements of Jesus' Time

a. *Preparation*

Display the overhead transparency titled "Religious Movements of Jesus' Time," and have the students refer to their maps titled "Galilee."

b. *Lecture*

The area around the Sea of Galilee was populated with different types of people. They were religious and nonreligious, Jews and Gentiles, rich and poor, farmers and merchants. Though it would be difficult to present a completely clear picture of all these groups, it is helpful to note the predominance of various groups in certain locations. Each group tended to gravitate to a specific area, but there were also exceptions. People traveled from one area to another to hear Jesus and other rabbis teach. Yet Jesus always managed to tailor His message so that it was appropriate for the beliefs and practices of the people of the particular area He was visiting.

c. *Discussion*

Using the overhead transparencies titled "Galilee" and "Religious Movements of Jesus' Time," point out the following information to your students. Then read the suggested scriptures together, and respond to the questions provided.

Northwestern Shore of the Sea of Galilee. This area was the home of the Orthodox Jewish people. Every town had its synagogue. The Pharisees, devoted to keeping God's Torah perfectly, predominated, and the people knew the Scriptures. There was a deep longing for the Messiah to come to relieve them of the burdens of the tax collectors and the debates of their scholars.

- Read Matthew 4:13–16, 9:1. Ask: Where was the "headquarters" for Jesus' ministry? Why do you think He moved here? Now read Matthew 10:5. What does this add to your answer?

- Read Matthew 11:20–24. Ask: Where were most of Jesus' miracles performed? Why was the reference to Sodom appropriate to this audience?

- Read Matthew 11:28–30. Each rabbi or teacher taught his disciples how Torah should be obeyed. The obedience was called "the yoke of Torah." Ask: Why was it meaningful for Jesus to describe His message in this way? To whom was He talking (unsaved people or those whose "yoke" was heavy, as some rabbis and Pharisees taught)? How can you apply this passage to your situation?

- Read Matthew 10:1–4, 19:28. Jesus chose 12 disciples. Other rabbis had disciples, but there is no record of anyone having just 12. Ask: Given the location of Jesus' ministry and the type of people who lived there, what do you think Jesus was communicating by choosing 12 disciples?

Northeastern Corner of the Sea of Galilee: Gamla. At the northeastern corner of the Sea of Galilee, poised on a mountaintop and protected on all sides by deep wadis, was the village of Gamla. Shortly after Jesus' birth, Judah of Gamla, a Pharisee, founded the Zealot movement. (The term *zealot* is often applied to all rebels who resisted Roman authority; technically, the term applies to those who belonged to the movement that originated at Gamla.) The Zealots espoused a strict creed: (1) God alone was to be served; (2) neither Rome nor Herod was a legitimate authority; (3) taxes were to be paid only to God; and (4) serving Rome, whether by choice or as a slave, violated God's supreme authority. Zealots violently resisted the authority of the emperor for nearly 100 years. They longed for a messiah who would raise a great army and totally destroy the Roman overlords. There is no record that Jesus ever visited Gamla, though He visited the other towns and villages in the area (Matthew 9:35). He did have interaction with the Zealots regarding their philosophy of using the sword to support the kingdom of God.

- Read Mark 3:18. Ask: Why would Jesus choose a Zealot as a disciple? What about His message would have been attractive to Simon? What would Simon have disagreed with?

- Read Mark 12:13–17. Ask: Why was the question of paying taxes to Caesar an issue? How would the Zealots have answered the question? (Note that Herod's party, the Herodians, supported paying taxes because they believed the Roman occupation was favorable for the Jewish people.)

- Read Matthew 8:4, 9:30; John 6:15. Ask: Why would Jesus ask people not to tell anyone about His miraculous power? To whom would such power be attractive? The Zealots would have been the ones most likely to misinterpret Jesus' messianic claims as being a political-military Messiah.

- Read John 18:40. Ask: The word used to describe Barabbas is the same as the word Josephus uses for the Zealots. The Sadducees and Herodians, being generally pro-Roman, vehemently disagreed with the Zealot campaign against the empire. Why would Pontius Pilate think Barabbas's release would not be popular? (Note that Jesus resisted any attempt to make Him an earthly king and taught a message of love and self-sacrifice—in strong opposition to the Zealots. At the end, Jesus' life was exchanged for that of a Zealot.)

Eastern Shoreline of the Sea of Galilee: The Decapolis. The Decapolis was an independent region of city-states established by Alexander the Great and strengthened by the Roman conqueror Pompey in 63 B.C. Several towns existed on the high plateau (today's Golan Heights), including Hippos (Susita), Kursi, and Gadara. The people of this area were quite pagan, worshiping Roman and Greek gods.

- Read Mark 5:1–17. Ask: Why might Jews believe that demons lived in this area? Why would pigs be raised if Jews thought pork to be unclean?

- Read Mark 5:18–20. Ask: What did Jesus tell the healed man to do? Compare this admonition with the one He gave in Matthew 8:4 and 9:30 and in John 6:15. Why this difference? (Possibly because the pagans did not have the messianic fervor and tendency to translate it into politics as did the people of the Decapolis.)

- Read Mark 5:12. The Romans sacrificed pigs to their gods, which the Jewish people considered demonic. Ask: Why would it have made sense to Jesus' Jewish disciples that the demons wished to enter the pigs? Why would the herders think only of the financial loss?

Southwestern Shoreline of the Sea of Galilee: Tiberias, Herod's Capital. Herod Antipas, who executed John the Baptist, built a beautiful city on the southwestern side of the Sea of Galilee. Tradition holds, with much support, that religious Jews would not live here at that time because it was built over a cemetery. The people who lived in the city were most likely secular Jews who supported the Herodian dynasty, in part because it gave them the economic and political power they enjoyed.

- Read Matthew 22:16; Mark 3:6, 12:13. Ask: What was Jesus' relationship with these pro-Herod people? Why would they be interested in taxes for Caesar?

- Read Luke 9:7–9, 13:31. Ask: Why do you think Herod wanted to kill Jesus? What threat was He to Herod and to the Herodians?

d. *Conclusion*

To wrap up this section, have your students think of examples in which modern-day people tend to interpret Jesus through their own belief systems. (For example, they might see Him as a revolutionary to justify their cause, or as a "gospel of success" teacher, or simply as a wise leader.) Ask: What cults exist based on a wrong view of Jesus? Why is it so important to understand Jesus' words correctly, as He intended? How can we prevent our own biases and desires from distorting His message?

6. Lecture: The Kingdom Is Here

a. To understand the overall perspective of Jesus' teaching, read Matthew 5–7 before class and encourage your students to do the same.

b. Have students refer to their maps titled "Galilee." Note the traditional location for the Sermon on the Mount and its proximity to the Sea of Galilee, Capernaum, and Chorazin. Be sure the class understands that we don't know the actual place where Jesus delivered the sermon, but that this is the right geographical location.

c. It is not possible to do a complete study of the Sermon on the Mount in one or two class sessions. The intent of this lesson is to help students understand that (1) the people of that time and place longed for the coming of God's Messiah and God's kingdom; and (2) the various groups who lived in Galilee had different ideas of what the Messiah and the kingdom would be. Therefore, Jesus came to make clear the true meaning of God's kingdom. We might see the Sermon on the Mount as His "blueprint" for kingdom living.

7. Key Points About the Kingdom of God

Review with your students these key points about the kingdom of God.

a. Was the Sermon on the Mount really one sermon?

- Some scholars say it is; others believe it is a compilation of Jesus' teachings given on several occasions. Luke places 34 verses of the sermon in other contexts. Matthew clearly viewed this material as the foundation of Jesus' teaching and therefore portrayed it as one message.

b. Does Jesus (and Matthew) intend this to be the institution of a new "people of God" as God designated Israel in the Old Testament?

- In Exodus 20, Israel began with God's Law on Mount Sinai. The 12 tribes received new revelation. Read Matthew 5:1. Jesus' kingdom began with God's "law" on a mountain. The 12 disciples received new revelation.

- Genesis, Exodus, Leviticus, Numbers, and Deuteronomy are the five building blocks given to the 12 tribes of Israel in the Old Testament. Matthew 5–7, 10, 13, 18, 24–25 are the five great discourses of Jesus in Matthew. They provide the building blocks for the community of Jesus.

c. What is the "blueprint" for the kingdom of God?

- Read Matthew 5:5,9,43–47. Ask: What would the Zealots have said? What would the Pharisees have said?

- Read Matthew 6:19–24. What was Jesus' view of wealth? What would the aristocratic Herodians have said?

d. From the scriptures you've just read, ask each student to select a verse that helps him or her understand how a person in Jesus' kingdom should live. (If your class is small, have students share their verses, and their reasons for choosing them, with the entire class. If your class is large, divide them into groups of five or six for this activity.)

e. Using a chalkboard or flip chart, have class members call out 10 key words they feel describe the kingdom of heaven (e.g., mercy, salt, forgive).

f. To sum up this section, ask: Based on our study, what is Jesus' kingdom to be like? How will those who follow Jesus live? Encourage your students to select one key word or verse to become their "motto verse" for the next month as they seek to be Jesus' disciples.

OPTIONAL — Digging Deeper I: The Way of the Sea *(30–50 minutes)*

HINT: *Lesson One, "Standing at the Crossroads," in Set 1 of this series, provides the Old Testament background for this* **Digging Deeper***. You may want to review that video and the curriculum that goes with it.*

A. Lecture

The land of Israel is important not only for *what* it is, but also for *where* it is. In Bible times, Israel was at the crossroads of the world, where the civilizations passed through because there was no other route. It was a land bridge between Mesopotamia (Persia, Babylonia, Assyria) and Egypt. These great empires depended on each other for trade. Since the Arabian desert was between them, the only trade route passed through Israel, a narrow corridor between the Mediterranean Sea and the desert to the east. This road is sometimes called the "Way of the Sea," or by its Latin name, the Via Maris. (Some scholars believe that this name refers to just one branch of the ancient road, not the entire route. That is possible, but it does not diminish the importance of the road.) The Via Maris was a vital trade route in Jesus' time. Rome, the dominant power in the west, desired trade with the eastern peoples. Traders of spices, gold, cloth, and other products followed the route to Palestine and to the seaports on the Mediterranean. King Herod constructed the massive harbor at Caesarea for exactly this purpose. The trade route still passed through Israel, which continued to be the crossroads of the world. The "Way of the Sea" was a busy road indeed.

B. Bible Exploration

Have a student look up and read each of the following verses aloud. After each verse is read, discuss the information provided.

1. Read Isaiah 43:12. God's mission for His people was to live *so that the world may know* that He is God. He placed Israel at the crossroads of the world so that all the nations would see Israel and, through Israel, see God.

2. Read Joshua 4:24; 1 Samuel 17:46; Isaiah 37:20. Many of the heroes of the Old Testament recognized the mission that Yahweh had given His people, and they pointed others to Him.

3. Read Isaiah 9:1–2,6. More than 500 years before Christ, Isaiah predicted that Galilee, which had endured brutal destruction at the hands of the Assyrians, would experience the renewal of God's light. And that light, Jesus Christ, would become known to the world because He lived by the "Way of the Sea."

4. Read Matthew 4:12–17. Jesus chose to live in Capernaum, which was not even a town in Old Testament times. Capernaum was a toll stop on the ancient Via Maris. Jesus was to live and teach at the crossroads of the world just as His ancestors had done.

C. Conclusion

Challenge your students by having them respond to the following: God often places His people at the crossroads of the world, not hidden in a back alley. Jesus the Messiah, our example, lived on the most heavily traveled road of the ancient world.

1. What are some ways in which we live at the crossroads of the world today?

2. What is there about your life that says to others, "The Lord is God" and "The kingdom of heaven is near"? Relate one example of someone whose life communicated this message to you, and one example of how your life communicated this message to someone else.

OPTIONAL — Digging Deeper II: Called to Be *Talmidim* (30–60 minutes)

HINT: Digging Deeper II *is a lecture that will enable you to share valuable insights into the nature of the rabbi-disciple relationship. You will also find Scripture references for students to read aloud and some questions to ask your students that will help them understand the material and apply it to their own relationship with Jesus Christ.*

Jesus called together many disciples at the beginning of His ministry. They were to be the group that would pass His teaching along to others. Some were part of the inner circle, numbering 12. Others were present frequently and traveled with Him, but they were not as central to His teaching. To understand Jesus' challenge to us to be His followers, we should understand the relationship between rabbi and disciple.

1. Was Jesus a rabbi? Read Luke 7:40, 12:13, 19:39, 20:27–28; Matthew 19:16, 22:35–36. Notice the diversity of people who believed Jesus to be a rabbi. The title means "Master" or "Teacher." "Rabbi" did not become an official office until after Jesus' time. In His day, it was a term of respect or a description of activity.

2. Did Jesus act like a typical rabbi? In His day, rabbis:

    - depended on the hospitality of others (Luke 8:3)

    - traveled, teaching outside or in synagogues, homes, and even the Temple courts (Luke 4:14–16; Matthew 5:1–2, 26:55; Mark 6:6)

    - were accompanied by their disciples (Matthew 17:24; Matthew 20:29)

    - taught in parables (Matthew 13:3)

    - encouraged their followers to take on the "yoke of Torah" (i.e., they would commit to obeying Torah as the rabbi taught) (Matthew 11:29–30)

    - chose disciples to be with them to learn (Matthew 10:1–4; Luke 5:27–28; Matthew 17:24; Matthew 20:29). It was unusual for a rabbi to have women following him (Luke 23:49).

3. What was a disciple? Read Matthew 10:24–25; Luke 6:40; John 8:31, 13:13–15. The word *disciple* is used to translate the Greek in the text. The Hebrew word in the culture is *talmid* (pl. *talmidim*). The Hebrew form stresses the relationship between rabbi (teacher) and disciple (student). A *talmid* is one who gives up his whole life to be with his teacher. The goal was not simply to know what the teacher knew, as it usually is in our educational practice. The foremost goal of any *talmid* was to become like the rabbi.

    - Ask your students to think of examples in which Jesus' disciples became like their Teacher. (For example, performed miracles, were killed for their faith, loved their enemies, etc.)

    - Jesus calls us to be His disciples (Matthew 28:19; John 8:31, 13:34–35).

    - Ask: Why is it important to *know* what Jesus said and did? Is this enough to be a disciple? Note that the Pharisees knew and *taught* the truth (Matthew 23:1–4). Why were they not disciples? (The key is to do what Jesus did and be like Him.)

4. Reread Matthew 10:24–25; Luke 6:40; John 8:31, 13:13–15. Ask your students to turn to a partner and relate an example of someone they know who is a faithful modern-day *talmid* of Jesus. Encourage them to elaborate on why they think this person is a good example.

5. Pose the following questions and give your students several moments to quietly contemplate their answers. Encourage them to be truthful with themselves. Have them ask themselves: Am I a true disciple of Jesus? Why or why not?

6. Have students gather in groups of three or four and close this session in prayer, asking God to forgive them for those times when their discipleship was based only on *knowing* the right things instead of also *doing* the right things. Encourage them to ask God for the knowledge and strength to become more like their personal Rabbi, the Lord Jesus Christ.

Step Two: "The Love Story"

1. Map Review

Display the overhead transparency titled "Galilee" while someone reads Matthew 11:20–24. Have your students refer to their "Galilee" maps as you point out the following:

> Capernaum
> Bethsaida
> Chorazin

Note (1) the distance these cities are from each other, and their proximity to the Sea of Galilee, (2) the fact that most of Jesus' miracles were performed in this small area, and (3) the people who lived in this "Gospel Triangle" were witnesses to a large portion of what Jesus said and did.

2. Guided Discussion: The Burden of Those Who Hear

a. *Lecture*

Jesus chose to conduct most of His ministry in a small area near the Sea of Galilee. Many people followed Jesus, listened to His words, and witnessed His miracles. Others simply turned away. Those who refused Jesus' message are the objects of this study. It is important to remember that not everyone in the area rejected Him. Most of the 12 disciples came from this area.

b. *Discussion*

Have a student read each passage. Then explore the questions asked and discuss the information provided.

- Read Matthew 11:20. What made Chorazin, Bethsaida, and Capernaum unique? Pretend that you are living back then and do not know what you know now. Would you have responded positively to Jesus' miracles and preaching? Why or why not?

- Read Matthew 11:21,23. What other cities are Chorazin, Bethsaida, and Capernaum compared to?

- Read Amos 1:9–10; 1 Kings 11:33, 16:29–32. What were the sins of Tyre and Sidon? What would be modern examples of such terrible behavior?

- Read Genesis 19:1–20 (especially verses 5–9); Ezekiel 16:4–50. What were the sins of Sodom? Name some modern examples of these sins.

- Read Matthew 11:21,23. For what did Jesus criticize the three cities? (Students should understand that these cities had seen most of Jesus' miracles, heard much of His teaching, and still did not respond.) Why was their penalty *more* severe than that of Sidon and Sodom, who were among the most evil peoples of the Old Testament?

- Who would fit the description of Chorazin, Bethsaida, and Capernaum today? (Who has heard all about Jesus and not responded?) Has Western civilization heard and known about God? Has it repented and lived for Him? Has our country heard and known about Jesus? Has it repented and lived for Him? Has your community heard and known about Jesus? Has it changed its values? If yes, in what ways?

- Have *you* heard about Jesus? Has it changed you? In what ways, specifically? (NOTE: Here is a strategic place to help your students realize that merely growing up in church or Sunday school, living in a religious home, or hearing as much about Jesus as the three cities did, does not make one truly His disciple. Anyone like that could be said to have "seen" most of Jesus' miracles and "heard" much of His teaching.)

- What is God's reaction to the person who hears and doesn't respond? Why do you think they will be judged more harshly than Sodom? What does this say to you today about how you should live?

c. *Summary*

It is easy to condemn Chorazin for seeing Jesus and not believing. What we don't recognize is that many of us know for a fact that He is Messiah and are faced with Him and His Word on a regular basis, yet we still don't respond in confession and obedience. That makes God angry. The sobering reality of our enlightened "religious" culture is that we have not repented. We face God's judgment as individuals and as nations.

d. *Prayer*

Challenge your students to reflect quietly and identify one area of their lives that they know is contrary to Jesus' teaching (what they have heard). Have the students spend a few minutes in private prayer, confessing their sins to God and promising Him that through His strength, they will hear and obey His Word.

3. Guided Discussion: Jesus Loves Me

a. *Lecture*

Displaying the overhead transparency titled "Chorazin," relate the following information to your students.

The ruins of Chorazin provide a setting to reflect on one of the many pictures Jesus used to describe His love for His people and His work on their behalf. Several times in His ministry, Jesus alluded to typical first-century marriage practices to illustrate His relationship to us. Not all scholars agree on the details of courtship and marriage practices in first-century Israel, so the practices presented in this section are those on which there is basic agreement. The important point for us to take away from this discussion is that Jesus often describes His love for us with the metaphor of a loving husband-wife relationship.

b. *Exploration and Discussion: The Household*

Displaying the overhead transparency "An *Insula*," relate the following information to your students. Then have them read the suggested Bible passages and respond to the questions provided.

People in Galilee often lived in family units, sometimes called *insulae* (sing. *insula*). Although not everyone lived in this way, it was common for people, particularly extended families, to combine several living units around an open courtyard.

It is possible that Jesus and His disciples lived in such a family compound in Capernaum (see Matthew 8:14, 12:46–13:1,36; Mark 2:1–2, 7:17). This is not definite, but the references to "house" and "home" and the size of the house needed for His disciples to live with Him make this likely. This practice provides the basis for one of the pictures of heaven (God's housing complex) and for the Bible's reference to household. "Household" means an extended family living together.

1. Read Matthew 10:24–25,36; John 4:53; Acts 11:14, 16:15,31, 18:8; Romans 16:10; Ephesians 2:19; 1 Timothy 3:15. Ask: What is added to each passage by the fact that each household represents an extended family?

2. Ask: What would be the advantages of living with your extended family? Encourage your class to imagine how family values could be passed to the next generation as children live and work daily with parents, grandparents, uncles, aunts, and cousins. In Bible times, there was also "pressure" within the family to live obediently before God so as not to dishonor the household.

3. Read Ephesians 2:19 and 1 Timothy 3:15 again. Ask: What does it mean that the church is God's household? What does this metaphor mean in our relationships with fellow Christians?

c. *Exploration and Discussion: Marriage*

The marriage metaphor is one of the most beautiful and compelling of Jesus' teaching ministry. In this section, we will further explore this metaphor and what it means to today's believers. Where Scripture references are given, have a student read the passage; then share the related information or pose the suggested question for discussion:

1. Read Ephesians 5:22–33; 2 Corinthians 11:2–3; Matthew 22:1–14; Revelation 19:7–9, 21:2.

   • Ask: What does this teach us about the nature of God's love? What does this teach us about how we should live?

2. An engagement in first-century Israel was as serious as marriage. Breaking an engagement required a divorce. The families agreed on a bride price (to compensate for the loss of a daughter), usually a large sum. The life commitment between bride and groom was sealed by drinking a cup of wine. With these customs in mind, read 1 Corinthians 6:19–20, Matthew 26:39–42, and Luke 22:20.

   • Ask: How does understanding the engagement custom of ancient Israel enhance your understanding of these passages?

3. The engaged bridegroom returned to his father's household and began to add a new living unit to the family compound—a practice mentioned in Jewish tradition. The young man would work tirelessly, eager to complete the dwelling so he could claim his bride. His father would oversee the work (perhaps because the bridegroom might be so anxious for marriage, he would do a poor job!).

   When the father determined everything was ready, he gave his blessing for the wedding ceremony to proceed. Generally, the engagement period was one year, though no one knew exactly when the wedding would take place (not even the bride and groom). With these customs in mind, read John 14:1–3, Matthew 24:36, and Matthew 1:18.

   • Ask: What is added to your understanding now that you know how the bridegroom went to prepare the new room in the household?

   • Ask: What is heaven? (God's household, which has many rooms for many brides.)

   • Ask: Where is Jesus, our Bridegroom? (Preparing our rooms in His Father's household.)

   • Ask: How does this information help you understand the nature of heaven? (It is a household of many rooms built around the Father's house, where all of us will live forever in one large community.) NOTE: Perhaps we should practice getting along better now!

4. The bride remained at home, eagerly preparing herself to be a good wife. She learned home-making skills from her mother and prepared for the wedding (she did not know the date). Read 1 Corinthians 6:19–20; Matthew 25:1–13.

   • Ask: What does the custom of the bride preparing eagerly for the wedding add to your understanding of each passage?

   • Ask: What is the purpose of our lives now? (To prepare to be Christ's bride.) Why is it important to be ready? (No one knows the time of the wedding.)

5. When the "wedding house" was ready and the father gave his approval, the groom brought his friends and family (often in the evening) to the bride's town. They would announce their coming with singing, dancing, and shouting (maybe even blowing a trumpet). The bride and her attendants would be taken to the new home together. Read Matthew 25:5–6; 1 Thessalonians 4:16–17; John 14:3.

- Ask: Now that we know about the custom of the "sudden wedding," what does this add to our understanding of these passages?

6. When they arrived at the groom's home, the bride and groom entered the wedding chamber (probably the prepared room), and in that private place, they would consummate their marriage. When it was consummated, the groom would tell his friend (the best man at modern weddings), who would announce it to the guests. Then the wedding feast would begin. Read John 3:29; Matthew 22:1–2; John 2:1–10; Revelation 19:7,9.

   - Ask: What can we learn from these passages about the time when we will be joined in spiritual marriage with our Lord Jesus?

OPTIONAL — Digging Deeper III: A Typical First-Century Jewish House
(35–70 minutes)

(*This section requires the use of the optional full-color overhead-transparency packet. For information on ordering it, see p. 243.*)

A. Lecture

It is difficult to picture the homes and everyday lives of people of Bible times. All that remains for us are the archaeological ruins. In Galilee, the ancient village of Qatzrin has been excavated and reconstructed. Though it dates to the centuries after Jesus' time, scholars believe that the buildings and artifacts they have found largely represent the practices of the first century. The homes were household complexes (*insulae*). Some have been reconstructed, using the original material where possible, and have been furnished with reconstructed household items. Viewing this village helps us picture the living conditions with which Jesus was familiar.

B. Visual Insights

The following overhead transparencies show a typical first-century Jewish home. Jesus probably lived in such a house.

Overhead Transparency 33. Building a Typical Galilean Home. The typical Galilean house was built of basalt (dark volcanic rock) with the stones carefully squared or "dressed" by a stonemason (sometimes translated as "carpenter"—see Matthew 13:55). The tools of the builder are displayed at the bottom of the picture. The wooden scaffold is used in the building process. Smaller stones wedged between the larger ones provided stability and strength. The courtyard in the foreground is located between the various rooms of the complex. It was paved with basalt stones as well. Sometimes, the exterior of the house was covered with mud plaster. The door frame of the house was made of stone ashlars (shaped stones) and was covered by a wooden door. The construction of the additional room on the house reminds the visitor of the bridegroom who returns to his father's household to prepare a place for his bride. Jesus would have been familiar with houses like this one because of His training as a stonemason and because He lived and taught in such homes throughout Galilee. (Houses in Chorazin, Bethsaida, and Capernaum are also built in this style and with this material). Some houses had a second story like this one.

Ask students to read the following Scripture passages aloud while this overhead transparency remains on display:

- Mark 6:3; Matthew 13:55
- John 14:1–3
- Matthew 8:14, 13:1; Mark 7:17
- Mark 1:33; Luke 13:24, 11:9

Overhead Transparency 34. A Galilean Kitchen. This kitchen is near the door of the house. A domed oven has been reconstructed; it was probably used for heating and cooking when the weather was cold. There would be similar ovens outside for use at other times. The outer part of the oven gathered the heat and smoke to be exited through the chimney. The fire was placed in the inner part. Animal dung, the pulp of pressed olives, and small branches were used for fuel. A cooking pot rests on the inner oven. The top of the outer oven was used for storage. To the left of the oven are household implements for food preparation. Note the various types of hand grinders used to make flour from grain (wheat for the wealthy or for special occasions; barley for others). The baskets were made from reeds or palm leaves and were used for gathering or storing food. The large stone jar on the left probably contained water carried from a nearby well. Dried onions hang from the ceiling. An engaged bride would spend much time here with her mother, learning the skills of collecting and preparing food.

The roof of this house is made of wooden beams covered with tree branches; on top of the branches is a layer of clay. Capernaum homes had this type of roof (the lame man's friends let him down through an opening in one of them), while those of Chorazin had stone slabs instead of branches. During rainy days, the clay would absorb water, sealing the roof so the rest of the rainwater ran off. Each year the roof needed to be repaired. In some cases, the roof became a "courtyard" where people worked and slept.

Have students read the following Scripture passages aloud while this overhead transparency remains on display:

- Luke 15:8
- Matthew 24:17; Mark 13:15
- Acts 10:9

Overhead Transparency 35. A Galilean Family Room. This room was the center of family life. It was probably used for eating, for storing food, and for socializing with extended family. Guests could be invited in if the weather was inappropriate for dining outdoors in the courtyard. A small wooden table stands in one corner. Wealthy people reclined as they ate, while poorer people sat on the floor or on small benches. Food was served on pottery plates or in pottery bowls. Apparently, Jewish laws of "clean" and "unclean" commanded that different pottery be used for various types of food (to prevent mixing meat and dairy, for example), so cleaning the serving and eating implements was important. Beyond the room is a small chamber in the floor, providing a cool area for storing grain, wine, or oil. Branches above provide a ledge for storing food items. The walls and floor are typical of the houses Jesus knew.

Have students read the following Scripture passages aloud while this overhead transparency remains on display:

- Matthew 9:10
- Mark 2:15
- Luke 5:29, 7:37, 10:7
- Matthew 5:15, 23:25, 26:23

Overhead Transparency 36. Household Implements. These four pictures show typical household items from first-century Israel.

The Sleeping Loft. Located on the second floor, this typical loft provided sleeping space for the family. The bed is a wood frame with rope stretched over it. The mat over the bed provided some additional comfort. In poorer families, people often slept on mats on the floor. If people traveled, their mats could be taken along. The walls are plastered with a mixture of mud and straw.

Have students read the following Scripture passages aloud while this overhead transparency remains on display:

- Luke 8:16
- Luke 11:7
- Matthew 9:2,6; Mark 2:4–12

The Lamp. The ladder goes up to the sleeping loft shown in the first photograph. Below is a typical "window" wall that allowed air circulation and more openness between rooms. In the window wall is an oil container made from the skin of a goat. Similar skins were used for carrying wine or water.

Above, on a ledge, is a small lamp typical of household lamps from first-century Israel. They burned olive oil and provided a small amount of light. Most people went to bed at sunset and got up at dawn. Honest people did not work after dark (hence the phrase "works of darkness"). The bridesmaids of Jesus' parable are described as having such lamps. The difficulty of providing light gave birth to a Jewish proverb Jesus quoted: Someone with a good eye is generous while someone with a bad eye is stingy. In that sense, Jesus said, the eye is the lamp of the body. A good eye provides light and a bad eye only darkness.

Have students read the following Scripture passages aloud while this overhead transparency remains on display:

- Matthew 9:17
- Matthew 25:1–8
- Luke 8:16
- Luke 15:8
- Luke 22:53; Romans 13:12; Ephesians 5:11

Provisions. Every home provided storage space for harvested food, as well as for additional possessions. Since life depended upon raising, preserving, and storing food, it was essential to store it so it wouldn't spoil or be eaten by rodents or insects. Some foods were hung from the ceiling. Other foods, such as grain, wine, and oil, were stored in large jars in cool places like this pit next to the main room of the house. For poorer families, the line between being able to eat and starving to death was this type of storage. Jesus encouraged people to live by faith that God would provide. Those who were obsessed with providing for the future to the point of hoarding earned His criticism.

Have students read the following Scripture passages aloud while this overhead transparency remains on display:

- 2 Kings 4:1–7; 1 Kings 17:7–14
- Matthew 6:25–26,31–33; Luke 12:18,24

The Storeroom. This storeroom was where the occupants kept their all-important farming tools. Most families needed to provide their own food. Small gardens, vineyards with grapes and olive trees, and some small livestock provided most of their diet. Hanging on the wall is a wooden plow; the iron point is on the floor below. The plow was pulled by a donkey or ox over the small fields used for growing grain.

Have students read the following Scripture passages aloud while this overhead transparency remains on display:

- Luke 17:7, 9:62

Also on the wall are a sickle, a winnowing fork, and a sieve for grain. The farmers cut the grain with the sickle, placed it on a hard stone surface (called a threshing floor), where it was crushed (threshed) by a small sled dragged by animals. Then the straw and grain mixture was thrown into the air on a windy day. The lighter straw and chaff blew away; the grain fell and was collected. Passing it through the sieve separated any chaff that remained.

Have students read the following Scripture passages aloud while this overhead transparency remains on display:

- Matthew 3:12
- Mark 4:26–29

On the far wall, other household items include reed baskets for storage, brooms, rope made from plant fibers, and an animal skin used as a churn for butter or cheese (it was hung and rocked for a long time to provide the churning action).

Have a student read the following Scripture passage aloud while this overhead transparency remains on display:

- Luke 15:8

C. Conclusion

This study gives us a mental picture of everyday life in Jesus' time. Seeing the common objects used by His culture helps us better understand the illustrations and examples He used in His teaching ministry. Because Jesus taught plainly and clearly—using references people could relate to—they were able to understand and embrace the kingdom of God He so generously offered.

Conclusion

Encourage your students to grasp the depths of Jesus' love for us based on the Bible's repeated metaphor of the loving husband and wife. Point out that our human marriages are flawed because we are sinners, yet many people experience great joy in marriage and recognize how incredibly wonderful a perfect marriage would be. That gives everyone the ability to comprehend what personal, powerful love Jesus has for us and what He wants us to have for Him.

Discuss together: (1) What does it mean to you that Jesus wants to be your spiritual husband? (2) How should you live every moment if you are "engaged" to Him?

Pray together, thanking God for His remarkable love through Jesus. Ask Jesus for the diligence to live as expectant "brides" preparing ourselves for Him.

THE RABBI

For the Teacher

It is difficult, if not impossible, for us to fully understand the world of Jesus. Fortunately, God's Word is clear even apart from such understanding. Yet there is great value in learning about the first-century Jewish world of Galilee because in doing so, Jesus' message becomes clearer still.

There are two main objectives in this lesson. The first is to recognize that Jesus taught and modeled a specific lifestyle as the kingdom of God. Contrasted with the Zealots who lived nearby, it becomes even clearer how different His approach was from theirs even though they, too, loved God. The second objective is to see Jesus teaching and acting like a typical rabbi of the day. To be sure, in some ways, He was unique—for example, the twists He would put on traditional parables. But in other ways, He was just like other rabbis of that time. Understanding this leads us to praise God for so carefully preparing for the coming of Jesus, and makes His message even clearer. And, as you will discover, it demands our total faith, like that of the ailing woman who touched the hem of His robe.

Many Western Christians are not familiar with the Jewish faith and its practices. Begin this lesson by asking your students if any of them know any religious Jewish customs. Ask them to briefly describe a custom they are familiar with that either enlightens their understanding of the Scriptures or is puzzling to them. Be sure to affirm that it was God's plan to place Jesus in the Jewish setting—that it was all according to His purpose.

Your Objectives for This Lesson

At the completion of this section, you will want your students:

To Know/Understand

1. The history and beliefs of the Zealots.

2. The story of the mountaintop city of Gamla.

3. The people who lived around the Sea of Galilee with whom Jesus interacted.

4. Synagogue history, practice, and structure as it existed in Jesus' day.

5. How a typical rabbi lived and taught in Jesus' time.

6. Why so many people called Jesus "Rabbi."

7. The importance of faith in seeking the power of God for their lives.

8. The meaning of *disciple* in the context of Jewish practice.

To Do

1. Commit to following Jesus' way, not their own desires, in their walk with Him.

2. Seek ways to be more faithful citizens of their country.

3. Find ways to impact others for Jesus and not be isolated from those who need Him.

4. Learn to appreciate the church as the community of faith and select a specific action to add to that community.

5. Make a decision to be a *talmid* (disciple).

6. Think of specific ways to show others their faith in Jesus and indicate to Him their belief that He is God's Messiah, their Lord.

How to Plan for This Lesson

Because of the volume of material in this lesson, you may need to divide it into several class sessions. To help you determine how to do that, the lesson has been broken into several segments. Note that the time needed may vary considerably depending on the leader, the size of the class, and the interest level of the class.

If you wish to cover the entire lesson in one session, you should complete Unit One, a discussion of major points in the video. It does not go into great depth. You may go into greater depth, or enhance your background knowledge as class leader, by selecting parts or all of the remaining material.

How to Prepare for This Lesson

Materials Needed

Student copies of the maps: "The Roman World"
                                  "Galilee"

Overhead transparencies: "The Roman World"
                                  "Galilee"
                                  "Gamla"
                                  "A Galilean Synagogue"
                                  "New Testament Chronology"
                                  "The Zealot Movement"

Student copies of the handouts: "The Zealots: No One But God"
                                  "He Went to the Synagogue . . ."

Video: **The Rabbi**

Overhead projector, screen, VCR

1. Make copies of the maps and handouts listed above for your students. (If possible, they should receive and read the handouts before the lesson.)

2. Prepare the overhead transparencies listed above. (You'll find them at the back of the book.)

3. Determine which **Steps** and which optional **Digging Deeper** sections, if any, you wish to use in your class session(s). NOTE: You can use these sections in any order you wish (e.g., you might want to use **Digging Deeper III**, but not **Digging Deeper I** or **Digging Deeper II**).

4. Review the geography of the lands of the Bible from the "Introduction."

5. Prepare your classroom ahead of time, setting up and testing an overhead projector and screen and a VCR. If you plan to hand out biblical references for your students to look up and read aloud, prepare 3x5 cards (one reference per card) to distribute before class.

Lesson Plan

UNIT ONE: Video Review

1. Introductory Comments

Jesus' ministry took place in a cauldron of conflicting ideas. Pro-Roman Herodians, religious Pharisees, pagans, and fiercely independent Zealots were in constant conflict over worldviews and belief systems. Jesus' message did not come in a vacuum; rather, it came, and must be understood, against the tumultuous political backdrop of His day. When we hear His message afresh, the way His audience did, it becomes even clearer, more relevant, and more powerful than before.

Since fellowship with God is the longing of every human heart, Jesus' message of restoration, forgiveness, and love attracted many. At the same time, others were repelled by the methods He proposed and the attitude toward others He commanded. Was He the Messiah? Ultimately, each had to choose.

In this lesson you will face the same choices. Jesus' message of loving your enemies, caring about others, and being willing to become more like Him is the setting for His claim on messiahship. Your acceptance of His claim depends on your willingness to obey His way of living in the kingdom of God.

2. Map Study: Gamla

Display the overhead transparency titled "The Roman World." Point out the following areas as your students locate them on their maps:

> Rome
> Judea
> Egypt

Display the overhead transparency titled "Galilee." Point out the following areas as your students locate them on their maps:

> Sea of Galilee
> Capernaum
> Decapolis
> Tiberias
> Gamla

3. Show the Video *The Rabbi* (*19 minutes*)

4. Guided Discussion: The Zealots and the Rabbi

a. *The Zealots*

The setting of this lesson is the fascinating city of Gamla, the home of the Zealot movement. Jesus knew Zealots, spoke to issues they were passionately interested in, and shared their total commitment to God alone. Yet He preached a message quite distinct from theirs. The contrast is enlightening.

1. Display the overhead transparency titled "Gamla," and point out to your students:

    - The isolated mountaintop
    - The packed houses on the slope of the hill
    - The defensive wall and tower
    - The synagogue

Ask: When is it appropriate to isolate ourselves from our world to be more godly, and when must we reach out with the message of Jesus? Would Jesus have approved of the Zealots' isolation? Do you think most Christians tend to be more like or unlike the Zealots?

2. Read Mark 3:18. The Zealots believed they should serve only God and must use every means to resist any other earthly authority, especially Rome. Violence was often their strategy against Rome or anyone who cooperated with Rome.

    Jesus had a Zealot for a disciple. Ask: How do you think a Zealot would have reacted to Matthew 5:5,7,9,14–16,36–48? Are there Christian groups like the Zealots today who use hatred and power to be heard? Who? Have there been such Christian groups in history? Why do you think it's so difficult to accept and live by Jesus' command that we love others even if we strongly disagree with them? What are some practical steps we can take to love others even though we disagree with them?

3. Read John 6:15; Acts 1:6; John 18:36. Many misunderstood Jesus' message and believed He came to establish a political-military kingdom. Ask: Would the Zealots have tended to miss His emphasis on a spiritual kingdom? Why or why not? If you had lived in that time, would you have recognized it? Why or why not? Can you think of examples of people who misunderstand Jesus today because they interpret His teachings through their own preconceived ideas? Have you ever discovered that you missed His point for the same reason? How did God correct you?

4. Read Matthew 22:15–22. Ask: What would have been the Zealots' response to Jesus? Is it ever right to serve an authority other than God? When? In our culture, how can one give total allegiance to Jesus and still serve human rulers? Is physical resistance to human rulers ever justified? If so, when—and who decides when it's appropriate?

5. Ask: Even though we have the benefit of 20/20 hindsight and can see how the Zealots were wrong, are there aspects of their belief system that we can admire? Why? Can you understand why they misunderstood Jesus' message?

b. *The Rabbi and the Synagogue*

Jesus participated in Jewish life as a rabbi, teaching and praying in synagogues.

1. Read Matthew 12:9–12, 13:53–57; Mark 1:21–28; Luke 4:16–30,31–37. Ask: What specific things did Jesus do in synagogues? Why do you think He went there so often?

2. Display the overhead transparency titled "A Galilean Synagogue" and point out:
   - The Torah scrolls
   - The platform where the reader stood
   - The benches where the important people sat
   - The place where the common people sat
   - Moses' seat

     Read Matthew 23:2,6; Mark 5:22,35–36,38; Luke 4:17–20, 8:41–49. Then note the following practices:

   - The reader sat in the Moses' seat because he was taking Moses' place in reading the Torah.
   - Scrolls were kept in the ark of the covenant.
   - The reader stood on the platform while reading.
   - The people sat on the floor and on the benches.

3. After you point out each of the activities of first-century rabbis below, ask a student to read the corresponding scripture. Rabbis:

- depended on others' hospitality (Luke 8:3)
- traveled as they taught (Luke 4:14–16)
- had disciples following them (Matthew 17:24)
- used parables (Matthew 13:3)
- urged followers to take the "yoke of Torah" (Matthew 11:29–30)
- had people welcome them into their homes (Luke 10:38–42)
- had a common treasury (Luke 8:3)
- often had many disciples (Luke 19:37)

4. What was a disciple? A disciple (*talmid* in Hebrew) was someone who not only learned from his teacher, but also tried to become *like* his teacher.

    Read Matthew 10:24–25; Luke 6:40; John 8:31, 13:13–15. Ask: How did Jesus' disciples become like their Teacher? Is Jesus' call for us any different from that of His disciples? Think of an example of someone you know who is Jesus' *talmid*—who is becoming like Jesus in some way. What character qualities can you identify that make that person Christlike? What is there in your life that indicates that you are Jesus' *talmid*?

c. *Prayer*

Spend a few moments in prayer together, asking God to help you be as devoted to Him as the disciples were to Jesus. Specifically, ask God to (1) motivate you to live by His way, not yours; (2) inspire you to make Jesus your Rabbi; and (3) guide you in becoming more like Jesus.

UNIT TWO
Step One: "Gamla and the Zealots"

1. Introductory Comments

Jesus chose to conduct His ministry around the Sea of Galilee. Capernaum, at the northwestern corner of the lake, is called His hometown. Not far away, perched on a rugged, steep hill, was the city of Gamla, home of the Zealots. These fiercely independent people were totally devoted to serving God. They believed it was appropriate to use violent resistance to remove the Roman yoke administered throughout the dynasty of King Herod. Jesus met these people, and they saw the displays of His power. One of them, Simon, was a disciple of Jesus. Jesus' message becomes clearer when we hear it contrasted with the Zealots' beliefs. This contrast helps emphasize the unique way Jesus called His followers to live.

2. Map Study: Gamla

HINT: *Begin this map study session by reviewing the geography of the overall region and working down to the city the lesson is dealing with—Gamla.*

Display the overhead transparency titled "The Roman World." Point out the following areas, and have your students locate them on their maps:

> Rome
> Mediterranean Sea
> Egypt
> Judea
> Caesarea

Display the overhead transparency titled "Galilee." Point out the following areas, and have your students locate them on their maps:

> Nazareth
> Capernaum
> Decapolis
> Galilee
> Sea of Galilee
> Gamla (note the distance from Capernaum, Jesus' hometown)
> Tiberias

3. Review the Overhead Transparency "New Testament Chronology"

Display the overhead transparency titled "New Testament Chronology." Highlight the following dates for your students:

586 B.C.	Babylonian Captivity of Judah
538 B.C.	Return to Israel
198–167 B.C.	Oppression under Hellenistic Seleucids
167 B.C.	Maccabee revolt
167–63 B.C.	Hasmonaean (Maccabee) kingdom
63 B.C.	Roman conquest of Judea
37 B.C.	Herod's reign begins
c.a. A.D. 27–30	Jesus' ministry
A.D. 66–73	First Jewish Revolt against Rome
A.D. 70	Jerusalem is destroyed

4. Show the Video *The Rabbi* (19 minutes)

5. Guided Discussion: Gamla and the Zealots

Ask your students to read the handout "The Zealots: No One But God" before the class session. Display the overhead transparency titled "The Zealot Movement" and note the history of the Zealots. If they have not done so, your students should read the handout "The Jewish Revolts" from Lesson Twelve.

a. *The Fortress of Gamla*

Display the overhead transparency titled "Gamla," pointing out the following:

- The isolation the mountaintop provided. Note the steep bank on the north side (right) and the narrow connection to the nearest cliff (foreground).

- The houses packed closely together on the south slope of the hill.

- The defensive wall blocking the only entrance to the mountaintop.

- The synagogue just to the left of the gate and behind the wall.

- The isolation of the fortress from the densely populated city and the religious center of the town.

The Zealots isolated themselves from the rest of the world. There is a constant struggle in the Christian community today between isolating ourselves, especially our children, from the world's unchristian values and reaching out to positively affect that world. For example, some people choose private Christian schools or home-school their children to protect them from ungodly influences.

Others see these secular schools as God-given ways to prepare children to live more obediently in (but not of) the world. Ask your students:

- How should we decide when it is right to isolate ourselves to be more godly, and when we should interact with the world to impact it for Jesus?

- Did Jesus approve of the isolationism of the Zealots? Why or why not?

- How are you like the Zealots in this regard? Unlike them?

b. *The Zealots*

The cultural setting of Jesus' ministry was not an accident. God planned the time and place where Jesus would present the kingdom of God. The Zealots, as part of the culture, had a purpose in that plan. Although we don't know God's mind, at the very least the Zealots' presence created a stark contrast to Jesus that made His message stand out even more. That may be part of God's purpose for this group's presence, and for their passion, during Jesus' ministry.

The following suggests some of the ways Jesus' ministry was in contact with Zealot thinking. Relate the following information to your students, review the Bible passages, and reflect on the questions provided.

1. Jesus chose Simon the Zealot to be His disciple (see Mark 3:18; Luke 6:15; Acts 1:13).[1] The fact that Simon is so designated may indicate the other disciples were not Zealots and even that Jesus was not in support of the principles of the Zealots. We do not know whether Simon gave up his support for Zealot tactics after joining Jesus. The constant tendency of the disciples to see the kingdom of God as a political entity may indicate Zealot influence on the whole group. Read Matthew 5:5,7,9,14–16,38–48, and discuss the following questions:

    - How would Simon have reacted to Jesus' message? Why?

    - Do you think Simon remained a Zealot after following Jesus? Could he have done so and still believed Jesus' message? Why or why not?

    - Are there any Christian groups or individuals today that remind you of the Zealots? Who are they? Can they hold these views and be faithful to Jesus? How?

    - How might Simon's presence (if he still held Zealot views) have helped make Jesus' message clearer?

2. Jesus' audience misunderstood his kingdom as human and political (John 6:15; Acts 1:6). His frequent teaching about the unique nature of His kingdom may have been intended to correct this Zealot belief so common in Galilee (John 18:36). Even the devil tempted Jesus to define His kingdom as human and political (Matthew 4:8–10). Discuss:

    - Why would Jesus' audience have misunderstood the nature of His kingdom?

    - If you were living then, do you think you would have understood Him correctly? Why or why not?

    - Can you think of examples in which Jesus has been misunderstood in our times because of preconceived ideas about Him?

3. Jesus frequently told people not to tell anyone about His miracles. Although the Bible does not reveal why, it is possible that one of His reasons was the Zealot misunderstanding that a powerful messiah would come to destroy the Romans (read Matthew 8:4, 9:30, 12:16; Mark 1:44, 5:43, 7:36; Luke 8:56). It is interesting that the miraculous healing in the demon-possessed man in the Decapolis led to a very different command (read Mark 5:19). It could be that the pagan Gentiles of the Decapolis were not affected by the messianic fervor of the Jewish Zealots and

were not as likely to misinterpret Jesus' message. Ask your students:

- Why do you think so many disregarded Jesus' command not to tell anyone? What would you have done?

- Do you agree that the command to keep quiet may have been due to the Zealot view that was so common? What other reasons could Jesus have had?

- Do you think there are ever similar times today, when God does something wonderful for you, but He asks you not to tell anyone? When? How would you justify silence?

- What message was the demon-possessed man to share? (Point out to your students that he did not go to a synagogue school or seminary for training. His task was simple: "Tell what God has done for you." If time allows, divide the class into groups of five or six. Give them five to 10 minutes to share together what God has done in their lives recently.)

4. The loaded questions asked of Jesus concerning taxes make sense in a world that included the anti-Roman Zealots and the pro-Roman Herodians. Read Mark 12:13–17; Matthew 22:15–22. Discuss:

- How do you think the Zealots responded to Jesus' answer? The Herodians?

- If the Zealots believed they were made in God's image, what did Jesus' answer mean for them personally?

- Is it right to serve an authority other than God? Why or why not?

- How can one give total allegiance to Jesus and still serve human rulers?

- Is violent resistance to human authorities ever justified? When? Who decides when this should occur?

- Was there anything in Jesus' ministry to indicate that there is a time and place for resistance? (See Matthew 21:12–17; Mark 11:15–18; Luke 19:45–47.) When are such actions justified? Would the Zealots have approved?

5. The misunderstanding concerning the nature of Jesus' kingdom (that it's nonpolitical and nonmilitary) surfaced frequently during His last week in Jerusalem. See how the following groups misunderstood:

- the disciples: Mark 10:35–45; Matthew 26:47–51

- the Romans: John 18:36

- the crowds: Matthew 26:55–56

- the triumphal entry: The crowds chanted "Hosanna," or "Lord, save us," and waved palm branches (which were sometimes connected with the Maccabee cleansing of the Temple). While there may have been some who recognized the salvation from sin Jesus proclaimed, many apparently did not. Their conduct led Jesus to weep and predict the ultimate result of following the Zealot approach to finding peace—violent destruction by the Romans, a fate that would arrive almost 40 years later. (See Luke 19:28–44; Matthew 21:1–9; Mark 11:1–10; John 12:12–15).

- Ask your students the following questions:

  a. What might have given the Romans the idea that Jesus was a Zealot? (He had a Zealot disciple; He came from Galilee; He was called a king; He was accused by the Sanhedrin; He drove buyers and sellers out the Temple; His triumphal entry; among other reasons!)

b. What does the fact that so many misunderstood Jesus tell you about the expectations of the people?

c. How, after being with Him, could the disciples still not understand?

d. Have you ever discovered you misunderstood (or refused to understand) something God said? How did you recognize it?

e. Jesus' love for His people led Him to weep when He recognized what the result of their methods and beliefs would be. Have you ever felt such compassion for people who refused to see Truth? (**HINT:** *If your students relate this question to the parent-child relationship, perhaps they'll gain a closer understanding of Jesus' personal sorrow as He wept for His children.*)

f. If Jesus came today instead of 2,000 years ago, for whom would He weep in our culture? Why? (Encourage students to explain their answers.)

6. At Jesus' trial and crucifixion, the Zealot threat became part of the process. Barabbas, offered in exchange for Jesus, is called an insurrectionist (Mark 15:7), a term used to describe the Zealots. The two "thieves" crucified with Jesus are called *lestai* in Greek (Mark 15:27; John 19:18), the official term for the Zealots. The Romans may have suspected Jesus of being the leader of the Zealots, though Pilate comes to recognize His innocence (Luke 23:4,22). Discuss with the class:

- Is there anything you admire about the Zealots? How could we maintain their zeal and total loyalty to God and be Jesus' followers? Would you be willing to give your life for your beliefs as they did?

- How was Jesus' zeal different from that of the Zealots?

- Now that you know more about the Zealot movement, how does their presence help you better understand Jesus' salvation message?

- Why is Jesus' way of sacrifice, devotion to God, and love for others the only hope of true peace?

- The Zealots separated themselves from others, were unconcerned about others, sometimes hurt people in God's name to accomplish their goals, and were more concerned about physical realities than spiritual condition. What can we do to be better disciples of Jesus and less like the Zealots?

6. Prayer

Spend a few moments in prayer together. Ask God to:

- help you be sensitive to the message of Jesus, hearing Him for what He claimed to be: our Savior and Lord.

- give you the desire and diligence to care for and love others while being passionately devoted to God.

- make you willing to reach out to others on Jesus' behalf and not isolate yourself from them—to be spiritually strong as you are in the world but not of the world.

Step Two: "Jesus the Rabbi"

1. Guided Discussion: The Synagogue

Synagogues were more than places where religious activities occurred. They were community centers, schools, courthouses, and even places where travelers stayed overnight. On Sabbath days, synagogues became the place the community gathered for worship in ways church members today would find familiar.

Local synagogues were at the center of Jewish life, especially in Galilee where belief in God flourished during the first century. If we understand the synagogue, we better appreciate the actions and words of Jesus that took place there.

To gain an understanding of the nature and significance of the synagogue, have students read the Bible passages suggested. Then pose the accompanying questions:

a. Matthew 4:23; Luke 4:15,16,44; Mark 1:21. Specifically, in which towns did Jesus visit the synagogue? How important was the synagogue to His ministry?

b. Matthew 12:9–12, 13:53–57; Mark 1:21–28, 3:1–5; Luke 4:16–37. What specific things did Jesus do as ministry in the synagogue? What was the reaction of the people? Of some of the Pharisees? Why would Jesus go to the synagogue so often? (Point out to students that the synagogue was the community center, the religious center, and the school.) Where should we take our witness for Jesus? What would be the equivalent of the first-century synagogue for us?

c. 2 Chronicles 36:17–19; Psalm 51:16–17; Isaiah 1:11–17. When the Temple was destroyed by the Babylonian army, the Jews could no longer worship God as they had for centuries. Based on passages like these, why would the Jews have focused on studying God's law instead? In what sense could one say that honoring and obeying God's law is like a sacrifice?

   Read Romans 12:1,9–21. In what way are Christians making a "sacrifice"? What are some of the laws we keep to offer ourselves as "living sacrifices" (v. 1)?

d. Matthew 23:2,6; Mark 5:22,35,36,38; Luke 4:17–20, 8:41–49, 13:14. What practices mentioned in the New Testament correspond to those mentioned in the video? Why did Jesus tell the people they must obey the Pharisees? Does that surprise you? Why or why not? (Sometimes Christians think that the Pharisees' theology was all wrong. It was not. They worked hard to be obedient to God. The problem was that they considered their human rules equal to God's and that they were hypocritical—teaching one thing and practicing another.)

   The Moses' seat was apparently the name given to the chair used in synagogues for the one who "sits" in Moses' place to read the words of Moses found in the Torah. Read Matthew 23:2–3. In what sense do we sit in the Moses' seat? Does this bring added responsibility?

   Who was Jairus? What type of person was he? What was the relationship between Jesus and Jairus? Does this tell us anything about Jesus' relationship with local synagogues?

   Read Luke 4:15. Why did the ruler (attendant or assistant) choose Jesus to read and speak in Nazareth? What passage was assigned for Jesus to read?

   Read Luke 4:21. What was Jesus' sermon? He may have said more, but the words recorded must have been powerful. Ask someone who is a good reader to reenact this sermon.

   It was customary in synagogues to stand while reading God's Word and sit while speaking about it (Luke 4:20; see also Matthew 26:55 and John 8:2). Why do you think they did this? Do you think we show the level of respect and awe for God's Word that was (and is) so evident in synagogues?

   The church was born from the synagogue. Like the synagogue, it was to be a community of people who live, learn, and pray together. Read Galatians 6:10; Ephesians 2:19. This description would have fit the synagogue well. Do we have this "community of faith" in our church? Why or why not? What could we do to make our church more of a community?

OPTIONAL — Digging Deeper I: Ancient Jewish Synagogues *(10–20 minutes)*

Display the overhead transparency titled "A Galilean Synagogue." The artist's rendering shows a typical synagogue design. Although earlier synagogues were small, simple rooms, they gradually became more elaborate as they developed into the community center of Jewish life: a place for prayer, school, legal courts, celebrations, and even lodging for travelers.

Outside each synagogue was a *mikveh* (pl. *mikvoth*), or ritual bath, for ceremonial bathing. This was done as a symbol that the worshipers had clean hearts as they entered the house of study and worship. This tradition was in keeping with the laws of the Torah regarding coming in contact with the dead (Numbers 19), body fluid (Leviticus 15), or other defiling objects such as idols. The *mikveh* must be hewn out of the rock or put in the ground. The water must be "living water," water that flows freely into the *mikveh* without being drawn. It is not known if Jesus used this ritual cleansing, partly because it is uncertain how widespread it was at His time. It appears likely He was familiar with this practice, as many *mikvoth* have been found from His day, including many near the Temple Mount in Jerusalem.

The congregation sat either on the floor or on the stone benches against the walls. The chief seats were those on the benches (Matthew 23:6). The common people sat on mats on the floor, which was usually paved but in some cases was dirt. Later, elaborate mosaics were used in synagogues.

The leader of the service would sit on a small, elevated platform that may have had a reading table, a menorah, and a seat (sometimes referred to as the Moses' seat—see Matthew 23:2). The Torah scrolls were kept in a chest called the holy ark, after the original ark of the covenant in which Moses placed the tablets of the Law. In the first century, these chests were portable; later, permanent cabinets were made. The columns in the interior held up the roof and also provided a balcony or gallery.

Next to the synagogue is the school where boys ages 5 through 12 were taught by the *hazzan* (synagogue ruler). Gifted students would continue their studies with a local rabbi or travel with an itinerant rabbi, learning to understand and apply Torah and oral tradition. The synagogue school also was the house of study for all the members of the community, just as the synagogue was the social center of the town.

It is likely that Jesus was familiar with synagogues like this one. Imagine Him sitting on the stone benches or on the floor; or on the *bema* (speaker's platform) with the Torah scrolls; or teaching in the school during the week. The synagogue was an important place for much of Jesus' ministry. In a beautiful way, it naturally integrated community life and worship. As such, it is the model for the church.

OPTIONAL — Digging Deeper II: More About Ancient Jewish Synagogues
(30–50 minutes)

(This section requires the use of the optional full-color overhead-transparency packet. For information on ordering it, see p. 243.)

Overhead Transparency 37. Synagogue of Gamla. The remains of this synagogue, one of the oldest found in Israel, are outlined in this photograph. It apparently functioned as a community center because no specifically religious artifacts were found in it. However, the *mikveh* (ritual bath) uncovered just outside (under the tin roof in the distance) led the archaeologists to conclude that it was a religious gathering place, hence a synagogue. Rows of steps or benches are found around the outside. They were used by the more important people of the community and the elders of the synagogue (Matthew 23:6). The floor in the center is unpaved. The common people of the community would sit on mats on the floor.

Columns around the outside supported a roof, apparently of wood, which was destroyed when the Romans devastated Gamla during the first Jewish revolt. The corner columns are heart-shaped (one can be seen in the lower left). The outside wall to the south (left) was destroyed so that the hillside of the steep mountain of Gamla can be seen, as can the wadi (dry riverbed) beyond.

The entrance to the synagogue is evident on the right. In the wall to the right of the entrance is a small enclosure, possibly the place the scrolls were kept (it cannot be seen in this photograph). On the far left is a small room that may have been the synagogue school, though the benches in it cannot be seen here.

The synagogue was about eight feet long and 50 feet wide. People cleansed themselves in the *mikveh* and entered from the west to join in the worship and readings of the synagogue. One can picture the joyful, thriving community of these religious Zealots praising God and seeking His guidance here on the hillside.

This synagogue was active when Jesus ministered at Capernaum less than 10 miles away. We do not know if He was ever here. Since "Jesus went throughout Galilee, teaching in their synagogues," it is quite possible. At the very least, this is similar to the synagogues in which Jesus did teach. The benches (chief seats), the *mikveh*, the study room, and the unpaved floor were often the locations for His teaching, His miracles, and His worship.

Overhead Transparency 38. Synagogue of Chorazin. Chorazin was one of the cities where "most of his miracles had been performed" (Matthew 11:20). Typical of Galilean towns of the time, the synagogue occupied a prominent place on an elevated platform in the center of town, symbolizing the importance of living in the presence of God. Just to the north (behind the photographer) was a *mikveh* for the ceremonial cleansing of the worshipers. Though the remains shown here date to the third or fourth century after Jesus, they retain the size, shape, and appearance of synagogues of His time.

This synagogue faced south toward Jerusalem, as all synagogues did after the Temple was destroyed in A.D. 70. Here you are looking from the north toward the south. The entrances are on the far side of the synagogue. Typically, synagogues of this time had three entrances. The hall shown here was 70 feet long and 45 feet wide. Three rows of columns, decorated with frieze, created a central "hall" and three "aisles." Parts of the reconstructed frieze, made of local basalt, can be seen. The column bases and the support base for them are in the original location. Remains of the decorative stone frieze and trim can be seen around the outside. The remains of stone benches can be seen on the west (right) under some of these stones.

It is possible that the synagogue had a balcony or gallery above the columns. Archaeologists found the remains of two decorated platforms located on the far end of the building. It is believed that they are the enclosed platform for the Torah ark and the reader's platform (bema). A replica of the stone Moses' seat is seen on the left at the far end of the synagogue (Matthew 23:2). Here the reader sat until it was time for the hazzan to bring the Torah scrolls to the reader, who would then stand to read (Luke 4:16–30).

Though these structures date from a time after Jesus, the practices in which He participated continued here. The inset shows the Moses' seat found in this synagogue. Made of local basalt, the seat has an inscription indicating that a man named Yudan made the chair and its raised platform for the people of Chorazin. It is possible Jesus sat in chairs like this one while He waited His turn to read in the synagogues of Galilee.

The Sea of Galilee is three miles south beyond the doorways. The ruins of the town of Chorazin are evident to the left beyond the synagogue. Jesus visited this town often, and He certainly was a part of the life of communities and synagogues like this one.

Overhead Transparency 39. Synagogue of En Gedi. This spectacular mosaic floor from a synagogue built in the second or third century was found at the oasis of En Gedi along the Dead Sea. The synagogue hall shown here is 45 feet long and about 30 feet wide. It follows the synagogue style found in Capernaum, Chorazin, and Gamla.

The rectangular structure in the floor background is the bema or reader's platform. The bases for columns around the outside are seen in the floor. This synagogue also faces toward Jerusalem, so it was built after A.D. 70.

The mosaic floor is among the most beautiful ever found. It is made of small stones of differing minerals that provided an array of colors. The artist who created it found white, black, reddish pink, red, brown, yellow, and blue-gray stones, which he carefully cut into tiny pieces (called tessera or tesserae). He then laid them in mortar, creating the designs seen here. Geometric designs form the outside borders. The center panel shows birds, peacocks, and grapes. The beauty and craftsmanship seen here emphasize how important the synagogue was to this community, just as it was important in Jesus' time.

Overhead Transparency 40. Aerial View of Capernaum. This aerial view shows the remains of Capernaum, a small village on the northern shore of the Sea of Galilee. ("Capernaum" comes from the Hebrew *Kfar Nahum*, which means "Nahum's Village"). Jesus chose this place as the hub of His ministry (Matthew 4:13) because it fulfilled prophecy that included His being on the main international road, sometimes called the Way of the Sea (Via Maris). Roman milestones still mark the road.

Jesus called Capernaum His hometown. Several of His disciples—Peter, Andrew, James, and John—were called to ministry here. Out of view to the left of this illustration was a small Roman garrison (see Luke 7:1–10), probably the home of the centurion whose faith Jesus commended. Capernaum was a small village (some estimate 1,200 people) of fishermen, farmers, and merchants—all religious and devoted to serving God.

The villagers' devotion to God is evidenced by the ruins of the synagogue of Capernaum, which date from three to four centuries after Jesus; but archaeologists believe the one from Jesus' time is beneath these ruins. The large hall on the right is the main hall. It is approximately 60 by 50 feet and faces Jerusalem. Benches have been reconstructed as they would have appeared in Galilean synagogues. Ordinary people sat on the stone floor. The large hall to the left may be a community center and probably contained the school. The size of this room helps us appreciate the importance the Capernaum citizens placed on their devotion to God and the study of the Torah. It seems only fitting that Jesus came here to proclaim His message of the fulfillment of the Torah.

Although there is no definite evidence as to which house was his, we know that Simon Peter did live in Capernaum (Mark 1:21–34; Luke 4:38–41), and it is clear that the early Christian community attached special significance to this location.

It was this town that first heard Jesus' message. The central location of the synagogue gives evidence to the deep religious convictions of the people to whom He ministered. Many became His followers.

2. Review: Called to Be *Talmidim*

This would be an appropriate place to discuss the material in **Digging Deeper II**, Lesson Fourteen.

OPTIONAL — Digging Deeper III: Around the Sea of Galilee *(35–70 minutes)*

If you have not done Guided Discussion 5, under Unit Two, in Lesson Fourteen, this would be an appropriate place to cover that material.

3. Lecture/Discussion: The Prayer Shawl

God commanded the people of Israel to wear tassels (*tsitsityot;* sing. *tsitsit*) on the corners of their garments (Numbers 15:38–39; Deuteronomy 22:12). Also, one of the threads in the tassel had to be blue. The wearing of tassels was significant not only because it would remind people to keep all of God's commandments, but also because the hem of a garment communicated the status or rank of the wearer. This may help explain David's cutting the hem of Saul's robe (1 Samuel 24:4). David was sorry for this act, which was a way of claiming Saul's throne—at least Saul seemed to think so (1 Samuel 24:20).

The Jewish people understood "corners" to be the front right and left and the back right and left of a shawl. The Hebrew word *kanaf* ("corners") can also mean "wing" or "extremity." Jewish tradition maintained that the blue thread was a reminder that Israel was royalty (blue was the color of royalty) because they were "a kingdom of priests" (Exodus 19:6). By Jesus' time, these tassels were widely worn and had taken on even greater significance.

Read the following Bible references together. Then point out the following information to your students and have them discuss the questions provided:

a. Read Numbers 15:37–41. Why were the Israelites to wear the tassels? The Septuagint, the ancient Greek translation of the Bible, translated the word *tsitsit* with a Greek word that is often translated as "hem." The distinguishing characteristic of a Jewish person's hem was a tassel with a blue thread. This helps us understand other references in the Bible. Discuss:

   • Is it a worthwhile practice for Christians to use symbols to remind us of God and His will? Why or why not? What symbols might we use?

   • Are there ways we could communicate to others our dedication to God by a symbol, just as the Jews did by wearing tassels? What are they? Should we do this? Why or why not?

b. Read Zechariah 8:23. The context is the coming day of the Lord, the Messiah. Why will the 10 Gentiles grasp the hem of the robe of one Jew? The hem refers to the edge of the garment with the tassels on it. It is probable that the verse also refers directly to the tassels themselves. The hem, with its tassels, will represent to the Gentile that God is with the Jew.

c. The Jews in the New Testament wore these tassels. There were two garments worn by Jews in Jesus' time: a tunic (a light robe) and a mantle (a heavy garment worn over the tunic). The tassels were apparently attached to the mantle, called *tallit* in Hebrew. This practice continues among religious Jews, who sometimes also fasten a tassel to an inner garment worn under a coat or shirt.

d. Read Matthew 23:5. Because the tassels reminded people of their obligations to God and were intended to direct others to God when Messiah came, some Jews apparently made their tassels quite long as a sign of their piety. What are some ways in which people today call attention to their piety? How can one live faithfully before God without becoming proud?

e. Read Matthew 9:20–22; Mark 5:24–34; Luke 8:43–48. The Greek word translated as "hem" is the word the Septuagint (Greek Old Testament) uses for *tsitsit* in Numbers 15:37–41. It would be appropriate to translate this episode in Jesus' ministry as touching the "tassel" of His garment.

   Apparently, in Jesus' time, these tassels held great meaning in Jewish tradition. The Bible teaches that the tassels represented God's command to obey His laws and the fact that God was with His people; the Jews also believed that the Messiah Himself would have "healing in His wings," represented by the tassels. When the woman grasped Jesus' tassels she was affirming Zechariah's message that God was with Him (Zechariah 8:23; see also Malachi 4:2). Her act was not a suggestion that Jesus' clothes had magical power but that God was with Him and that He was truly the Messiah. In other words, it was an act of faith to touch the hem or tassel and not His sleeve or some other part of His clothing. Jesus affirmed this as well (Mark 5:34).

f. Read Numbers 5:1–2. Notice that people with the condition the ailing woman had were isolated from the community because they were considered unclean, even if they were not responsible for the condition. That meant this woman was probably ostracized by most people and was therefore lonely. Discuss:

   • Have you ever felt shunned and unworthy as this woman must have felt? What did you do? Can you imagine her joy when Jesus' healing touch enabled her to fully rejoin the community? Have you had a similar experience? Relate it to the group.
       Read Matthew 9:29; Mark 10:52. What other examples can you think of where faith was essential to the working of Jesus' power?

   • Can lack of faith lead to God being unwilling to work His power? (See Matthew 13:58.)

   • Is it necessary for people today to have faith if God's power is to work effectively through them? Can lack of faith result in an absence of His power?

   • How could we indicate our faith that Jesus is Messiah and His power is sufficient—as the woman did by grasping His hem?

4. Prayer

Spend a brief time in prayer. Ask God to help you see Jesus more clearly every day. Ask for the faith to grasp His tassels—to live in total conviction that He truly is Messiah with the power to work miracles in your life.

Conclusion

It is amazing that God planned the cultural setting of Jesus' ministry so carefully. The presence of the Zealots made His message of love and sacrifice such a clear contrast to the misguided hopes of the Zealots. His actions as a typical Jewish rabbi provided the perfect setting for Him to proclaim His message in the synagogue and through the teaching practices and style of a Jewish rabbi. But the most important reminder for us is that we must believe in Him. We must have the faith of the nameless woman who believed in Jesus and His power. Through her simple faith, God performed a miracle. He does no less for us.

Notes

1. Some suggest that the reference to Simon as a "Zealot" means only that he was zealous. Though that is possible, it is unlikely. The use of the term would have been most clearly understood in that time and place as a "member of the Zealot movement." For the sake of our study, this will be considered to be the most likely possibility.

THE ZEALOTS: NO ONE BUT GOD

Lesson Fifteen
Handout #1

The history of impassioned defense of freedom and the right to serve God alone was vivid in the collective memory of the people of Jesus' day. Only 150 years earlier, the deeply religious supporters of the Hasmonaeans (Maccabees) called the Hasidim (meaning "pious ones") had gladly taken up swords against the pagan oppression of the Seleucid Greeks to defend their right to worship God. The Roman masters of Jesus' time were less oppressive, but the lack of status of a free nation and the frequent conflict over the pagan values of these foreigners led people to remember the heroes of the past whose trust in God and readiness with the sword had become God's instruments of deliverance.

TORAH AND KNIFE

The Pharisees, passionately devoted to God, were apparently content to condemn idolatry and strive to separate themselves from all religious contamination. Though on occasion they became the object of brutal repression for their stubborn refusal to accept any of the pagan practices of the emperor, they seem to have been reluctant to use violence to advance their cause (at least until after Jesus' time).

The Zealots had a different view of serving God.[1] Occasionally the Romans conducted a census of their subject lands to determine the taxable resources of these peoples. To the Jews who believed they and their land belonged to Yahweh, a census reminded them that they were the "possession of Rome." The fact that the censuses were ordered by Roman emperors (thought to be divine and worshiped in some of the Gentile towns of the land) added to the bitterness of the Jews toward taxation. They belonged to God and were not to honor anyone else but Him. How could they serve these pagans, even with their taxes?

In about 45 B.C., a Jewish patriot named Ezekhias (Hezekiah), from Trachonitis (east of Galilee), led a band of freedom fighters against the Romans and their supporters. Apparently, he was captured by Herod the Great and executed. In the intervening years, thousands of like-minded Jews were caught and crucified as examples to the population. Herod himself was so brutal in repressing these people that he was summoned to Jerusalem to answer to the religious council, the Sanhedrin, for his conduct. Under pressure, the Sanhedrin freed him, and many paid with their lives when Herod solidified his rule.

After Herod's death, many of the Galilean supporters of Hezekiah attempted to create resistance against Herod's sons. This too was brutally put down. In A.D. 6, Judea was officially incorporated into the Roman empire. A census was ordered, and Quirinius, governor of Syria, carried out the order so that the new province could be appropriately taxed. The priests in Jerusalem urged restraint and cooperation with the Romans; but Hezekiah's

LESSON FIFTEEN **117**

son Judah of Gamla (the isolated mountaintop city northeast of the Sea of Galilee) urged violent resistance. A popular Pharisee named Zadok, also from Galilee, supported Judah. The Zealot movement was founded. The well-known Pharisee Gamliel recorded the early history of Judah and his movement: "Judas the Galilean appeared in the days of the census and led a band of people in revolt. He too was killed, and all his followers were scattered" (see Acts 5:37). He was probably killed by Herod Antipas, who also murdered John the Baptist (Matthew 14:1–12).

Both Judas and Zadok were devoted to the Torah as the only guide for righteous living before God. They based their zeal for God on the action of Phinehas, Aaron's son, recorded in Numbers 25:7–13. Phinehas is praised for his zeal, which imitated the zeal of God (Numbers 25:11,13). The fact that Phinehas, a priest of God, used a spear became the basis for what Zealots considered a divine command to use violent action to defend God's name and destroy unfaithfulness to Torah among the Jewish people. This interpretation would lead to a long history of violent acts against Rome and brutal conflict between the Zealots and the Jews they believed cooperated with the pagan empire.

ZEALOT BELIEF

The philosophy of the Zealot movement was simple: There was only one God, and Israel was to serve Him alone; the Torah and other writings of the Bible were the only guide to righteous living; and serving the emperor in any way, whether in worship, slavery, or paying taxes, was apostasy against God.

Josephus, who knew the Zealots, described their passion for freedom as unconquerable because they would serve no one but God. Violent resistance was considered a God-ordained responsibility. Since they believed God was on their side, they knew that they would triumph in the end. This led to their reputation for incredible bravery and tolerance for suffering.

The Zealots lived by the most strict conformity to the Torah. And they refused to acknowledge anyone as king, since "you shall have no other gods" (Exodus 20:3). Galilee in particular was influenced by these defenders of freedom. They were committed to the Scriptures' promise of a coming anointed one who would be a great military leader and king, like David of times past. They knew they would soon prevail over the detested Romans and their collaborators, the Herodians (Jews who supported the Herods) and the Sadducees.

JESUS AND THE ZEALOTS

Jesus chose Galilee for His ministry, using Capernaum as His home base. Though several miles from Gamla, the hotbed of Zealot fervor, Capernaum certainly was influenced by the Zealot passion for freedom and the anticipation of a Messiah. The presence of this fierce devotion to God in Galilee had both direct and indirect influences on Jesus' ministry. (1) One of His disciples was Simon the Zealot (Mark 3:18).[2] (2) Jesus often needed to correct His audience's interpretation of His message as political rather than spiritual (John 6:15; John 18:36; Acts 1:6), and on several occasions, He urged those who experienced His power not to report the miracles, possibly to prevent such misinterpretation (Matthew 12:16; Mark 1:44). (3) The Zealots expressed great interest in Jesus' answer to the query about paying taxes (Mark 12:13–17). (4) The Romans apparently considered Jesus to be part of the Zealot movement (John 18:36). And (5) Barabbas, probably a Zealot, was offered in exchange for Jesus (Mark 15:15), and Jesus was crucified with two who are described by a Greek word officially used for Zealots (Mark 15:27).

Jesus' message was made clearer by its contrast with the Zealot perspective so pervasive in Galilee. This may have been part of God's plan to confront people with a faith choice among radically different alternatives. Would they accept a suffering Messiah (Isaiah 53:1–10) whose kingdom demanded a lifestyle of loving one's enemies, forgiving transgressors, (Matthew 5:21–24,38–47), and being peacemakers (Matthew 5:9)? Or would they seek a messiah who would violently overthrow their oppressors to establish a new political empire (John 18:36; Acts 1:16)? Would they recognize that true peace comes from forgiveness of sins rather than from military conquest?

THE END OF THE ZEALOTS

Judah, the founder of the Zealot movement, was executed. His sons Jacob and Simeon were both crucified approximately A.D. 48. Another son, Menahem, seized the fortress Masada at the beginning of the Jewish revolt (A.D. 66) in the first true military action of that war. The Roman weapons found there equipped the Zealots who led the revolt. Menahem, probably thought to be the Messiah, commanded the rebel forces until he was murdered by another Zealot, bringing to mind the words of the true Messiah: "All who draw the sword will die by the sword" (Matthew 26:52). A descendant of Judah, Eleazar Ben Jair, fled to Masada and assumed command of the forces there.

John of Gischala, another Zealot, futilely defended Jerusalem and the Temple Mount against the Romans. Again the words of Jesus, who wept when people did not embrace the kind of peace He offered, came true (Luke 19:41–44). The Romans threw the Zealots and their children off the city wall to their deaths, and destroyed the Temple and the city.

In A.D. 73, the Romans, under the command of Titus, laid siege to Masada. Eleazar, a descendant of Judah of Gamla, and his Zealots held out until there was no hope. They chose to kill their families and each other rather than serve anyone but God. With that mass suicide, the Zealot movement came to an end.

NOTES

1. In popular use, the term *Zealot* refers to all Jews who resisted Rome and Jewish collaborators. Technically, the name refers more narrowly to the party, or "philosophy" as Josephus calls it, rooted in the movement led by Judah and Zadok.

2. Some suggest that the reference to Simon as a "Zealot" means only that he was zealous. Though that is possible, it is unlikely. The use of the term would have been most clearly understood in that time and place as a "member of the Zealot movement." For the sake of our study, this will be considered to be the most likely possibility.

"HE WENT TO THE SYNAGOGUE . . ."

The New Testament records more than 10 occasions on which the ministry of Jesus took place in the synagogue. The Gospels record that "Jesus went throughout Galilee, teaching in their synagogues." Yet the Christian reader rarely ponders the significance of such an apparently common structure so central in Jesus' ministry.

The synagogue provided a ready platform for the teaching of Jesus and later the apostle Paul. In that way, it proved to be a significant part of God's preparing exactly the right cultural practices for His Son's ministry. But more than that, Jesus, His disciples, and Paul (as well as most early Jewish followers of Jesus) went to the synagogue to worship. The synagogue was not simply a place to share God's Word, but also an important part of the Jewish people's relationship to God. It might surprise modern Christians to discover that many church practices are based on synagogue customs that Jesus followed. Understanding the synagogue and its place in Jesus' life and teaching is an important step in hearing His message in the cultural context in which God placed it.

THE ORIGIN

There are many theories of the origin of a gathering place called synagogue. The Greek word means "assembly" and is used in place of the Hebrew word meaning "congregation" or "community of Israel." Originally, it probably referred to the gathered people and over time came to refer to the place of assembly as well. It is never used to refer to the Temple, which was God's dwelling place and not primarily a place of assembly for the community. No one but Levites and priests could enter the Temple proper. All members of a Jewish community could participate in the community life of the synagogue.

Some Jewish traditions hold that there were places of assembly for the study of Torah during the time of the Temple of Solomon. At the most, the Old Testament indicates that the practice of prayer, with or without sacrifice, which was to be so central to the synagogue, had already begun (Psalm 116:17; Isaiah 1:11,15; 1 Samuel 1:10ff).

The beginning of the assembly of people for the purpose of study and prayer (the Jewish way of describing worship) appears to be the Babylonian exile after the destruction of the first Temple. Jewish scholars believe Ezekiel's reassuring promise that God would provide a "sanctuary" (11:16) for His people is a reference to the small groups that gathered in their homes during the exile to recall God's covenant, His law, and especially the redemptive promises of the prophets. It is likely that these godly people, having learned a hard lesson about the importance of obedience to God, assembled regularly to study His Torah to prevent the sins of their ancestors from being repeated. A group of experts in the law and its interpretation taught and studied in small associations at humble locations called "houses of study." These places of study, and the reflection on the need to be obedient, are the roots of the synagogue—a sanctuary to inspire obedience to God.

In spite of the later emphasis on prayer and study in the place of assembly, it is likely the main focus of the early gatherings of Jewish people was simply the need to maintain their identity as a people living in a foreign and pagan country. That the synagogue began as the center of the Jewish social life is confirmed by the fact that it was the community center in the first century as well. The synagogue was school, meeting place, courtroom, and place of prayer. In some towns, the synagogue may even have provided lodging for travelers. It was the place where small groups of Jewish students assembled for Scripture reading and discussion of the Torah and oral tradition. This meant that worship and study, friendship and community celebration, and even the governing of the community were all done by the same people in the same place.

It appears that the early church patterned itself after the synagogue and continued the same practice of living and worshiping together as a community, often in private homes (Acts 2:42–47). The modern "assembly" of Jesus' followers would do well to remember that the roots of the church are in a community living and worshiping together. Worship (prayer) was a natural extension of the life of the community.

SYNAGOGUES OF JESUS' TIME

By the first century, a synagogue was found in many (some say most) of the towns and villages of Galilee. The Gospels specifically mention those of Nazareth (Matthew 13:54) and Capernaum (Mark 1:21). Archaeological evidence is scant for those early synagogues, though later ones left much more substantial remains. Typically, they were built on the highest point in town or on a raised platform. As long as the Temple stood in Jerusalem, synagogues apparently did not face Jerusalem.

In some cases, the front facade had three doors. Inside there were benches on three sides of the room. There was a small platform where the speakers or readers would stand, and it is possible that a small menorah (a seven-branched candlestick), like the one in the Temple, stood on that platform. The floor was usually dirt or flagstones, and common people probably sat on mats on the floor, while the important people sat on the stone benches (Matthew 23:6). In later synagogues, elaborate mosaics with a variety of designs covered the floor. (None exist from Jesus' time.)

There might have been a seat for the reader of the Torah called the Moses' seat, because the Torah recorded the words of Moses (Matthew 23:2). The Torah scrolls and the writings of the prophets were probably kept in a portable chest and brought to the synagogue for worship. Only later do permanent Torah cabinets (called the holy ark) appear. Outside was a *mikveh* (ritual bath) for the symbolic cleansing required for entrance into the synagogue.

The synagogue, a kind of democracy, was governed by local elders. Males 13 or older could belong to the synagogue. A local ruler, called the *hazzan*, was responsible for maintaining the building and organizing the prayer services (Mark 5:22,35–36,38; Luke 8:41–49, 13:14). The *hazzan* was often the teacher of the synagogue school, especially in smaller villages. He would announce the coming Sabbath with blasts on the shofar (ram's horn). Although the *hazzan* was in charge of worship services, the prayer leader, readers, and even the one who delivered the short sermon could be any male member of the community. All were recognized as being able to share the meaning of God's Word as God had taught them in their daily walk with Him. Even boys over 13 could be granted permission to read or speak. In this way, the community encouraged its youngest members to be active participants in its religious life. (Jesus' encounter with the wise teachers in the Temple courts was unusual not so much because of His age, but because of the wise questions He asked and the profound answers He gave—see Luke 2:41–47.) The *hazzan* also cared for the Torah scrolls and other sacred writings and brought them out at the appropriate times (Luke 4:17–20). Priests and Levites were welcome to participate in synagogue life, including worship, but they had no special role except that only priests could offer the blessing of Aaron from the Torah (Numbers 6:24–27) at the end of the service.

SYNAGOGUE AND SABBATH

While the synagogue building functioned as a community center, school, court, and place of study during the week, on the Sabbath it served as the place where the assembly met for prayer.[1] When the first three stars could be seen on Friday evening, the *hazzan* blew the shofar to announce that the Sabbath had begun. The people gathered at twilight to eat the Sabbath meal in their homes. All the food was already prepared because no work was permitted during this time.

The following morning, the community gathered in the synagogue building. The service began with several blessings offered to God. The congregation recited the Shema: "Hear, O Israel: The LORD our God, the LORD is one" (Deuteronomy 6:4). The Torah scrolls would be brought out by the *hazzan* and would be read in several portions, sometimes as many as seven. Different people would be invited forward to read a portion. The readings were determined according to a set schedule, so the reader would have no choice of the passage read.

Following the Torah portion, a section from the prophets (called the Haphtarah) would be read by another reader. After all readings, a short sermon would be offered, often by a person recognized for his insight and wisdom—though visiting speakers were common. Any male member of the community was eligible to speak. The sermon was apparently quite short (Jesus spoke only a few words—Luke 4:21). The service ended with a benediction using the Aaronic blessing found in the Torah (Numbers 6:24–26), if a priest was present to offer it.

Jesus spent much time in synagogues (Matthew 4:23). He taught in them (Matthew 13:54), healed in them (Luke 4:33–35; Mark 3:1–5), and debated the interpretation of Torah in them (John 6:28–59). Clearly, He belonged to the community of the synagogue, because when He visited Nazareth, He was invited to read the Haphtarah (Luke 4:16–30). This is a remarkable example of God's preparation, as the passage Jesus read was exactly the passage that explained His present ministry.

The early Christians continued to attend synagogues, though with a new interpretation of the Torah, now that Jesus had been revealed as Messiah (Acts 13:14).

The new community of Jesus was born out of the synagogue. Believers were to become assemblies, not single individuals seeking God alone. We address God as "our Father" because we are His assembly. We are one body because we are made that way through Jesus (1 Corinthians 12:12–13). In our fractured, broken world, with all its self-preoccupation, the model of the synagogue, the picture of the community of God, presents an alluring message. We would do well to understand the synagogue of Galilee.

THE SYNAGOGUE SCHOOL

Boys went to school; girls did not. Students probably attended school in the synagogue and were taught by the *hazzan*. Study began at age five or six in elementary school, called *bet sefer*. The subject was the Torah and the method was memorization. Since the learning of the community was passed orally, memorization of tradition and God's Word were essential.

At first students studied only the Torah. Later they began to study the more complicated oral interpretations of the Torah. Question-and-answer sessions between teacher and student were added to the memorization drills. The more gifted students might continue after age 12 or 13 in *beth midrash* (meaning "house of study," or secondary school). Here began the more intense process of understanding and applying the Torah and oral tradition to specific situations. The truly gifted would leave home to study with a famous rabbi to "become like him" as a *talmid* (disciple). Although their discussion and study might be held in the synagogue, these disciples would travel with their rabbi, learning the wisdom of Torah and oral tradition in the daily situations they faced.

By the time a person was an adult, he knew most of the Scriptures by heart. If someone recited a passage, the audience would know whether it was quoted accurately or not. Jesus, in keeping with His culture, would simply begin with "It is written . . . ," knowing His audience would recognize an accurate quote.

The Mishnah (the written record of the oral traditions of Jesus' time and after) recorded that the gifted student began study of the written Torah at age five, studied oral traditions at age 12, became a religious adult at 13, studied the application of Torah and tradition at 15, learned a trade at 20, and entered his full ability at 30. Although this may represent conditions after Jesus, it is significant that He came to Jerusalem at age 12, already wise; then He learned a trade from His father until His ministry began at age 30. His life seemed to follow the education practices of His people quite closely. Did He attend the schools? Learn from great rabbis? It is quite likely He did. Being addressed as "Rabbi" frequently indicated someone who had learned from a rabbi. He certainly selected a group of students who followed Him, learning as they went. And everywhere His audience had the knowledge of the Bible on which Jesus so often based His teaching.

NOTES

1. Christians describe the church activity of formal interaction with God as "worship." Jews describe the same activity in synagogues (or, in Bible times, in the Temple) as "prayer." In Jesus' parable, the tax collector and Pharisee go to the Temple to pray (Luke 18:10). Their activity certainly included prayer, for going to the Temple to pray meant going at the time of worship and sacrifice. The Temple is called the House of Prayer (Isaiah 56:7; Luke 19:46), meaning "the place of worship."

LANGUAGE OF CULTURE

For the Teacher

Most Christians know that Jesus lived in a rural, agricultural setting in the back country of Galilee. They realize that His main audience was composed of peasants with an occasional aristocrat from Jerusalem thrown in. To show that this may be true, ask your students to describe briefly the type of people Jesus ministered to. See if anyone suggests that Jesus interacted with the highly cultured, sophisticated world of royalty and the theater. If no one mentions this fact, point out that only recently has archaeological research begun to help us broaden our view of the diverse groups of people with whom Jesus lived.

This lesson will help students recognize this part of Jesus' world and will highlight His ability to speak in concepts and "word pictures" they understood. Jesus used the world of high culture to enhance His message for those who knew that world or lived in it. This meant that what He said and did could be understood by a wide range of people. He spoke a language that many people understood. He spoke the "language" of his culture. That made Him a master teacher.

Ask your students: Do Christians speak in words and ideas our culture understands? Must we find a way to faithfully communicate the message of Jesus so that it can be understood by those who don't know the "Christian jargon" of Bible stories? Can we do that without compromising the message? Those are the issues and questions that are primary to this lesson.

Your Objectives for This Lesson

At the completion of this section, you will want your students:

To Know/Understand

1. The history and archaeology of Sepphoris.
2. The location of Sepphoris.
3. Why Jesus lived in Nazareth.
4. The beautiful analogy of Christianity as an olive tree.
5. The trade Jesus learned.
6. The nature of Jesus' relationship with Herod Antipas and the lessons to be learned from it.
7. How Jesus used the images of the world of culture to communicate the gospel.
8. How Jesus used the practices of the theater to teach about sincerity.
9. Why God hates hypocrisy.

To Do

1. Learn to be more aware of Christianity's Jewish roots.
2. Plan to produce fruit as a branch on God's tree.

3. Learn to communicate the message of Jesus more clearly by communicating in language the culture understands.

4. Commit to being genuine in their religious practice.

5. Look for specific people they have been insensitive to, in their desire to be true to their beliefs.

6. Support people who communicate Jesus' message through means that speak the "language of our culture."

How to Plan for This Lesson

Because of the volume of material in this lesson, you may need to divide it into several class sessions. To help you determine how to do that, the lesson has been broken into several segments. Note that the time needed may vary considerably depending on the leader, the size of the class, and the interest level of the class.

If you wish to cover the entire lesson in one session, you should complete Unit One, a discussion of major points in the video. It does not go into great depth. You may go into greater depth, or enhance your background knowledge as class leader, by selecting parts or all of the remaining material.

How to Prepare for This Lesson

Materials Needed

Student copies of the maps: "The Roman World"
                                 "Galilee"
                                 "The Kingdom of Herod the Great"

Overhead transparencies: "The Roman World"
                                 "Galilee"
                                 "The Kingdom of Herod the Great"
                                 "New Testament Chronology"
                                 "The Herod Family Tree"
                                 "The Olive Tree"
                                 "Sepphoris Theater"

Student copies of the handouts: "In Herod's Footsteps: The Dynasty Continues"
                                     "Pharisees or Sadducees?"

*Video: **Language of Culture***

Overhead projector, screen, VCR

1. Make copies of the maps and handouts listed above for your students. (If possible, they should receive and read the handouts before the lesson.)

2. Prepare the overhead transparencies listed above. (You'll find them at the back of the book.)

3. Determine which **Steps** and which **Digging Deeper** sections, if any, you wish to use in your class session(s). NOTE: You can use these sections in any order you wish (e.g., you might want to use **Digging Deeper III,** but not **Digging Deeper I** or **Digging Deeper II**).

4. Review the geography of the lands of the Bible from the "Introduction."

5. Prepare your classroom ahead of time, setting up and testing an overhead projector and screen (for the overhead transparencies) and a VCR. If you plan to hand out biblical references for your students to look up and read aloud, prepare 3x5 cards (one reference per card) to distribute before class.

Lesson Plan

UNIT ONE: Video Review

1. Introductory Comments

Jesus' world included many different kinds of people. Yet Jesus effectively communicated His message to all of them because He was familiar with their culture and could speak in ways they understood. One class of His culture was the wealthy aristocracy, who usually had a Hellenistic (Greek), humanistic outlook on life. Jesus knew how to speak to them so they could clearly understand what He was saying to them. This lesson will help you understand this sophisticated, cultured element of Jesus' world and teach you how to be more like Him in finding ways to communicate better about Jesus to your own culture.

As you view the video, pay careful attention to the remains of Sepphoris. It will help you understand more clearly Jesus' world and message.

2. Show the Video *Language of Culture* (21 minutes)

3. Map Study: Sepphoris

HINT: *With your students review the maps listed. Identify the key locales and work toward the city this lesson is dealing with—Sepphoris. This will enable students to become familiar with the settings of biblical events and to be able to identify specific locations.*

Using the overhead transparency titled "The Roman World," point out the following areas and locations, and have your students find them on their maps.

> Mediterranean Sea
> Rome
> Judea
> Caesarea

Using the overhead transparency titled "Galilee," have your students find the following areas and locations on their maps.

> Caesarea
> Jerusalem
> Masada
> Bethlehem
> Sea of Galilee
> Galilee and Perea (the territory of Herod Antipas)

Using the overhead transparency titled "The Kingdom of Herod the Great," have your students find the following areas and locations on their maps.

> Capernaum
> Tiberias
> Nazareth
> Sepphoris

Be sure to point out the geographical proximity of Nazareth and Sepphoris.

4. Guided Discussion: Jesus and the Herods

a.   Read Matthew 2:19–23; Isaiah 11:1; Romans 11:21. Apparently, the word *Nazareth* comes from the Hebrew word for "branch" or "shoot." After moving to this town, Jesus was known as the Nazarene, or the Shoot or Branch, thus fulfilling prophecy (see also Isaiah 53:2). The image is

- Israel is the stump.

- Jesus is the branch growing from the stump.

- Those who believe in Him grow naturally from Him or are grafted into Him.

- They bear fruit because they are nourished "in" Him.

   Ask your students the following questions:

- Why is fruit a symbol for the Christian life?

- Describe someone you know who is clearly grafted into Jesus because of the fruit of his or her life. What is the fruit he or she is producing?

- Why are our Jewish roots important for us as Christians?

b. Read Matthew 14:1–12; Luke 8:3, 9:7–9, 13:31–33, 23:6–12. Ask your students the following questions:

- What effect did his execution of John the Baptist have on Herod?

- What was Herod's attitude toward Jesus after he had John killed?

- Whose funds supported Jesus? Where did they originate? Who actually was supporting Jesus? Think of another example of God using evil intent for good.

- What was Jesus' attitude toward Herod? Can you think of anyone else He criticized by name?

- How could someone be so close to Jesus and not believe in Him?

- Why is it important to respond to Jesus when we have the opportunity?

- Who appeared more powerful—Jesus or Herod? Who really was?

- Who or what appears the most powerful today? Who really is the most powerful?

   Point out to your students that Herod built the beautiful city of Sepphoris, which today lies in ruins. Jesus' city, on the other hand, is still growing and will last forever.

c. Read Luke 19:11–27. Herod Archelaus was given one-third of the kingdom when his father, Herod the Great, died. Archelaus immediately went to Rome to ask for more land. The Jews sent a delegation to ask Caesar to appoint someone other than Archelaus to govern them, but Caesar ignored their request and appointed Archelaus anyway. Upon returning to Israel, Archelaus promptly rounded up the delegates and their families and had them executed.
   Jesus grew up in the shadow of the Herod family, whose capital, Sepphoris, is three miles from Nazareth.
   Ask your students to respond to the following questions:

- What are the similarities between the parable and Archelaus's life?

- What would be the effect of patterning the parable after real life?

- How would it affect the audience?

- What does this tell you about Jesus' ability to communicate? About His awareness of the world of royalty? About His awareness of His audience?

- How would you apply this principle when communicating Jesus' message to our culture?

d. Read Matthew 6:2–4, 6:16–18, 23:23–31. Jesus used the word *hypocrite*, which means "actor," 18 times. Paul didn't use it at all. Religious Jews spurned the theater and everyone attached to it because they considered it pagan. Yet there are many individuals in Jesus' audience who were not religious or Jewish. Jesus' use of theater images would speak clearly to them.

Ask your students the following questions:

- What point was Jesus trying to make when He used theatrical images and terms such as "hypocrite" in His teaching? (NOTE: Actors were announced with trumpets and painted their faces to portray different characters.) What does God think of an "actor" when it comes to religious faith? How can we keep our religious practices from becoming empty routine?

- What is significant about Jesus' use of theater concepts to communicate truth?

- Who in the audience would have understood these images? Who might have been offended?

- What does this tell you about Jesus' desire to communicate His message to everyone? What lessons can we learn from this?

- What would correspond to the "theater" in our culture (i.e., something that is secular but could help communicate Jesus' message more clearly)?

- Give an example of Christians using communication styles that speak only to ourselves and not to our culture. How could you (your church) communicate Jesus' message more effectively to the culture around you?

- In what ways, if any, could you compromise the message by using contemporary language or methods?

e. Prayer: Spend a few moments in prayer, asking God to help us learn to communicate His message of salvation through Jesus more effectively to our culture and world.

UNIT TWO
Step One: "Growing Up in Nazareth"

1. Introductory Comments

Jesus grew up in Nazareth, a small village in lower Galilee. Nearby was one of the glorious cities of His day, Sepphoris. Usually the emphasis in studies of Jesus is His ministry among Galilean peasants and fishermen. This lesson investigates His relationship with the more sophisticated culture of His day—the theater and the aristocracy—and His use of its imagery in His teaching. God carefully prepared the time and place of Jesus' work on earth. Understanding all the elements connected with these two things makes Jesus' message clearer and more challenging to our world today.

2. Map Study: Nazareth and Sepphoris

HINT: *With your students review the maps listed. Identify the key locales and work toward the cities this lesson is dealing with—Nazareth and Sepphoris. This will enable students to become familiar with the settings of biblical events and to be able to identify specific locations.*

Using the overhead transparency titled "The Roman World," point out the following areas and locations, and have your students find them on their maps.

Mediterranean Sea
Rome
Egypt
Judea
Caesarea

Using the overhead transparency titled "Galilee," have your students find the following areas and locations on their maps.

> Capernaum
> Gamla
> Tiberias
> Nazareth
> Sepphoris
> Valley of Jezreel

Be sure to point out the geographical proximity of Nazareth and Sepphoris, and the two cities built by Herod Antipas—Tiberias and Sepphoris.

Using the overhead transparency titled "The Kingdom of Herod the Great," have your students find the following areas and locations on their maps.

> Caesarea
> Jerusalem
> Masada
> Bethlehem
> Sea of Galilee
> Herod Archelaus's territory—Judea, Samaria, Idumaea
> Herod Antipas's territory—Galilee and Perea
> Herod Philip's territory—Gaulanitis
> Decapolis

3. Review the Overhead Transparency "New Testament Chronology"

Using the overhead transparency titled "New Testament Chronology," highlight the following dates for your students:

63 B.C.	Roman conquest of Judea
37 B.C.	Herod's reign begins
4 B.C.	Herod's death
4 B.C.–A.D. 6	Archelaus rules Samaria, Judea, and Idumaea
4 B.C.–A.D. 39	Herod Antipas rules Galilee and Perea
c.a. 6 B.C.	Jesus' birth
c.a. A.D. 27–30	Jesus' ministry
A.D. 66–73	First Jewish Revolt against Rome
A.D. 70	Jerusalem is destroyed

4. Show the Video *Language of Culture* (21 minutes)

5. Guided Discussion: Growing Up in Nazareth

a. *Why Nazareth?*

Read Luke 1:26–28; Luke 2:1–7; Matthew 2:13–15,19–23. Ask your students to respond to the following questions:

- Why did Mary and Joseph go to Bethlehem?
- Why did they go to Egypt?
- Why did they return to Nazareth?

Point out the following:

- They must have been gone several years.
- They may not have planned to return to Nazareth at all (Matthew 2:22–23).
- God's plan was that prophecy should be fulfilled.

Read Matthew 2:22. Display the overhead transparencies titled "Galilee" and "The Herod Family Tree," and point out:

- where each of Herod's sons ruled,
- when Archelaus's rule began and ended,
- that Nazareth is in Antipas's and not Archelaus's territory.

b. *The Branch*

According to Matthew 2:23, a prophecy was fulfilled by Jesus' return to Nazareth—"He shall be called a Nazarene." Scholars have long discussed the relationship of Nazareth to this prophecy. There are several opinions. The following is believed by many (including the author) to be the best possibility.

Read Matthew 2:21–23. What are the specific words of the fulfilled prophecy? Matthew said Jesus returned to Nazareth to fulfill "the prophets" (2:23). No prophet speaks these specific words, so what prophecy is being fulfilled? There are probably several.

Read Mark 14:67, 16:6; Matthew 21:11, 26:71; Luke 4:34, 18:37, 24:19; John 1:45, 18:5,7, 19:19. The word *Nazareth (Nazarene)* is part of Jesus' identification. The Greek word translated *Nazareth (Nazarene)* is most likely based on the Hebrew word *netzer,* a word frequently used in the Old Testament for the royal line of David. It means "branch" or "shoot."

- Isaiah 11:1–3 (verse 1)—"shoot"
- Isaiah 53:2—uses a different Hebrew word but has the same meaning: "shoot" or "root"
- Other passages use the idea of a growing plant for the Messiah:

> Jeremiah 23:5—branch
> Jeremiah 33:15—branch
> Zechariah 3:8—branch
> Zechariah 6:12—branch

Clearly, *Nazareth* means "branch" or "shoot." Thus someone from there would be a *Nazarene.* Jesus the Nazarene, meaning "Jesus the Branch," would clearly link Him to the Old Testament prophecies that the Messiah would be the branch out of Jesse's stump.

Read Revelation 22:16. Jesus is the root from David.

Read Romans 11:17–21. There are many lessons in this passage. One beautiful picture is the relationship between the Jewish people, Jesus, and Christians.

- Israel is the stump (Isaiah 11:1)
- Jesus is the shoot from the stump in dry ground (Isaiah 53:2)
- Christians (Gentiles) are the grafted branches (Romans 11:17)
- We get our spiritual "nourishment" from the roots and the "shoot" (Romans 11:17–18)
- God cut down the tree (vine) once because it didn't produce fruit (Isaiah 6:13, 10:33, 53:2; John 15:1–8,16)

Conclusion: One way to view this beautiful biblical metaphor is:

- Israel is the root of the Christian faith.
- Jesus is the shoot that became the new tree or vine.
- Believers are the branches that must bear fruit for Him.
- Branches that don't bear fruit are pruned.

- The fruit is attached to the vine and the roots.

Ask your students the following questions:

- Why is "fruit," or Christian living (see Galatians 5:22; John 15:8), necessary? ("Fruit" is being Jesus' disciple.)

- Think of an example of someone who is "grafted onto Jesus" because of the fruit he or she produces.

- What specific area of your life is unfruitful? If you can, share your answer with the person next to you. What will you do to bear fruit?

- What does it mean that Jesus is "the branch" (Nazarene, *netzer*)?

- What is one reason God made sure that Mary and Joseph went to Nazareth?

c. *Prayer*

Read Acts 24:5. Early Christians were called Nazarenes—"people of the Branch." The Hebrew word for "Christian" is *Notzri* (pl. *Notzrim*). We are still known as "people of the Branch," or "people of the Messiah." Pray that our fruit may show that we are rooted in the Jewish soil of Jesus and grafted onto Him, our Branch.

OPTIONAL — Digging Deeper I: The People of Nazareth *(10–20 minutes)*

Who were the people of Nazareth? Archaeological research and details in the Bible provide only a few known facts about them; much can only be surmised.[1]

- Nazareth is not mentioned in the Old Testament. It probably did not exist then.

- Excavations suggest a small population, possibly 200 at most. It was probably a small "daughter" city of a larger nearby town.

- An archaeological find in Caesarea mentions a family from the town. The spelling indicates that the word *Nazareth* derives from *netzer*, or "branch."

- Essenes referred to themselves as a "shoot planted by God," a similar use of this concept.

- It is likely that the people of Nazareth settled here before New Testament time. Based on their name and their Davidic lineage, they thought the Messiah might come from them because they were the "shoot" town. This may explain why His family wanted Jesus to return there (Mark 3:20–21). It would also help explain why the people of Nazareth were so angered when He refused to do a miracle in their town but would elsewhere (Luke 4:23–30).

- The Nazarenes' belief that the Messiah would come from their town may lie behind the distaste with which others referred to Nazareth (John 1:46). One of the reasons Jesus was despised (Isaiah 53:3) may have been His association with "disliked" Nazareth.

- They had a synagogue and were religious (Luke 4:16–30).

OPTIONAL — Digging Deeper II: The Olive Tree *(20–40 minutes)*

Use Overhead Transparency 17, "The Olive Tree," at the back of the book, to illustrate this lesson.

NOTE: This section covers the same material as Guided Discussion 5, pp. 132–133, except it goes into greater depth.

Jesus was the shoot from Jesse's stump and the branch of God. He is the vine and we are the branches. This image of grape vines and olive trees comes from the agriculture of Israel. The olive tree can become a beautiful metaphor for Jesus, His messianic task, and our relationship to Him, as the following items show.

1. Olive trees grow very old. When they get so old that the branches no longer produce, the farmer cuts the branches off, leaving only a massive stump, several feet wide and high. Soon new shoots grow out of the old stump. Most are trimmed, and the remaining shoots become branches and produce great amounts of olives. Sometimes new branches are grafted onto the old stump.

    - Read Matthew 3:10, 7:19. In the Old Testament, God cut down Israel for not bearing fruit. He will do the same to those who are the new branches.

    - Read Isaiah 11:1. Like the olive branch, a new shoot came out of Jesse's stump. That shoot is Jesus. He is rooted in God's Jewish people but is a new shoot.

    - Read Romans 11:11–24. Gentile Christians are not "natural" branches out of the stump; they are grafted. But they too can be "pruned" if they do not produce fruit.
      Ask students to respond to the following questions:

      a. Who is the "farmer"?

      b. Where are our roots?

      c. Who is the shoot, now become a huge branch onto which Gentiles believers are grafted and Jewish followers of Messiah are attached?

      d. What will happen if these branches don't bear fruit?

      e. Why is it crucial to understand and appreciate our Jewish roots?

      f. What might you do to better understand the Jewish roots of your faith?[2]

      g. Why has there been so much anti-Semitism in the history of the church? (See Lesson Seventeen in this book.)

      h. Read Matthew 1:1. The title given to Jesus—*Christ* from the Greek and *Messiah* from the Hebrew—means "Anointed." In one sense, that title is related to the olive tree because the Old Testament prophets and kings were anointed with oil, probably olive oil (see Exodus 29:7 and 1 Samuel 16:13). This title is used more than 375 times in the New Testament. The olive tree producing its precious oil is a metaphor for the Messiah, God's Anointed.

2. Conclusion: From the overhead transparency, help your students see the relationship between Jesus, Israel, and Christians.

    - The roots are Israel.

    - The stump is Israel (note its size). The faces are the artist's rendering of Abraham and Sarah, the parents of the Jewish people.

> - The large boughs are Jesus, the Shoot or Branch.
> - The branches are the believers in Messiah. Note that the leaves are people.

d. *Guided Discussion: Learning a Trade*

Little is known about Jesus' life in Nazareth. According to Luke 2:40, Jesus grew in wisdom and strength. Matthew 13:55 tells us Joseph's occupation. Mark 6:3 indicates Jesus learned His father's trade.

1. The Greek word *tekton* is translated as "carpenter." It can mean one who builds with wood, but its general meaning is a craftsman who builds with any material, including stone and wood. It is unlikely that trades in biblical times were as specialized as they are today. The *tekton* was able to build with whatever material was available.

   Anyone who visits Israel knows that little was (or is) built from wood since no wood is available. Wood was used for doors and roof beams, but most building was done with local stone. In spite of generations of pictures of Jesus in a wood shop, the text of the Bible and the culture would indicate He spent as much or more time building with stone. The "stonemason" in Israel today, who spends countless hours sitting or kneeling shaping stones, is probably closer to the trade Jesus knew than the modern carpenter.

2. Herod built Sepphoris on a huge scale. Its palace, theater, roads, water system, and much more made it the jewel of his kingdom. Most of the buildings were made of local limestone with plenty of imported marble. Many builders were needed to complete it.

3. Nazareth was three miles away from Sepphoris. Since it was built during Jesus' early life, did He work there? Did Joseph? To answer yes is pure speculation. Yet from our perspective, it is certainly possible. At the least, we can say Jesus the *Tekton* could have watched the most magnificent example of His trade slowly being built.

4. The picture of Jesus learning the building trade, working with wood and stone, adds meaning to His use of construction images in His teaching. Read each passage and respond to the questions:

   - Matthew 16:18. Where will Jesus build His church? With what? (*Peter*, which means "stone"?)

   - John 2:19–22; Mark 14:58. Seeing the spectacular stone construction of Herod's Temple, Jesus made this claim. He knew what went into its construction, and so did His audience. He was speaking of His body but used the analogy He was familiar with—that of building. Which was more spectacular: If He rebuilt the Temple or raised His body from the dead? Why?

   - Luke 14:28–30. What did Jesus compare becoming His disciple to? What was His point? How might He have been familiar with building towers?

   - Matthew 21:42; Acts 4:11–12. What part of the building is Jesus? What does this say about His role? (He is the capstone or cornerstone, which means the final piece holding it all together.)

   - 1 Peter 2:4–8. Who (or what) is Jesus in the analogy of a building? (Living Stone, Cornerstone, and *Builder.*) Jesus the *Tekton* is a builder of His building—the church, God's people. In what sense is Jesus building today? With what (or with whom)? How can you be a part of His building, being shaped by Him? In what sense are you also building with Him? Describe something you are now doing that contributes to His building.

5. Prayer: There was Herod, the greatest builder of stone Israel ever saw. His magnificent buildings now lie in ruins. Then there was Jesus, a humble stonemason who left no stone buildings we know of. His building, constructed on the foundation of His disciples, with Himself as the

cornerstone, is still being built today. And we, His followers, have the great honor of being the living stones that form the walls, floors, and so on, of the building. Jesus' building will never be ruined; it will last forever.

Spend a few moments in prayer, thanking God for bringing Jesus the Stonemason into our lives so that we can be His living stones and part of His everlasting kingdom.

Step Two: "Jesus in Culture—Sepphoris"

1. Introductory Comments

In this section, we're going to focus on the theater in Sepphoris, Herod Antipas's magnificent city. Sepphoris (*Zippori* in Hebrew, which means "bird") is perched like a bird on top of a high hill about three miles north of Nazareth, Jesus' boyhood town. Sepphoris is surrounded by fertile, farm-dotted valleys and has an abundant water supply. A main branch of the international trade route (sometimes called the Via Maris) runs nearby.

Sepphoris has been an archaeological treasure trove. More important, it has been a window into a new element of Jesus' world—a Greek-Roman world of Hellenistic ideas, wealth, and power. Sepphoris's ruins, not all from Jesus' time, include a theater, an immense water system, a colonnaded roadway, beautiful mosaic floors, and much more. Be sure your students appreciate the magnificence of this city because it is crucial to their fully understanding what will be discussed here.

2. Guided Discussion: Jesus and Sepphoris

a. *History of Sepphoris*

Display the overhead transparencies "New Testament Chronology" and " The Herod Family Tree." Then point out the following information to your students.

- Sepphoris is mentioned in several ancient sources from the Hasmonaean period.

- Israel was conquered by the Romans, and the Roman commander Pompey designated Sepphoris as the district capital of Galilee.

- The people of Sepphoris resisted Herod, who destroyed the city and slaughtered its inhabitants in 37 B.C.

- The people of Sepphoris, led by the Zealots, revolted in 4 B.C. after Herod's death; the city was conquered again by Romans.

- Herod Antipas became king of Galilee and rebuilt Sepphoris as his capital in 4 B.C.

- Jesus was born c.a. 6 B.C. and grew up in Nazareth, 3 miles away from Sepphoris. It is not known exactly when Jesus and His family went to Nazareth, but it must have been approximately 4–2 B.C. He began His ministry sometime before A.D. 30. The exact amount of time Jesus spent in Nazareth is not known, but it must have been a significant amount since He was known as Jesus *of Nazareth.*

   Ask your students to discuss the following:

   1. Describe Sepphoris based on the video *Language of Culture.* Make sure they point out the mosaics, colonnaded street, and theater. Let students give their reactions.

   2. How might the proximity of this great city have affected life in Nazareth?

3. Does it surprise you that Jesus grew up in the shadow of one of the most modern secular cities, the capital of a member of the powerful Herod family? Why or why not?

4. Why have we tended to view Jesus' world as that of the peasant?

b. *Jesus and the Herods*

Refer to the overhead transparency "The Herod Family Tree" as needed in this section. Students should read the handout "In Herod's Footsteps: The Dynasty Continues."

Jesus' life and the lives of the Herods were intertwined in an amazing way. Herod the Great searched for Jesus and tried to kill Him when Jesus was still a baby (Matthew 2:1–23). Archelaus's treachery brought Jesus to Nazareth to fulfill prophecy (Matthew 2:23). Herod Antipas killed John the Baptist and tried to kill Jesus. Few families came so close to the Messiah and yet remained so far away. Herod Antipas built Sepphoris, the city where the video for this lesson was filmed. His relationship to Jesus was typical of the Herods.

Have your students read the passages and answer the questions that follow.

- Matthew 14:1–12; Mark 6:14–29. Why did Herod kill John the Baptist? What opportunity did Herod miss?

- Mark 6:14–29; Matthew 14:1–2; Luke 9:7–9; Luke 13:31–33. What effect did John's execution have on Antipas? What was Antipas's subsequent attitude toward Jesus? What opportunity did Antipas miss?

- Luke 8:3. How was Jesus' ministry financed? Where did Joanne get her money? From whom did Cuza receive his salary? Who, in effect, was financing Jesus' ministry? Can you think of other examples in which God uses evil for good?

- Luke 13:31–33, 23:6–12; Matthew 14:13. What was Jesus' reaction to John the Baptist's death? What was Jesus' attitude toward Herod? Can you think of anyone else Jesus criticized by name? What do you think was Jesus' reason for refusing to answer Herod? How can someone be so close to Jesus (and eternal salvation) and not only turn Him down but attempt to destroy Him?

- Matthew 22:16; Mark 3:6, 12:13. It is likely that the Herodians were aristocratic Jews, supporters of Herod and thus pro-Roman. Apparently, they lived in Galilee, mainly in Tiberias, and so were right across the Sea of Galilee from Capernaum, Jesus' hometown. They were also only a few miles from Gamla, where the anti-Roman, anti-Herod Zealot movement began. Probably, the Herodians wanted Jesus removed because of their fear that He might start a popular uprising and the Romans would then replace Antipas with a more effective ruler. Once Antipas was dethroned, the Herodians would lose their position as well. The Sadducees (the priestly aristocracy) had the same fear for themselves (John 11:49–50).

  Did it help or hurt Jesus' ministry to have such opposition? Why? Why is there always opposition to God's work? Relate an experience when you tried to serve God and a follower or followers of the evil one opposed you. Did God intervene?

- Conclusion/Discussion: (1) Why is it important to respond to Jesus when we first meet Him? (2) How do you think God's purpose was accomplished in Herod? (3) In what sense do Jesus and Herod represent the two great powers in the universe? Who appeared more powerful at the time? Who really was greater? Is the same true today (i.e., evil appears more powerful than good)? Relate some examples to the class. (4) Who are the Herods of our day? (5) Is there anyone in the class who has experienced persecution? How is that similar to what Jesus experienced under Herod? (6) Read Luke 13:31–33 again. What comfort is this passage?

- Prayer: Spend some time in prayer. Ask God to help you recognize Jesus and follow Him. Ask for deliverance from the "Herods" of our day, and pray for those who face daily persecution so that they may be strengthened by the knowledge that Jesus is greater than any Herod.

OPTIONAL — Digging Deeper III: Herod Antipas, the Fox *(15–30 minutes)*

In an article entitled "That Small Fry Herod Antipas, or When a Fox Is Not a Fox," Randall Buth explained that the fox in Jewish culture was more than an example of craftiness. Frequently, the fox was compared with the lion. Lions are powerful; foxes are small and weak, though they may act like lions. Great people are like lions; petty people who put on airs, pretending to be greater than they are, are like foxes. In this sense, saying "How do you, a fox, dare voice an opinion when there is a lion present?" would mean "How do you—a nobody, a pretender, a wimp—dare speak when a truly wise person is present?" Dr. Buth quoted many such examples. A fox is somebody who acts big and talks big but is really a "nobody." A lion can make good on his talk because he is truly strong.

This is probably Jesus' meaning in Luke 13:31–33. Possibly referring to the fact that Herod was popularly called "King" when he was only a tetrarch, Jesus implied that Herod was simply an impostor, a weak pretender, a fox. Jesus said, "I'm really the one in control because I will do exactly what I plan to do."

Ask your students to read Luke 13:31–33 and answer the following questions.

1. What verses support the possibility that Jesus is calling Herod a "nobody"? What thoughts support the idea that Jesus is saying "I am in total control"?

2. It is possible that craftiness was also associated with the fox. Do you find anything in the passage that suggests Jesus is calling Herod crafty?

3. If Jesus is using *fox* in the cultural sense suggested above, calling Herod a fox is an extraordinary insult. Why might Jesus have made such a strong statement? Is there ever a time for such strong language for a Christian? If so, when?

4. How can we still love our enemies? What was Herod's crime?

5. Do you find irony in the fact that Herod lived so close to Jesus? (Sepphoris, his first capital, is three miles from Nazareth, where Jesus grew up; Tiberias, his later capital, is six miles from Capernaum, where Jesus lived during His ministry.) If God prepared the time for Jesus' coming, what is the reason for Herod and Jesus being so close throughout Jesus' ministry?

3. Guided Discussion: Cultural Images in Jesus' Teaching

It is clear that Jesus used the people, places, events, and activities of His time as object lessons, parables, and metaphors in His teaching. That was the Jewish way. The Greeks thought and taught abstractly. Theory, definition, and logical systems of thought were important to them. The Hebrews, on the other hand, put their ideas into concrete language. They used "word pictures" and stories to convey their views. Thus, Jesus spoke of salt and light; He was bread, living water, a shepherd; His followers were to become fishers of men and branches producing fruit. These concrete lessons make it easy to remember Jesus' words and add power to His teaching. The images Jesus used came from the rural, largely agricultural world of His time, particularly Galilee.

But there was another source for these images and examples. Jesus often used word pictures from the aristocratic world of His day—a world of culture, wealth, tax collectors, kings, and even the theater. We seldom picture Jesus as part of that world. It is impossible to know how much He participated in it in spite of the many banquets He attended. Yet He was familiar enough with that world to use slices from it to portray the lessons He taught. He could communicate clearly to those in His audience who knew that world. He could speak the language of culture. That made Him a master teacher and His teaching clear and powerful. This study will consider two elements of the world of wealth and power that were part of Jesus' teaching: royalty and the theater.

There are many locations at which Jesus and His disciples might have learned of the society of wealth and power. Jerusalem, Caesarea, and Damascus were not far from where they traveled and taught. But right in Galilee were two cities of great glory: Tiberias and Sepphoris. Sepphoris was only three miles from Jesus' boyhood town of Nazareth. Tiberias was only six miles from Capernaum, where Jesus centered His ministry. Although both cities must have given Jesus and His audience an abundance of material that could be used in teaching and learning, we are going to focus on Sepphoris.

a. *Introduction*

Display the overhead transparency titled "Galilee," and locate the cities of Sepphoris and Nazareth. **HINT:** *If you have the optional full-color overhead-transparency packet, display the overhead transparency titled "Sepphoris: Bird on a Hill." The description of the city in* **Digging Deeper V** *of this lesson also provides an excellent illustration.*

Point out to your students the following facts about Sepphoris:

- It was located on a hill that was visible for miles around.

- It was laid out in the latest Roman pattern with a colonnaded street leading to the forum.

- It was crowned by Herod's elaborate palace.

- It was home to one of the largest theaters of the day.

- It was Hellenistic in culture, with a gymnasium, an elaborate water system, and probably a bathing complex.

- The only king Jesus had recorded contact with was Herod Antipas, the builder of Sepphoris. (Jesus was certainly familiar with the other kings in the Herod family.)

b. *Jesus and the King*

Jesus used images from the royal court for two categories of lessons: parables and analogies. Divide the class into small groups and assign each group a category or example within a category. Ask each group to discuss the questions and report back to the larger group with a summary of their discussions.

Parables

1. Luke 19:11–27. Have someone read aloud the sections entitled "Herod's Will" and "Herod Archelaus" in the student handout "In Herod's Footsteps: The Dynasty Continues." Then have the group answer the following questions:

   - What similarities are there between the life of Archelaus and Jesus' parable?

   - Do you think this is just coincidence? Why or why not?

   - Why would Jesus make His parable so similar to a real-life example? How would it help His audience?

   - What does this example indicate about Jesus' audience? About Jesus? (Hopefully, students will point to their awareness of the world—of Herod's kingdom—around them.)

   - How does this parable indicate familiarity with the royalty of the day? What does it teach?

2. Luke 14:25–33. Remind this group that Herod Antipas had recently gone to war with Aretas, his father-in-law and king of Nabatea, because Antipas had divorced Aretas's daughter. Antipas lost badly.

   - What point is Jesus making?

   - How does the "king" example support His lesson?

- Does the parable have similarities to Antipas's life? Do you think this is coincidence? Would Jesus' audience have understood Jesus' lesson better because they were familiar with real situations like the one in Jesus' story even if Jesus Himself did not have a specific example in mind? Why?

- How does this parable support Jesus' use of the royal world of His day as examples?

Analogies

1. Matthew 11:2,7–11; Luke 7:25.

   - What was occurring in John's life that involved "kings"?

   - What image does Jesus use from the royal court?

   - What does Jesus assume His audience knows?

   - What is His point? Why is it communicated so effectively? (Because people understood His example.)

2. Mark 10:35–45; Matthew 20:20–28.

   - What "royal" practices are mentioned?

   - What is the point of the analogy? What is the "royal court" an example of?

   - How does knowledge of the Herods help you understand the purpose of this teaching example?

   - How does this analogy indicate familiarity with the royalty of the day? What does it teach?

Conclusion

Bring the small groups back together. Ask them to give summaries of their discussions. Then discuss:

- Why was Jesus able to communicate so well with so many different people in His culture? (He spoke a "language" they understood because it was part of their experience. He reached different types of people by using different cultural experiences.)

- How would you apply this principle to your life? Why is it important to communicate God's truth in words and pictures our culture understands?

- In what ways do Christians speak a "language" foreign to the culture around us? Is this Jesus' way?

- What are some things we need to be familiar with in our culture to communicate effectively with it?

- Can the gospel be explained differently to different people? Ask students to think of examples in which we must know someone's world to communicate with them (e.g., teenagers and adults, different races or ethnic groups, people of religious or nonreligious backgrounds).

- Jesus conformed His teaching to the worldview of His audience. Can you think of an example of His teaching that fit an agricultural world? A fisherman's world? The world of the aristocrat?

- Why do we hesitate to speak to our culture in a language it would understand? (Perhaps we're afraid that we may "weaken" the content of Jesus' message?) How can this be prevented?

NOTE: Teachers might recommend the book *Roaring Lambs: A Gentle Plan to Radically Change Your World,* by Robert Briner (Grand Rapids: Zondervan, 1993). Briner makes a powerful case for learning to speak to a desperate culture in ways it understands. The book is replete with examples and recommendations.

c. *Jesus and the Theater*

Students should review the handout "Pharisees or Sadducees?" Then point out the following information.

Herod the Great popularized the theater in Palestine as part of his campaign of Hellenization. He built theaters in Caesarea, Jerusalem, Jericho, Samaria, and Sidon. The plays were the latest in Greek-Roman drama, including comedy and tragedy. Bawdy and often obscene, they were frequently about gods and goddesses and mocked honorable and sacred things. The Jewish religious community considered them immoral, and the Talmud taught that one should not go to theaters because sacrifices were made to pagan gods. Rabbi Simeon Ben Pazi was reported to have said, "Blessed is the man that has not walked to the theaters." That seems to have been the belief of those devoted to Yahweh.

It is important that your students understand there is *no* evidence that Jesus participated in or attended the theater. But there is clear evidence He was familiar with this part of the culture, and by speaking its "language," He could communicate with those who knew it, including the pagans of the Decapolis (many Decapolis cities had theaters).

Display the overhead transparency titled "Sepphoris Theater," and point out the following information to your students:

- The stage was over 150 feet wide and 25 feet in depth.
- The floor of the stage, now gone, was probably made of wood.
- The theater could seat over 4,000 spectators.
- There was a colonnade around the back with a roof over the spectators.
- Many in Jesus' audiences were familiar with the theater.
- Jesus used the word for "stage actor"—*hypocrite*—18 times. Paul didn't use it at all.
- Actors would "paint" their faces to portray different characters or emotions.
- Leading actors would be announced with trumpets.
- The pantomimes of the actors were often dramatic exaggerations.

Discussion: Ask the students how each of the following examples is related to the stage actor. Then ask what the point of the teaching is.

- Matthew 6:2–4
- Matthew 6:16–18
- Matthew 23:23–31
- Luke 6:41–42

    1. Who would be considered a hypocrite today? Why is it so difficult to act on what we believe?

    2. How do we keep our religious practices from becoming empty routine?

Conclusion: The following questions may raise difficult issues for Christians struggling to be distinctive in a secular world. The intent is *not* to modify or change God's message. The purpose is to use Jesus' example to find ways to speak in a "language" (words, methods, media) that our culture speaks so our message is understood.

- What lessons can we draw from Jesus' use of theater images?
- What would correspond to the theater in our culture? (Media? Popular music? Movies? Theater?)

- How can being knowledgeable about the elements of popular culture enhance our ability to communicate the gospel's unchanging message?

- Is it appropriate to use a means of communicating the message of Christianity if that means is also used by the secular (pagan) culture around us? Is the means inherently sinful? Why or why not?

- How might Christians use the following to communicate the gospel:
    1. Popular music
    2. Theater
    3. Movies
    4. Television
    5. Computer

- Give some examples in which Christians' use of their own "language" (words, methods, media) makes it difficult for an "outsider" to understand God's message.

- Read 1 Corinthians 9:19–22. What is Paul teaching? How is it similar to Jesus' use of the "stage actor" to communicate His message?

Prayer: Spend a few moments in prayer, asking for the devotion to God that avoids compromising His truth. Ask God for a love for others that makes us ready to communicate God's love in ways they understand. Ask Jesus for the wisdom to know how to speak the language of our culture and for the courage to be faithful to His truth.

OPTIONAL — Digging Deeper IV: The Pharisees (15–35 minutes)

Jesus strongly condemned the hypocrisy of the Pharisees, who did not practice what they believed and taught. It might be appropriate to help students understand that in spite of His strong words, Jesus did not condemn all Pharisees. In fact, in some ways it is unfortunate and unfair to these people that they have become synonymous with uncaring legalists and phonies. Please point out that this observation is not intended to water down Jesus' words or to defend those He criticized. It is simply to say there is more (in the Bible) to the picture.

If they haven't already, students should read the handout "Pharisees or Sadducees?" Then review the following:

1. Read John 3:1–2, 7:50. Some Pharisees supported Jesus, inviting Him to dialogue and eat with them.

2. Read Matthew 23:2–7. Jesus commanded His followers to obey the Pharisees but not imitate their hypocrisy.

3. Read Matthew 23:13–28. Jesus criticized the hypocritical Pharisees (as they themselves did) and the "leaven" of the Pharisees. He never criticized them for being Pharisees.

4. Read Luke 13:31. The Pharisees, in trying to protect Jesus, warned Him that Herod wanted to kill Him.

5. Read Mark 12:34; Acts 15:5. Some Pharisees were not far from God's kingdom, and others entered while remaining Pharisees.

6. Read Acts 23:6; Philippians 3:5. Paul remained a Pharisee after becoming a follower of Jesus.

Discussion: Ask your students to respond to the following questions:

- Do you think there is value in trying to balance your view of the Pharisees? Why or why not?

- Why were Jesus' strongest condemnations for those who were the most religious and devoted to God? Is hypocrisy among the devoted followers of God worthy of greater condemnation than other sins of that day (such as the theater, the games of the arena, pagan sacrifices in the Decapolis)?

- What can you learn from this about Jesus' reaction to Christians who say one thing and live another?

- Who today practices religious things they do not mean? Can you think of some examples in your own experience that Jesus would condemn?

- Jesus criticized the Pharisees because their interpretations sometimes disregarded the needs of people (see Matthew 23:23). Do Christians today get so caught up in being right (about politics and religious views) that people with needs are ignored? Are we hypocrites if we have the "right" theology but do not care about others? What would Jesus say?

Conclusion: The Pharisees whom Jesus criticized deserved every word. But they struggled just as we do to have the right beliefs and religious practices. Yet they were insincere, proud, and insensitive to others while they did it. We can learn as much from the Pharisees' mistakes as we can from their devotion to God.

OPTIONAL — Digging Deeper V: The Theaters of Jesus' Day *(20–45 minutes)*

(This section requires the use of the optional full-color overhead-transparency packet. For information on ordering it, see p. 243.)

More than any other person, Herod the Great was responsible for bringing the theater to Israel. His campaign to make Hellenism (humanism) the worldview of his people included several theaters—at Caesarea, Jericho, Jerusalem, Samaria, and Sidon. The ruins of these structures remain. The Gentile and largely Hellenistic populations of the Decapolis made the theater an important community institution. Many places, including Susita and Beth Shean, near the area where Jesus ministered, had theaters. Sepphoris, built near Nazareth at the time of Jesus, had a theater, though not all experts believe it was completed at that time. Certainly, the theater, often in opposition to the God-centered worldview of the Jews, was an important influence in first-century Israel. This section will help students appreciate the glory of some of theaters of Jesus' world and the influence they had on the culture.

Overhead Transparency 18, Sepphoris Theater, and Overhead Transparency 41, Sepphoris: Bird on a Hill. The first overhead transparency is an artist's rendering of the theater at Sepphoris; the photograph shows the remains of Sepphoris today. This glorious city, on a hilltop in Galilee, is slowly being uncovered by archaeologists. The name *Sepphoris* is the Greek translation of the Hebrew *Zippori*, which means "bird." According to Jewish tradition, this name was used because, as seen here, the town looks like a bird perched on the hill. Nazareth is three miles to the left. The fortress on the top of the hill was built centuries later.

Herod Antipas built a fortified tower, a palace, and a forum on this hilltop. The theater, which was probably renovated after Jesus' time, had a diameter of approximately 225 feet and seated 4,000 people. The spectators sat on stone seats that were fitted into grooves in the bedrock. Though it is unlikely Jesus attended this theater, He probably saw it and others in Galilee. His use of the word *hypocrite* (which means "stage actor") indicates the familiarity of His audience with this cultural institution. The city of Sepphoris probably had 25,000 or more inhabitants while Jesus was growing up in Nazareth, a village of about 200 people.

Overhead Transparency 42. The Theater at Caesarea. Herod's love of Hellenistic culture and his desire to introduce it to the Jewish nation is illustrated clearly by the theater at Caesarea. Apparently, this structure was built outside the city because its obscene and bawdy performances may have created an offense among religious Jews. The theater seen here has been reconstructed for use in modern times and shows the splendor and size of theaters in the Roman world. In Herod's day, it seated approximately 4,000 spectators on stone benches similar to the reconstructed ones shown here. The floor of the orchestra (the semicircular space in front of the stage where the important people sat in Roman times) was colorfully painted stone in Herod's time and later paved with marble. The front of the stage (orchestra wall) was painted stone imitating marble. There are six wedges of seats. The square place for the governor's seat can be seen midway in the center wedge. The Bible records the death of Herod Agrippa I (Acts 12:19–23), which Josephus recorded taking place in the theater. It is also possible that Paul was interrogated here by Felix (who was married to Drusilla, Herod the Great's granddaughter) and Festus, as well as Agrippa II and Berenice, his sister (Acts 24–26).

This theater illustrates the glory of the Hellenistic lifestyle. It was seductive and overwhelming to the Jewish people. It was resisted by the religious community. An ancient rabbi named Yitzak is quoted in the Megilla, a collection of Jewish sayings, as believing that Caesarea and Jerusalem could not prosper at the same time. Either one or the other would be in ruins. This was his way of teaching that the values represented by Caesarea (and its theater) were antithetical to those of Jerusalem (and the Temple). Followers of Jesus today would do well to remember the rabbi's words as they seek to hold to the values of Jesus that conflict with the Hellenism of today—secular humanism. Ask your students for examples in which we compromise our values with the secular values of our culture. How do we affect our culture as we participate in it but resist its effect on us?

Overhead Transparency 43. The Theater at Beth Shean. (NOTE: *If you have the optional full-color overhead-transparency packet from Set 1, Overhead Transparencies 26, 27, and 28 are of Beth Shean as well. Their descriptions are given in Lesson Four,* **Digging Deeper I.**) This spectacular theater was built during the Roman period in the Decapolis city of Beth Shean, known also by its Greek name, Scythopolis. It was more than 360 feet in diameter and seated over 7,000 people. As seen here, one tier of seats remains. The black basalt foundations of the second tier are still visible, but the foundations of the third tier are gone (the bases for them remain—see Overhead Transparency 44, "Scenes from the Theater," below). The ruins of Beth Shean are in the foreground.

The Decapolis region, largely Gentile and pagan, was governed by Rome, not by the Herods. Jesus frequently visited these 10 city-states, where He attracted many followers. His use of "hypocrite" as a descriptive term would have been clear to people of this region, who attended theaters like this one.

Overhead Transparency 44. Scenes from the Theater. Upper left: The stage of the theater in Beth Shean. Though covered by wooden panels today, it was originally covered with stone. It is built on arches with drainage channels beneath it. Behind the stage stood the *scaenae frons,* a backdrop for the stage, including a row of granite and marble columns and stone panels shown here. This provided the set or scenery for the presentations. The size of the columns, imported from great distances, illustrates the glory of these first-century theaters. The orchestra "pit" (seating for dignitaries or for the orchestra) was paved with marble, most of which has been plundered over time. The ruins of the city are seen beyond the stage. The Old Testament *tel* of Beth Shean, a mound composed of layers of civilization, is in the distance.

Lower left: The remains of the first tier of seats can be seen. The elaborate stone benches are fitted into foundations cut into bedrock on this first section. The seats are carefully shaped with a lip edge for spectators' comfort. On the far end of the row, several seats have been reconstructed. Seats in the front row, along the orchestra pit, had backs on them (both the backs and the lips have broken off over time) to provide extra comfort for the important people who sat here.

Upper right: This closeup shows the somewhat decayed and broken seating stone on the left. The fine craftsmanship of the *tekton* (i.e., "carpenter") who carved it is seen along the bottom. On the right, a modern stone has been cut to show the shape of the original. The care with which thousands of these stones were cut for this structure highlights the theater's importance in Jesus' world.

Lower right: The black basalt piers were the support structure for the now-gone second tier of seats. The entrance vaults allowed spectators to enter the theater beyond the foundations. If you look carefully, you will see the top of the foundation beginning the arched vault that would have gone over the dirt path in the foreground. In the distance, one pier on which this vault rested can be seen. This vault supported the third tier of seats, also gone, which would have been above the dirt path and the stones on the right. This tier would have gone all the way to the hill on the far right. This enormous theater, the largest found in Israel, must have drawn people from miles around, including those who would have heard Jesus teaching about "hypocrites" and the importance of sincerity in one's faith. The lesson would have been clear to the patrons of the Beth Shean theater.

Conclusion

The lesson of Sepphoris is a real challenge. We are to be involved with our culture so we can teach about Jesus and yet not compromise His message. We must follow Jesus' example and speak in a language our culture will understand so that we will bear the fruit that He desires. The only way we can accomplish that task, however, is if we are grafted onto Jesus and are nourished by Him and by our Jewish roots. Only then will we be genuine in our faith and sensitive to those around us. Speaking a language unknown to culture hides the message. Jesus spoke the language that was needed to be understood. We must do the same.

Notes

1. Bargil Pixner, *With Jesus Through Galilee* (Rosh Pina, Israel: Corazin Publishing, 1992). This book contains an excellent treatment of the cultural-historical background of Jesus' ministry.

2. Marvin Wilson, *Our Father Abraham: The Jewish Roots of the Christian Faith* (Grand Rapids: Eerdmans, 1993), is an outstanding treatment of the Jewish background of Christianity.

IN HEROD'S FOOTSTEPS: THE DYNASTY CONTINUES

Herod lay dying in his opulent palace in Jericho. He had been seriously ill for a long time. From the description in Josephus's writings, Herod had gangrene, severe itching, convulsions, and ulcers. His feet were covered with tumors, and he had constant fevers. The stadium of Jericho was filled with loved and important people from around his land who were to be killed at the moment of his death, lest no one mourn when he died. It didn't seem to matter that they would not be mourning for him.

As he lay on his deathbed, Herod's thoughts may have turned to the rabbis and their students whom he recently had executed for tearing down the Roman eagle from the Temple gate because it violated God's law against images. Perhaps he reflected on his beloved wife Miriam's two sons whom he had drowned in the palace swimming pool next door. He could have remembered the execution of his favorite son, Antipater, only days ago for plotting against him—Antipater, the one who was to take his father's place. Or maybe he thought about the 45 members of the Sanhedrin he had murdered, or the hundreds of family and staff whom he suspected of plotting against him, or the thousands of subjects who died in his brutal campaign to claim a country they believed he had no right to rule. It is possible Herod also recalled—though only briefly—the massacre of a few boy babies in a town near his massive fortress Herodion, soon to be his tomb.

HEROD'S WILL

As he lay dying in Jericho, Herod revised his will to reflect the execution of his son Antipater. Archelaus—his son by Malthace, his Samaritan wife—was given the best territory: Judea, Samaria, and Idumaea. Herod Philip—son of Cleopatra, his fifth wife—was to rule the area northeast of the Sea of Galilee: Gaulanitis, Batanea, Trachonitis, and Auranitis. Herod Antipas, another son of Malthace, was given Galilee and Perea. Shortly after completing this will, Herod died and was buried with pomp and circumstance in the Herodion, overlooking the fields of Bethlehem.

Greedy for more territory, Herod's sons went to Rome to ask for additional lands. A delegation from Judea and Jerusalem, fed up with the Herod dynasty, also went to Rome to request that the emperor, Augustus, appoint someone else to govern them. While they were gone, the country was in turmoil. Still upset over Herod's assassination of the rabbis and their students, Jews rioted in Jerusalem on Pentecost. The Roman governor from Syria came with soldiers, and fighting flared around the country. Judah, a Zealot from Gamla, seized Sepphoris and plundered the armory and palace.

Roman troops brutally put down the revolt. Jerusalem was reclaimed from the rebels, and more than 2,000 of them were crucified. Sepphoris also was retaken, and the inhabitants—those who survived at least—were sold into slavery.

Finally, Augustus made his decision. To the great disappointment of nearly everyone, he honored Herod's will. The land would belong to Herod's three sons, though none of the brothers was made king. Archelaus was made an ethnarch, a position slightly higher than tetrarch, which his brothers received.

It was 4 B.C., and Joseph and Mary learned this news in a dream (Matthew 2:19–23).

HEROD ARCHELAUS

Archelaus ruled in Jerusalem for 10 years. He hunted down the delegation that had gone to Rome, and as a true son of his father, he executed them and their families and confiscated their property. Archelaus had all Herod's evil qualities, and his reign was as bloody as his father's had been. In A.D. 6, another delegation of Judeans risked their lives and went to Rome to accuse Herod of breaking the emperor's command to govern peacefully. Archelaus was summoned to Rome and exiled to Gaul—at which point he promptly disappeared from history. Judea, Samaria, and Idumaea were named the Roman Province of Judea, to be subject directly to Rome under a military prefect ominously given full power to inflict the death penalty. Coponius was appointed the first prefect; Pontius Pilate came later. Judea no longer gave allegiance to the Herod family.

During Archelaus's short, bloody reign, Joseph and Mary, who had fled to Egypt during Herod the Great's reign because he had tried to kill their baby, were told by God that Herod was dead (Matthew 2:1–23). It was safe for them to return home. When they came to Judea, where they apparently planned to settle (maybe in Bethlehem?), they heard about Archelaus and decided they would not risk facing another bloodthirsty Herod's fear of losing his throne (Matthew 2:22). They skirted his territory and settled in Nazareth, under Herod Antipas's rule, thereby fulfilling prophecy (Matthew 2:23).

People did not soon forget the cruel Archelaus. Years later, the bloody beginning of his reign would provide the basis for a clever though probably dangerous parable (Luke 19:11–27). Jesus, however, would conduct His ministry under the watchful eye of Archelaus's younger brother.

HEROD PHILIP

Herod Philip received the territory north and east of the Sea of Galilee. This area was large but fairly poor. Philip was a peace-loving tetrarch, an excellent administrator, and a just ruler. The majority of his subjects were Gentiles, which may have spared him the burden of having to deal with the internal struggles of the Jewish people and the constant appearance of one self-proclaimed messiah after another.

Philip established his capital at Caesarea Philippi, expanding a largely pagan town and building a temple to its gods. Jesus later brought His disciples here to impress upon them the reality that His church would become the dominant community in the world (Matthew 16:13–20). It was in this pagan setting that Peter professed Jesus as *the* Messiah.

Philip also built a city—named Julius—near or on the site of Bethsaida, close to where the Jordan River enters the Sea of Galilee. Jesus' disciples Peter, Andrew, and Philip came from this town (John 1:43–44).

Herod Philip married his niece Salome, daughter of Herodias and a noted dancer, according to his brother (Matthew 14:1–12). After a reign of 37 peaceful years, Philip died and was buried at Julius.

The rule of his half brother, Herod Antipas, wasn't as peaceful. Antipas was the only Herod to meet the Messiah.

HEROD ANTIPAS

History's View

Antipas is remembered as an outstanding ruler who brought peace and prosperity to his land for more than 40 years. His territories of Galilee and Perea were among the most religious in Israel. Antipas tried to avoid offending his Jewish subjects and their commitment to the Torah—for example, by refusing to mint coins with images on them. Both the Pharisees and the Herodians (a largely upper-class, secular group that probably formed during his reign) supported him.

Just three miles from Nazareth, Antipas built the magnificent city of Sepphoris, which functioned as his capital. The boy Jesus certainly must have watched Sepphoris being built on a hill north of His hometown. Perhaps He even worked there, since many of the builders (carpenters) in the area contributed to Sepphoris's construction.

Herod Antipas's greatest project was the city of Tiberias on the shore of the Sea of Galilee. Constructed near hot springs, it was one of the most beautiful cities in Galilee. It had the best of everything, including a stadium, hot baths, and a great palace. The religious Jews of the area (where Jesus ministered) were unwilling to enter Tiberias because it was supposedly built over a cemetery and was therefore defiled according to Old Testament law (Numbers 5:2). The city was probably completed shortly before Jesus moved to Capernaum a few miles away. Tiberias was clearly visible to the citizens of Capernaum (as well as to the Zealots at Gamla, who hated Herod with a passion that only religious commitment can create).

Throughout most of his life, Antipas had the support of Tiberius, the Roman emperor for whom his capital was named. When Tiberius died, Antipas's rival and relative, Herod Agrippa (Agrippa was Antipas's father's grandson), accused him of plotting against Rome. Caligula, the new emperor, exiled Antipas and claimed his property. At this point, Herod Antipas passed quietly from history.

The Bible's View

The Bible presents a very different picture of this son of Herod the Great. According to New Testament writers, Antipas was a scheming weakling who was the archenemy of Jesus of Nazareth. Antipas had married the daughter of the Nabatean king Aretas. During a visit to his brother Philip (not the Herod Philip who was king in the north), Antipas fell in love with Herodias, Philip's wife. Antipas divorced his wife and married his brother's wife while Philip was still alive. Because this was forbidden by law (Leviticus 18:16), Herod Antipas incurred the bitter opposition of the religious Jews he ruled, including a desert preacher named John whose mission, to prepare a way for the Lord in the wilderness, had no room for such blatant disobedience—and by the king no less (Matthew 14:1–12; Mark 6:14–29). John's call for turning from sin, symbolized by baptism, was popular with religious Jews, who expected the Messiah at any time. If the way (i.e., everyone living by God's law) was prepared, Messiah would certainly arrive.

John's harsh criticism of Antipas struck a nerve. He was arrested and imprisoned. On the occasion of Herod Antipas's birthday, Herodias's daughter Salome (who would later marry Herod Philip) danced provocatively and obtained Antipas's favor. Her mother encouraged Salome to ask for John's execution, for she too was obviously tired of being publicly criticized by this popular figure. Trapped, and probably not entirely sober, Herod Antipas concurred, and John was beheaded. (Some scholars place the execution at Tiberias, barely five miles from Jesus' town of Capernaum.) The event was to haunt Herod. The Jewish people loved John and hated Antipas. The king, believing John was indeed a genuine prophet, feared the consequences until nearly the end of his life (Luke 23:6–12).

To make matters worse, his divorced wife fled to her father, King Aretas, who declared war on his unfaithful son-in-law. Herod was defeated, an event his subjects attributed to his breaking God's law. Caligula sent an army to rescue him and protect his kingdom. But this was the beginning of the loss of Roman support. Herod Antipas's ungodly marriage eventually led to his downfall despite the execution of his critic. John's execution also brought opposition from another, greater Jewish rabbi.

ANTIPAS AND JESUS

Herod Antipas was the only member of his family to come face-to-face with Jesus. His father, Herod the Great, had lived close to Jesus' birthplace in Bethlehem and had even searched for the baby (Matthew 2:1–18). But apparently Herod had never met Jesus. Philip lived only a few miles from the area where most of Jesus' miracles were performed (Matthew 11:20–21), but there is no record of the two men meeting. Antipas, on the other hand, spent years trying to meet Jesus and finally had an opportunity.

After John's murder, Herod and Jesus were in constant opposition.

Jesus criticized Antipas by name (Mark 8:15; Luke 13:31–33), calling him "that fox"—the cultural equivalent of "wimp." When the two men finally did meet in the courtroom where Jesus was on trial for His life, Jesus refused to speak to Herod (Luke 23:9). Herod mocked and abused Him (Luke 23:11; Acts 4:27), thereby missing his opportunity for salvation. In the end, Antipas was no better off than his father or brothers.

Antipas's life was haunted by his execution of John and the appearance of Jesus. He feared that Jesus was John raised from the dead (Mark 6:14–16; Matthew 14:1–2; Luke 9:7–9). Nevertheless, he plotted Jesus' death (Luke 13:31–33), of which the Pharisees warned Jesus.

Jesus' execution proved to be far more earth-shattering than John's, but Herod didn't live long enough to learn that reality.

THE OTHERS

Herod Agrippa I

Herod the Great loved his wife Miriam more than anything. When he had her executed for a supposed affair, his grief knew no bounds. Yet he executed her son without a second thought. Ironically, her grandson, Herod Agrippa I, continued the Herod dynasty: He governed territory formerly belonging to Philip (the area north and east of the Sea of Galilee) from A.D. 37–41 and was king of Judea from A.D. 41–44. While in Rome for his education, Agrippa became friends with Caligula, who as emperor, was Agrippa's supporter. When Caligula died, the new emperor, Claudius, continued to support him, and for a short time, Agrippa's territory was nearly equal to that of his grandfather.

Agrippa also knew about Jesus. He determined that the followers of Jesus, his uncle Antipas's nemesis, must be stopped. Agrippa killed the disciple James and imprisoned Peter and others (Acts 12:1–19). Agrippa's frustration must have been as great as Antipas's, because Peter disappeared. Proving he was a full-blooded Herod, Agrippa had the guards executed.

Later, Agrippa went to Caesarea to celebrate a festival in honor of the emperor Claudius. Receiving the adulation of the admiring crowds, Herod was struck down—a victim of family pride (Acts 12:19–23).

Herod Agrippa met Jesus' disciples and heard the gospel. His son, Agrippa II, refused to go even that far.

Herod Agrippa II

Herod Agrippa II was 17 years old when his father fell dead in Caesarea. Like his father, Agrippa II was educated in Rome. In A.D. 50, Caesar appointed him king over a small fraction of his father's territories. He had some authority over Jerusalem and was allowed to appoint the high priest.

Agrippa II did much to advance the Hellenistic culture in his kingdom. When the Jewish revolt against Rome began in A.D. 66, he tried to persuade his subjects not to fight the Romans. At that point, he fully supported Rome and was even wounded in the battle for Gamla, near Jesus' town of Capernaum. When the Romans finally defeated the Jewish rebels, Agrippa II invited the legions to Caesarea Philippi to rest and celebrate.

In Acts 21, the Roman commander of Jerusalem arrested a "rabbi," Paul, who had created a riot on the Temple Mount. To make sure that Paul, a Roman citizen, received a fair trial and was not lynched by an angry mob, the officer sent him to Caesarea (Acts 24). Governor Felix, who was married to Agrippa's sister Drusilla (granddaughter of Herod the Great, daughter of Agrippa I), left office before a sentence was passed. He was succeeded by a man named Festus. When Agrippa II and his sister Berenice (granddaughter of Herod the Great, daughter of Agrippa I) came to Caesarea, Festus invited them to Paul's arraignment (Acts 25). Agrippa asked to hear Paul's defense (Acts 25:22). Both Berenice and Agrippa heard a ringing proclamation of the good news of Messiah, Jesus of Nazareth, who had been born near Herod the Great (who tried to kill Him), who had preached near Herod Antipas (who tried to kill Him), who had been tried by Antipas (who sentenced Him to die), and who had founded a new movement of Jews and Gentiles (whom Agrippa I tried to kill). Festus thought Paul was mad (Acts 26:24), and Agrippa II, though fascinated, was not persuaded (Acts 26:28). He and Berenice determined that Paul was not guilty but allowed him to be sent to Caesar in Rome (where Paul too would be killed).

SO CLOSE

There have been few families in history who came so close to the greatest message the world has ever heard. One after another, the Herods met or knew of Jesus and His followers. One after another, they killed or tried to kill anyone connected to Him. How anyone could be so close and yet so far is hard to understand. Maybe the Herod family, who were descended from Esau and Edom, simply fulfilled the prophesies (Genesis 25:23; Numbers 24:17; Obadiah 8–21).

The most powerful family of kings Israel had known for many years had the opportunity to meet and serve the King of the universe. Instead, they exemplify the ultimate fate of those who do not recognize the Messiah. They lived only for themselves and not so that the world may know "that there is a God in Israel" (1 Samuel 17:46).

PHARISEES OR SADDUCEES?

THE ORIGIN OF THE PHARISEES

The Maccabees' struggle against oppression by the Hellenistic Seleucid Greeks was ultimately a triumph of God's people over those who exalted human beings as supreme (167 B.C.). Among the Maccabees' strongest supporters was a group called the Hasidim, or the "pious ones." These Torah teachers and scholars joined Judah Maccabee and his rebels because the Seleucid authorities had outlawed the study of Torah. The Hasidim are called the "mighty warriors in Israel" in 1 Maccabees. Though noted for their fierceness in battle, ultimately they were devoted to obeying God alone in everything they did.

After the Maccabee victory and the cleansing of the Temple, the Maccabees' successors, known by the family name Hasmonaean, soon became as Hellenized as the Greeks they had fought earlier. That presented a problem for these "mighty warriors." Some apparently opted to continue to battle the influence of paganism, whether it belonged to Jews or to pagans such as the Romans, who came in 63 B.C. Around the time of Jesus' birth, this rebel group became a formal movement under the leadership of Judah of Gamla. They called themselves the Zealots.

Others decided that violence would not work. They believed that God had allowed (even caused) the foreign oppression because of the failure of His people to obey the Torah. This group believed that one should devote oneself to complete obedience to every detail of law—and to separate oneself from all influences or people that might interfere with that devotion. These Jews took the name "separated" or "the separatists" (*perushim*)—"Pharisee" in English. They committed themselves totally to God and assumed the responsibility to lead Israel back to Him.

THE BELIEFS OF THE PHARISEES

The Torah was of great importance to the Pharisees. It was the focus of every part of their lives. They believed that Moses had given a two-part law: the written law of the Torah itself and additional oral commandments that had been passed through generations to help the faithful understand and apply the written law. The Pharisees continued to interpret and expand the Torah to cover every possible occurrence of unfaithfulness to the written law. This oral law became a complex guide to everyday life often beyond the comprehension of the average person. Yet its intent was to help people understand Torah, much as a creed or catechism is intended to help summarize and interpret the Bible today. It is important to recognize that the word "law" can mean either (or both) of these "Torahs" when used in the Bible. It is often the oral Torah that Jesus criticized, though He kept it in many respects.

The Pharisees had many beliefs in common with Jesus and the New Testament. They believed in the physical resurrection of the dead (the Sadducees did not) and a coming day of judgment followed by reward or punishment. They anticipated the Messiah at any moment. They believed in angels. They recognized a combination of free choice and divine control in human life. They thought of God as all-wise, all-knowing, just, and merciful. They taught that He loved His people, calling them to a life of obedience. The Pharisees believed that everyone had the power to choose good or evil, and the Torah must be his or her guide.

Because their lives revolved around the study of the Torah, the Pharisees made the synagogue their community center, though they supported the Temple as well. There were more than 6,000 Pharisees by Jesus' time, and they were the dominant influence on the people's spiritual lives. The "yoke of Torah" (or method of obeying) taught by the Pharisees was a heavy burden, sometimes obscuring the very law they sought to obey. The Pharisees desired to raise the spiritual character of the Jewish people to help them draw nearer to God (Psalm 73:28, 34:18; see also James 4:8 for a New Testament expression of the same idea).

HYPOCRITES AMONG THE PHARISEES

Most of the Pharisees were godly men who tried to be totally devoted to God in a hostile world without resorting to the violence of the Zealots. They were greatly persecuted by the Hasmonaeans and Herods, and they disagreed strongly with the Sadducees, whose theology and Hellenistic lifestyle conflicted with the Pharisees' desire to submit totally to God.

Among the Pharisees, not all were godly and righteous. Though they set high moral standards, not all of them measured up. The Misnah, the written record of their oral law, contains many criticisms of the "sore spots" among them who were "plagues of the Pharisaic party" (Mishnah Sot. 3:4, 22b). Some were so zealous for their oral interpretations that they violated the very letter of Torah. Others were so focused on obedience that they did not notice or care about the needs of those around them (a problem still significant in many churches today). This overemphasis on tiny details of obedience, particularly to human tradition, at the expense of the care and concern for others that the Torah itself demanded (Deuteronomy 10:19) was harshly condemned by the truly faithful among the Pharisees.

It is quite unfortunate, then, that history perceives this group as hypocrites and stubborn, uncaring religious fanatics who rejected

Jesus. Though it is unlikely this view will ever change, it is important to note both Jesus' strong condemnation of certain Pharisees and the specific application of that condemnation. Jesus never criticized anyone for *being* a Pharisee. He criticized "hypocritical Pharisees" (Matthew 23) and those who were "leaven" among the Pharisees and spoiled the whole group (Matthew 16:6,11). Jesus instructed His followers to *obey* what the Pharisees taught (Matthew 23:2–3) but not to practice their hypocrisy (Matthew 23:3–7). Many Pharisees supported Jesus, frequently inviting Him to their homes (Luke 7:36, 14:1, 11:34) and even warning Him that Herod wanted Him killed (Luke 13:31). Some were not far from the kingdom of God (Mark 12:34) and others entered it as Pharisees (Acts 15:5). Paul spoke and wrote proudly that he *is*, not *was*, a Pharisee (Acts 23:6; Philippians 3:5).

This should not be interpreted as defending those who rejected and hated Jesus or worked for His arrest and conviction. Nor does it deny that Jesus strongly condemned the hypocritical Pharisees (most references to them make this point). It is intended to say that Jesus pointed out sin, especially hypocrisy, wherever He found it. To paint all Pharisees with the brush of legalism and hypocrisy is unfair and incorrect. Many of them were a powerful force for good among God's people. In many (perhaps most) respects, the theology of early Christians was similar to that of the Pharisees, including the fact that both groups worshiped in synagogues.

THE ORIGIN OF THE SADDUCEES

The Sadducees also had their roots in the time of the Hasmonaean dynasty. After the Israelites returned from the Babylonian Captivity, it was the tradition that the high priest must be of the tribe of Levi, the family of Aaron, and the family of Zadok, Solomon's high priest (1 Kings 2:35; Ezekiel 40:46). Descendants of this family (called *Zedukim*, or "Sadducee" in English) were the Temple authorities throughout the time before Jesus was born. Descendants of Zadok and their supporters, many of them priests, were also called Sadducees. They were wealthy and politically active (having the favor of the Romans and the Herods), and they were a large majority on the Sanhedrin. This gave them far greater influence than their small numbers justified (some scholars believe there were fewer than 1,000 actual Sadducees). They also controlled the economy of the Temple, for which they were criticized by the Essenes and confronted by an angry Jesus. Apparently, many were Hellenistic in lifestyle, though faithful to the Temple rituals.

THE BELIEFS OF THE SADDUCEES

The Sadducees were definitely the conservatives of the time. They held that only the written Torah was authoritative, rejecting the oral law completely—even holding the prophets and other writings of less value than Torah. They opposed the Pharisees in every way they could up to the time the Temple was destroyed in A.D. 70. They denied a bodily resurrection and most of the Pharisaic doctrine of angels and spirits. They held completely to the letter of Torah with no room for the creative applications of the Pharisees. This was especially true in cases involving the death penalty. Extenuating circumstances made no difference.

The Sadducees' authority was one of position and birth, unlike the Pharisees, whose authority was based on piety and knowledge. They hated the Pharisees, believing the synagogue and study of the Torah and its interpretations as a form of worship undermined the Temple ritual. They frequently dealt brutally with anyone who undermined the Temple, its economy (their income), and its ritual—and with Roman support they were capable of severe punishment. The Sadducees offered worship that brought God down to the people. In their eyes, worship was an act of homage to the divine ruler, not an exercise in understanding. Their power was largely based in Jerusalem and Judea through the Sanhedrin, the ruling religious council, used by the Romans and Herods as the instrument to govern the Jewish people.

The Sadducees had the most to lose because of Jesus. Any popular movement jeopardized not only their place as the majority on the Sanhedrin, but also the support of the Romans who ruled through it (John 11:49–53), a fact that would have profound consequences. This was the one group most likely to wish Jesus removed from the scene.

The early church, now a growing movement, faced a similar reaction from the Sadducees (Acts 4:1, 5:17), although a large number of priests who became believers in Jesus probably were Sadducees (Acts 6:7).

When the Temple in Jerusalem was destroyed, the Sadducees ceased to exist.

MISGUIDED FAITH

For the Teacher

The emphasis of this series has been God's call for us to be witnesses for Him. The Old Testament people were called to live on the crossroads of the world so others would learn to know God by watching them. Jesus gave the same command to His followers. We are to be salt and light to the world. Others who see us will learn of Him and God, His Father. Unfortunately, Christians do not often live in ways that allow others to see God in their lives. Begin by asking your students if any of them have known someone who rejected God because of the poor example of a Christian. You should come prepared to give an example as well.

This lesson focuses on the Crusades, a significant period in history when Christians behaved in a way that turned others from God. Be careful to indicate to the students that not all Crusaders were bad, and some good did come from the Crusades. But unfortunately, the overall conduct of these Christians, done in the name of Jesus and the sign of the cross, was not consistent with Jesus' commands. Great damage was done to the reputation of Christianity in that part of the world, especially among Jewish and Muslim peoples. Jesus' name was defamed as well.

Impress upon your students how easy it is for Christians to find other ways to live for God than those Jesus taught. It's imperative that we always stay close to our Jewish Rabbi and His teachings so that others may know Him through us.

Your Objectives for This Lesson

At the completion of this section, you will want your students:

To Know/Understand

1. The geography of the northern Jordan Valley.

2. The basic history and conduct of the Crusades.

3. The effect the Crusades had on people in the Middle East.

4. Why people still judge Christianity by how Christians conducted themselves during the Crusades.

5. The failure of the Crusaders to understand the people they ruled.

To Do

1. Commit to following Jesus' methods for bringing His message to the world.

2. Plan to stand against anything that might communicate that Christianity is what the Crusaders lived.

3. Become more sensitive to how others perceive Christianity.

4. Examine our lives to ensure that we present God to others as He has revealed Himself to be.

How to Plan for This Lesson

Because of the volume of material in this lesson, you may need to divide it into several class sessions. To help you determine how to do that, the lesson has been broken into several segments. Note that the time needed may vary considerably depending on the leader, the size of the class, and the interest level of the class.

If you wish to cover the entire lesson in one session, you should complete Unit One, a discussion of major points in the video. It does not go into great depth. You may go into greater depth, or enhance your background knowledge as class leader, by selecting parts or all of the remaining material.

How to Prepare for This Lesson

Materials Needed

Student copies of the maps:	"The Roman World"
	"Galilee"
Overhead transparencies:	"The Roman World"
	"Galilee"
	"New Testament Chronology"
	"Belvoir"
Student copies of the handout:	"Soldiers of the Cross"

Video: **Misguided Faith**

Overhead projector, screen, VCR

1. Make copies of the maps and handout listed above for your students. (If possible, they should receive and read the handout before the lesson.)

2. Prepare the overhead transparencies listed above. (You'll find them at the back of the book.)

3. Determine which **Steps** and which **Digging Deeper** sections, if any, you wish to use in your class session(s). NOTE: You can use these sections in any order you wish (e.g., you might want to use **Digging Deeper III,** but not **Digging Deeper I** or **Digging Deeper II**).

4. Review the geography of the lands of the Bible from the "Introduction."

5. Prepare your classroom ahead of time, setting up and testing an overhead projector and screen (for the overhead transparencies) and a VCR. If you plan to hand out biblical references for your students to look up and read aloud, prepare 3x5 cards (one reference per card) to distribute before class.

Lesson Plan

UNIT ONE: Video Review

1. Introductory Comments

The Crusades are not an easy subject to teach. Westerners have rarely looked at them through the eyes of Jews and Muslims. They are not a pleasant chapter in the history of Jesus' people. Unfortunately, they do shape others' perceptions of us and Him. These holy wars illustrate how easy it is to justify methods and attitudes other than those commanded by Jesus because one believes the cause is right. Hopefully, this unit will drive students back to Jesus as He truly proclaimed Himself to be—Savior, not Warrior. Just as important, it may encourage them to model their attitude and behavior after His. Only when we do that will we be able to reclaim the right to be salt and light, reflecting Him to a dark world.

2. Map Study: Galilee

HINT: *Begin this map study session by reviewing the geography of the overall region and working down to the area the lesson is dealing with—Galilee.*

Using the overhead transparency titled "The Roman World," point out the following areas and have your students locate them on their maps.

> Rome
> Mediterranean Sea
> Egypt
> Judea
> Caesarea

Using the overhead transparency titled "Galilee," point out the following areas and have your students locate them on their maps.

> Nazareth
> Capernaum
> Galilee
> Sea of Galilee
> Jezreel Valley
> Beth Shean (Scythopolis)
> Belvoir

3. Show the Video *Misguided Faith* (13 minutes)

4. Guided Discussion: Jesus and the Crusaders

   a. In His ministry, Jesus never backed away from confrontation when furthering God's message. Have students read the following passages and note whom or what He confronted.

- Mark 5:1–10
- Matthew 15:21–28
- Matthew 16:21–23

Ask your students to respond to the following questions: (1) What can we learn from Jesus' examples of not being afraid to confront? (2) If you feel comfortable, give an example in which you backed away from confrontation.

b. Jesus' tactics in confronting people were to show love, kindness, and self-sacrifice. He asks His followers to do the same. Have students read the following verses and relate the guidelines to godly living given in each passage.

- Matthew 5:5–7
- Matthew 5:13–16
- John 13:34–35

  Ask your students to respond to the following questions: (1) Did Jesus follow these guidelines? (2) Do you know anyone who does? How do their actions and attitudes affect other people? (3) Why is it so hard to follow these guidelines? (4) Why is there so much hatred and dissension among Christians?

c. The Crusaders followed different methods of trying to convince others to follow Jesus. Ask the students to evaluate the Crusades from what they saw in the video by answering the following questions: (1) What were the Crusaders' motives? What were their methods? Did any good come from this unfortunate episode in history? (2) What would Jesus have said to the Crusaders? (3) How can we restore Christianity's damaged reputation? (4) Are we guilty of the same things? Do we ever harm Jesus' reputation? How? (5) Should we use language that reminds people of the Crusades? Why or why not? (6) What lessons can be learned from the Crusades?

d. Discussion/Prayer: Ask if there are any Jews in the group who might agree with the reputation the Crusades have among their people. Ask the students to respond by sharing their views of Jesus and His methods.

  Then spend time in prayer together, asking God to forgive you for those times you dishonored Him; to give you His Spirit so you may live as Jesus taught and present His claims faithfully to others; and to give you the opportunity to tell Jews and Muslims your desire to disown the evil parts of this chapter in the history of Christianity.

UNIT TWO: "They Will Know We Are Christians"

1. Introductory Comments

Jesus gave clear instructions for His followers to continue the mission He had begun. They were to build His church, feed the hungry, clothe the naked, and care for the lonely. The kingdom of God would not fail. The method Jesus used to carry out this mission is equally clear. He gave a stirring call to be peacemakers and servants so His people would be salt and light. The Old Testament call to live for God so *that the world may know* was still in force. But not everyone in Jesus' day agreed. The Zealots preferred to bring about God's kingdom with the knife, and the Pharisees believed only single-minded dedication to Torah would accomplish the task. These two groups failed to see the foundational truth of the kingdom of God that Jesus demonstrated when He went to the cross: "Greater love has no one than this, that he lay down his life for his friends" (John 15:13).

Tragically, the Christian community Jesus created has also failed at times to follow Jesus' methods in spreading the news of salvation. At times in Christian history, the Essene call for isolation and separation from the world won the day. Often the Zealot call for violence and hatred to bring the kingdom has been the predominant message proclaimed. It is the latter that has done the most damage to the kingdom Jesus preached. Violence, sometimes in Jesus' name, has built walls between Christians and Jews. These incidents have damaged the reputation of the Rabbi of Galilee in serious ways. The subject of this lesson is the need to follow Jesus completely. We must be as committed to the methods He wants us to use as we are to the message of salvation He died to provide. If we are to be His disciples, we must become like Him in every way. And that is often not easy or popular.

We don't have the space or the time here to undertake a study of Jewish-Christian relations over the last 2,000 years. Instead, we're going to concentrate on a tragic example of how Jesus' message and methods can be warped when human beings lose sight of God and go their own way. We're going to look at the Crusades and the negative consequences they had on furthering the cause of Jesus. Students should be encouraged to delve deeper into this sad episode of anti-Semitism in our Christian tradition. They should view this as a growing experience that will enable them to rededicate themselves to the message Jesus taught and lived. Hopefully, it will also motivate them to begin to build bridges between us Christians and those we've wounded by our sinful behavior. Only then will we be able to show them the true Jesus as He revealed Himself to be.

2. Map Study: Galilee

HINT: *Begin this map study session by reviewing the geography of the overall region and working down to the area the lesson is dealing with—Galilee.*

Using the overhead transparency titled "The Roman World," point out the following areas and have your students locate them on their maps.

> Rome
> Mediterranean Sea
> Egypt
> Judea
> Caesarea

Using the overhead transparency titled "Galilee," point out the following areas and have your students locate them on their maps.

> Nazareth
> Capernaum
> Galilee
> Sea of Galilee
> Jezreel Valley
> Beth Shean (Scythopolis)
> Belvoir

3. Review the Overhead Transparency "New Testament Chronology"

Using the overhead transparency titled "New Testament Chronology," highlight the following dates for your students:

c.a. A.D. 27–30	Jesus' ministry
66–73	First Jewish Revolt against Rome
70	Jerusalem is destroyed
131–135	Bar Kochba Revolt (Second Jewish Revolt)

In addition, review the following dates not on the chronology:

A.D. 315	Constantine forbids Jews from proselytizing
439	Jews are denied the right to hold public office or build new synagogues
600	Pope Gregory forbids Jews from eating with Christians
613	Forced baptisms in Spain (Jews who refuse are expelled and their children under seven are given to Christians)
632	Byzantine emperor Heraclitus I forces Jews to be baptized or be killed
1075	Pope Gregory VII prohibits Jews from holding office in Christian countries
1096	First Crusade (Jewish communities are slaughtered across Europe and Israel)
1145	Second Crusade (mobs kill Jews throughout Europe)
1170	Third Crusade (Jews are killed across Europe)
1198	Pope Innocent III begins Fourth Crusade and orders Jews killed to atone for Jesus' death (Jews must wear badges)
1291	Crusaders leave Palestine
1320	Shepherd's Crusade (120 communities of Jews are slaughtered in Europe)
1933–45	Nazi Holocaust

4. Show the Video *Misguided Faith* (13 minutes)

5. Guided Discussion: Jesus' Methods

a. *Introduction*

There were many voices in Jesus' time proclaiming the solution to the problems of the day. Help your students understand these different voices.

- The Pharisees taught that national obedience to the Torah was the only way to bring God's blessing and possibly even the Messiah. Obedience in the tiniest detail became an obsession for this group.

  Jesus was also committed to obedience, but an obedience that put God above all else.

- The Essenes separated themselves from the world to wait for God to act.

  Jesus taught a theology similar to theirs, but He surrounded Himself with other people, ministering to and loving them.

- The Zealots believed that violence was an appropriate means to bring about God's kingdom in Israel. They believed it was their duty to throw off the chains of the hated Roman rule by every means possible, even if it meant murdering every Roman soldier and Jewish collaborator.

  Jesus told His disciples to love their enemies.

- The Herodians and Sadducees preached a message of cooperation with Rome so that they could maintain the status quo and be able to continue to exist peacefully.

  Jesus' message had no room for compromise of God's law to keep peace.

b. *Discussion: Confronting Evil*

Have your students read the following passages and answer the questions that follow.

1. Mark 5:1–10 (see also Matthew 8:28–34; Luke 8:26–37)—point out that the "other side" of the Sea of Galilee is the Decapolis, a pagan land believed by some religious Jews of Jesus' day to be controlled by demons.

    - Where did Jesus tell the disciples to go? What was the reputation of this area?

    - Whom did Jesus meet when He got there? What was His reaction?

    - Based on this story, what was Jesus' course of action against demonic powers?

    - Where might we meet demonic forces in our times? What should our reaction be?

    - Think of a specific instance when you saw evil being directly confronted. What happened?

2. Matthew 16:13–20

    - Where does Jesus take His disciples? (This, too, was a pagan city.)

    - What is Jesus' promise for His new church?

    - What are gates supposed to do for a city? Do gates ever act offensively (i.e., attack)?

    - If the gates of hell will not overcome (conquer, triumph over) the church, who does Jesus say is attacking whom? What is the task of the church? Give an example of how this might be done in a specific case. Relate the example to the class.

3. Matthew 15:21–28; John 4:1–26,39–42

    - What was the reputation of Phoenicia? Tyre and Sidon were cities in Phoenicia. (Read 1 Kings 16:31; Isaiah 23:17; Matthew 11:21.)

    - Why did Jesus go there?

    - What was His strategy for the pagan people?

    - What lesson is there for us in His example? Who would correspond to the people of Phoenicia today (pagan, immoral, often the enemy of God's people)?

    - How should we respond to these people? (Jesus deliberately went to the most evil people because He knew they were in most need of His message.)

4. Matthew 16:21–22; Luke 9:21–22,51, 13:22, 18:31–33

    - How did Jesus act, knowing He was going to suffer and die and that it would happen in Jerusalem?

    - Read Luke 9:51 again. The Greek literally says, "He strengthened or set His face for Jerusalem." It means He was completely committed to what He was doing. What does it mean to you that Jesus was determined to go to Jerusalem, knowing He would be killed?

    - How did Jesus respond to great opposition and even the threat of death?

5. Matthew 10:17–42, 28:19

    - To whom must Jesus' message be brought by His disciples?

    - What will be the reaction?

    - Should that reaction stop the disciples from carrying out Jesus' orders?

    - Reread verse 34. What does Jesus mean? Does He intend His followers to use the sword? What in the text indicates that that is not His meaning?

- Why does Jesus' message bring conflict? Whom or what does the conflict involve? Give an example of a conflict you have faced because you brought Jesus' message to someone.

6. Conclusion: Have your students answer the following questions.

   - Was Jesus confrontational in His ministry? Did He back away from the people who needed His message?

   - Were His confrontations violent? What governed the way He treated people?

   - How can a Christian be confrontational in Jesus' name?

   - Think of two times when your Christian community avoided confrontation. Tell them to the class. Why did they occur? What should (could) have been done instead?

   - Think of a time when you as an individual avoided a confrontation by not bringing Jesus' message. Discuss a few of these examples as a group. Why did you avoid confrontation? What could you have done differently?

   - How can Jesus' followers today be confrontational, yet still bring the love of Jesus?

7. Prayer: Take a few moments to pray together, asking God for the courage to do what He wants even if it means confronting opposition and the power of evil.

c. *Discussion: Jesus' Tactics for Bringing the Kingdom*

Students should read the handout "Soldiers of the Cross" before beginning the following discussion.

Jesus displayed God's love. He came to be a sacrifice for the sins of the world. He loved us so much that He was willing to die for those who didn't even care about Him. God, who could have destroyed all opposition with legions of angels, chose to have His Son change the world with a confrontational love that reached out to meet the needs of the people He met. Jesus' sacrifice will be the subject of the next set of lessons. In this section, we are going to consider Jesus' call for His disciples to follow His example. Often people of the Middle East respond to the presentation of Jesus by saying, "If the history of Christianity is what He is about and depicts what happens if you follow Him, then we are not interested." It is up to us to change this incorrect view. We must conduct our daily lives in such a way that we reflect the true Jesus and His gospel to those who have been blinded by ignorance or pain.

Read each of the following passages and ask the students whether they live by these commands. Have them give specific examples of when they abide and when they fail.

- Matthew 5:5–7
- Matthew 5:13–16
- Matthew 5:23–24
- Matthew 5:38–42
- Matthew 5:43–48
- Matthew 6:14–15
- John 13:34–35
- John 15:9–17

Ask the class to respond to the following questions:

1. Is it possible to live that faithfully? Do you know anyone who is faithful (recognizing, of course, that no one is perfect) to these teachings of Jesus? What are they like? What do others think of them?

2. Give an example of someone who failed to live by Jesus' standards and turned someone away from Christianity.

3. Why is there so much dissension and hatred among Christian groups? What kind of example is this to others?

4. What impression do we give to non-Christians with our divisions and bitterness toward other followers of Jesus?

d. *Guided Discussion: The Crusades and Their Tragic Legacy*

This discussion explores a sensitive subject: the impact of the Crusades on Christianity's, as well as Jesus', reputation. The purpose of this section is not to fully understand or critique the Crusaders as a historical movement; rather, the goal is to discover whether they were faithful to the methods Jesus described and exemplified for His followers.

TEACHER'S NOTE: Please explain to the class that there are other aspects to the Crusades than those covered here. Some Crusaders were fine Christians, and some of those whom they fought were barbaric in their oppression of Christians (and Jews) in the holy land.

The Crusades also had some positive results. The gospel reached new areas, though primarily by the clergy who came after the Crusaders and not by the knights themselves.

It is important for students to realize that the Crusades did great damage to the cause of Christianity among both Jews and Muslims. Even today our faith (and our Messiah) is judged according to the "soldiers of the cross." It is hard for us to imagine how strong an impact this historical episode still has in the Middle East today, influencing people's perceptions of Christianity.

Western Christians should seek two goals in the Middle East today: (1) to destroy the distortion of Jesus and His message that Muslims and Jews often have, and (2) to help people understand that in many ways the Crusaders and their actions did *not* represent Jesus' way.

Ask the class to spend a few minutes evaluating the Crusaders and their methods of bringing the gospel from what they viewed in the video.

- What were the Crusaders' motives for going to the holy land?

- What were the tactics they used once they were there?

- What have been the long-term effects on Muslims and Jews and their attitude toward Christianity?

- What would Jesus have said of the Crusaders and their methods?

- Read Matthew 26:51–54; Luke 22:47–51; John 18:10–11. What is the difference, if any, between using political and military power to enforce God's laws of justice and using that same power to force people to become Christians?

- Why would Crusaders kill Jewish people all over Europe if their intent was to free the holy land? What has been the long-term result?

- Why is hatred a dangerous motive for doing anything, even good things? Did Jesus ever do anything out of hatred?

- What modern hatreds might be tempting to Christians today? How can we be confrontational for the gospel but retain the tactics and motives Jesus commanded?

- How could you communicate to a Jewish friend that you do not agree with the violent approach of the Crusaders? Ask class members to think of a Jewish acquaintance (maybe there are Jews in the class) for whom a discussion of this video might offer an opportunity to renounce what these holy wars stood for.

- Since we represent Jesus to others and claim to live according to His commands, (1) Why is it so important that we live by His words? and (2) What are we guilty of if we distort His way?

- The legacy of the Crusades was to turn people away from Jesus because the Crusaders brutally slaughtered many innocent people in Europe and the Middle East, creating a deeply rooted distrust and dislike for Christianity. The very word *Crusade* conveys to those in the Middle East everything destructive from that time.

  Think of ways Christians unknowingly link themselves to the Crusades and hence create barriers that prevent others from being attracted to Jesus. (For example: evangelism crusades, Crusader hymnals, military imagery) Should we limit our use of these terms because they distort Jesus' message? Why or why not? Are there better terms we can use?

- Read Matthew 17:24–27; Romans 14:19–21; 1 Corinthians 9:19–23. Would it compromise the gospel for Christians to be sensitive to history? What would Jesus say about using Crusade terms? What would Paul say? NOTE: Some students may believe they are not part of the church responsible for the Crusades, so this does not apply to them. Remind them that to non-Christians, all Christians are part of the same movement, just as to us, all Muslims appear to be part of the same body. Thus, we need to be aware of their perceptions of Christianity and the Crusades even if we are not personally responsible for what happened centuries ago.

- Are there other ways we might communicate to Jews or Muslims that we still have the intolerant and hateful attitudes of the Crusaders? Give specific examples.

- What can you do to communicate to them that Jesus' way is not the way of the sword?

- Prayer: Spend a few moments in prayer. Ask God's forgiveness for the times your hatred or intolerance might have given someone the wrong idea of Jesus and His way. Ask God for an opportunity for you to share with a Jewish person your sadness about this history and your determination to be different as you follow Jesus.

OPTIONAL — Digging Deeper I: The Fortress of Belvoir (*20–35 minutes*)

(Part one of this section requires the overhead transparency labeled "Belvoir." Part two requires the use of the optional full-color over-head-transparency packet. For information on ordering it, see p. 243.)

A. Lecture

The fortress of Belvoir was built in the twelfth century by the Knights of the Order of the Hospitalers. Belvoir's function was to protect the eastern side of the Crusaders' kingdom. The name *Belvoir* is French for "beautiful view." Perched on a hill 1,700 feet above the Jordan Valley, the fortress offers a breathtaking panorama. It is also isolated from roads and communities in the area. From A.D. 1180–1184, Belvoir saw fierce battles between Crusaders and Muslims, who were unable to take the fortress. In 1187, after the stunning defeat of the Crusader army at the Horns of Hattin, nearby Belvoir was besieged again. The 50 knights and 400 soldiers resisted for over a year. Eventually, they surrendered and departed for Europe. The Muslims destroyed the fortress so it could not be reused. It stands today as a monument to the Crusaders' ability to make magnificent fortresses. It is also a reminder of their brutal, unchristian tactics done in the name of Jesus and the cross. Their cruelty and self-imposed isolation from the people were in complete contrast to Jesus' message. As modern-day Christians, we must learn from their mistakes. We must make sure that our tactics are those of Jesus, and we must not separate ourselves from our culture but be involved in it so that we can communicate the gospel to others.

B. Visual Insights

The following overhead transparencies show different views of the fortress of Belvoir.

Overhead Transparency 19. Belvoir. The fortress of Belvoir has both an outer fortification and an inner castle. A moat, hewn out of the same bedrock quarried to build the castle, encircles the structure on three sides. Towers stood in each corner and in the center of the outer walls so the archers could be closer to anyone trying to attack the fortress. Small postern gates led from each tower into the moat, enabling the knights to attack anyone trying to undermine the walls. The entrance is on the east. A huge outer tower defended the gate area.

Inside the outer wall was a smaller fortress, or keep. It consisted of four vaulted walls (enclosing two stories) and a courtyard. Cisterns for water were dug beneath the vaulted rooms. The upper-story rooms were plastered and painted with colored frescoes. There was also a church on this floor. It was made of limestone and not basalt, like the rest of the fortress. Its chapel measured about 25 by 55 feet. One of the stones found there was formerly used as a lintel in a synagogue and has a menorah carved on it. This seems appropriately symbolic. The Crusaders destroyed the worship centers of other faiths to build their own. In the process, they lost the opportunity to influence the world they lived in and damaged the reputation of Christianity for generations to come.

But did Jesus call His people to be fortress builders or community builders? That is the question posed by Belvoir.

Overhead Transparency 45. Jordan Valley from Belvoir. Belvoir is located on the western side of the Jordan Valley. It is in a group of hills known as the Issachar Plateau just north of Beth Shean. This photograph is of the Jordan Valley looking northeast. Down in the valley, the channel where the Jordan River flows can be seen just beyond the ponds. In the background are the Gilead Mountains (Elijah came from there) and part of the region of the Decapolis. The Sea of Galilee is barely 10 miles to the north, also in the valley.

The Jordan Valley is very fertile. The road from Galilee to Jerusalem, the one Jesus followed on His way to Jerusalem and death, passes through the valley. The fortress (ruins on the left) was built on this high hill partly to control the road below and partly to "protect" the Crusaders from the local population. Obviously, this position isolated the knights and soldiers so that, even if they had wanted to, they were unable to exert any daily influence on the people in the valley below. Given the Crusaders' brutal conduct toward Jews in Europe and the Middle East and toward the Muslims they fought, it is clear they did not follow Jesus' teachings to "love your enemies" (Matthew 5:38–48) or to be the "salt of the earth" (Matthew 5:13). The Crusaders were a "city on a hill," though certainly not in the way Jesus intended (Matthew 5:14). Did Jesus, who often passed this hill on the road below, look up and know the fortress would be there one day? Did he grieve for the European Christians who would so misunderstand His message? The lesson of Belvoir and the Crusades must lead us always to follow Jesus in the ways He taught. Only if we live *in* our culture will we be able to influence it for Jesus.

OPTIONAL — Digging Deeper II: Who Is Responsible for Jesus' Death?
(10–15 minutes)

A. Lecture

Have a student read aloud Matthew 27:11–26. Note especially verse 25.

Matthew recorded the fierce anger and hatred directed toward Jesus as His "trial" progressed. When Pilate, already in trouble with his Roman superiors, indicated that he believed Jesus was innocent of the charges and that he didn't want to order Him killed, the mob accepted responsibility for Jesus' death sentence. They willingly took Jesus' "blood" on their own heads and the *heads of their children*. This verse has been used to justify nearly 2,000 years of persecution of Jewish people. To put it bluntly, the Crusaders (and many other Christians through the centuries) hated Jews because they believed they were responsible for killing Jesus.

But is that appropriate? Did God place the blame for Jesus' death on that Jewish mob and their children? Did those people speak for all Jews? If we are to overcome the legacy of the Crusaders, we need to address this fundamental reason for Christian hatred of Jews.

B. Guided Discussion

Have your students read the following passages and answer the questions.

1. John 11:45–53, 18:12–14,19–24; Matthew 26:69–74. Who arrested and interrogated Jesus? Why at night? Why a plot? What appears to be the popular view of Jesus and His teaching? (See Mark 11:18; Luke 19:47, 20:19,39, 21:37–38, 22:1–6; Acts 5:17–18,25–26; Matthew 21:46, 26:3–4.) Even if God were holding the Jewish people responsible (note Luke 23:34), would they have been held guilty?

    Help students see that many people were sympathetic to Jesus. If they hadn't been, the Temple authorities (especially the Sadducees and Caiaphas, the high priest) could have just had Him arrested. Obviously, the plotters knew that there was enough support for Jesus that His arrest would cause problems. The point is not to excuse those who actually rejected Jesus or treated Him so unjustly. The issue is whether "all" Jews agreed with these instigators and whether they represented "all" Jews. Most Jews probably had nothing against Jesus.

2. Matthew 27:11,27; Luke 18:32, 23:2,24–25,47; John 19:1,16. Who executed Jesus? Why didn't the Sadducees who arrested Him do it?

    Help students see that the Jewish crowd pressured the Romans to crucify Jesus. However, the Romans were responsible for wielding justice in Israel, especially in capital offenses. From a legal standpoint, then, the Romans were responsible for Jesus' execution. Yet we do not hold all Italians responsible. Why? There were far fewer followers of Jesus among the Romans than among the Jews. The point is not to excuse anyone who rejected Jesus' claims. That is God's concern, not ours. Nevertheless, the *Romans* actually crucified Jesus.

    Read Luke 23:34. Even if the Jewish mob had not called down a curse on themselves and their children, would they have been held responsible?

3. Ezekiel 18 (especially verses 1–4, 19–20, 30). Does God judge children for their parents' sins? The results of sin can affect future generations (see Exodus 20:5—even here the punishment, or effects of it, are to three or four generations); but Ezekiel clearly taught that each person is responsible to God for his or her belief or unbelief. With that in mind, even if the Jewish leaders had accepted responsibility for Jesus' death, would God have held their descendants responsible?

Read Romans 10:1, 11:1,11–12,25–29. Did God "give up" on Israel?

4. John 1:29, 3:16, 10:10–18, 12:23–27, 15:13–15, 19:30. Why did Jesus die? Who sent Him to die? On whose behalf did He die? Was He forced to die? Whose "sins" were responsible for His death? Have you ever sinned? Who is responsible for Jesus' death?

Conclusion/Prayer: Clearly, from the preceding discussion, we can see that anti-Semitism is unbiblical. Ask each student to pray silently for a few moments as he or she reads the following:

Jesus died because of my sins. I am responsible. Even if not one other person had ever sinned, Jesus would have had to die. Thank You, God, for not cursing those responsible for Jesus' death, because then I, too, would be cursed. Thank You so much, God, for Your love and mercy.

OPTIONAL — Digging Deeper III: Isolation versus Involvement
(30–45 minutes)

The Crusaders never blended into the Middle Eastern way of life. They built their castles on high hills far away from the people they ruled. Though they dominated the political scene, they had little influence on the people's daily lives. They were, in a sense, irrelevant to the culture around them.

Today two ancient roads still lead up to Crusader fortresses. Each is several miles long over difficult terrain. Visitors to Israel who decide to walk these roads learn, with their feet, how isolated the Crusaders were from the people around them. One of the major contentions of this curriculum series is that God called His people to live on the crossroads of life so that the world may know that our God is truly God. (If you have Set 1 of this series, see Lesson One, Step One, for more information.) Not only did the Crusaders abandon the self-sacrificing methods Jesus taught His followers, but they also isolated themselves from the world instead of living in it. The following brief exercise reminds us of our call to be involved in our culture.

Read the following passages, summarize what each commands, and then for each, ask these questions: Did the Crusaders follow this command? How should we live so we obey God's words?

- Isaiah 43:12
- Matthew 15:29–31
- 1 Peter 2:11–12
- Matthew 28:19–20
- Matthew 5:13–16
- 2 Corinthians 1:12
- 1 Corinthians 9:19–23

Ask your students to respond to the following questions:

1. Why is it easier to be isolated and defensive as a Christian? (Always fearing attack, the Crusaders waited for others to come to them.)

2. Is the Christian community isolated or involved in today's culture? Your church?

3. Are you living in the world as a witness or are you hiding from it?

4. Is the Christian community relevant to our world? Or like the Crusaders, do we build

churches and develop theologies and strategies that isolate us and protect us from the world, making us irrelevant to our culture?

5. How could your church become more relevant to the needs and concerns of your community?

Conclusion

The Crusades are a sad chapter in our Christian history. They have damaged Jesus' reputation, built walls between Christians and people of other faiths, and helped create a defensive, isolationist mentality in the Christian community. Encourage your students to commit themselves to being caring, loving followers of Jesus who reach out to others. Though we must always defend the truth, we do this out of concern for those around us to whom we must be light and salt. Help your students think of opportunities to indicate to Jews and Muslims that we do not condone the methods the Crusaders used to proclaim God's news of salvation. Their way was not Jesus' way. Christians follow Jesus' way of love, kindness, and self-sacrifice. Encourage your students to demonstrate Jesus' way to those whose history includes oppression by "Christians." Then as a class, pray that God will inspire His church to become more involved in the culture around it. Jesus' message is desperately needed in the world today. God gave it to us, not to hoard in our hilltop fortresses, but to give away to those in the valley below.

SOLDIERS OF THE CROSS

Lesson Seventeen

Handout #1

Pope Urban II, in an impassioned speech before thousands of people in Clermont, France, on November 27, 1095, called upon all true Christians to free the holy land from the Muslim infidels, who had invaded it centuries before. Christian pilgrims were not able to visit holy sites, including the Church of the Holy Sepulchre, the most sacred of all shrines. This sparked a period of violent conflict between the Christian Europeans and the Muslims of the Middle East. Thousands of knights, serfs, peasants, and even a few kings sewed the sign of the cross on the front of their tunics, hung it on their shields, and went to war for Jesus Christ. The Jews, without a country, found themselves caught in between.

THE HOLY WARS

The First Crusade

The First Crusade began at Clermont, France. The knights (surprisingly few in number) were accompanied by mobs of farmers, shopkeepers, and other fortune seekers as they left France on their way to Germany and then the holy land. Throughout Europe, there were many towns and cities with prosperous Jewish communities; some had been there for hundreds of years. The sight of these wealthy communities ignited a fire of hatred among the Crusaders. Why should the "killers of Christ" be allowed to live in peace and good fortune at home while the soldiers of the cross traveled across Europe to their probable deaths? The leaders of the Crusade promised they would avenge the crucifixion in blood. Though some of the clergy who were among the Crusaders tried to prevent the massacre, the size of the mob and its frenzy were unstoppable. In Speyer, Worms, Mainz, Cologne, and a host of other German cities, the slaughter began. Men and women, young and old, it didn't matter—they were all brutally killed. Synagogues filled with Jews seeking safety from the mobs were locked and ignited. The people inside were burned alive. Hundreds were offered a choice: convert or be killed. Almost all remained faithful to their beliefs. Many committed suicide as the knights and the unruly mob came into their towns. All across Europe, one massacre followed another. Few of these thousands of victims put up any resistance to the soldiers of the cross. The Crusades had been launched in blood.

The slaughter did not stop in Europe. It continued wherever the Crusaders went, occasionally including Orthodox Christians who had the misfortune to dress or look like Muslims. Tens of thousands of Muslims were also killed.

Finally, the Crusaders reached Jerusalem, and on July 15, 1099, they captured it. A terrible massacre ensued, with few Jews or Muslims surviving. Those who did were sold into slavery. The streets were red with

LESSON SEVENTEEN **171**

blood. Christianity had earned a reputation that would last a long time. It was not the military campaign or the ruthless treatment of the Muslim soldiers that gave Christianity its negative image. It was the treatment of civilians, particularly women and children. All this was done under the sign of the cross and in the name of Jesus.

The slaughter of the local populace left few people to work the farms and run the local economy. The knights built their great European-style castles on high hills, far from roads and even water, and they soon became places of refuge and escape. Eventually, they became prisons. Having traveled thousands of miles to win the holy land and the infidels to God's truth, the European conquerors had no gospel to offer their subjects. The Crusaders never understood the land, and their isolated fortresses made them irrelevant to its people. Jesus would not have recognized these soldiers who came to spread His kingdom. For they knew little of the methods He taught and the way of sacrifice He walked.

The Second Crusade

The Second Crusade was not much different from the first. In 1144, an itinerant monk began traveling around Europe urging soldiers to destroy the Jewish communities of Germany to avenge Jesus' crucifixion. Though a brave few raised their voices against this madness, it happened anyway. Though probably less extensive than the First Crusade, the slaughter of innocent people in Jesus' name only added to the horrible legacy of the Crusades.

The Third Crusade

Spared the horrors of the first two Crusades, the Jewish communities in England were not so fortunate when the third one began. Jews in York, Lynn, Norwich, Stamford, and other towns were massacred. Thus England, too, joined the roster of countries whose Christian armies distinguished themselves in their brutality against the "infidels," even if they were Jewish and citizens. The slaughter continued for nearly 200 years.

The Shepherds' Crusade

The Crusades formally ended in 1291 with the loss of the holy land. But a few years later, European Jews were subjected to the "Shepherds' Crusade." Nearly 40,000, mostly teenage "Crusaders" pillaged, killed, and burned their way south across Europe. Some sources indicate 150 communities of Jews were exterminated by these soldiers of the cross.

ORIGIN OF THE HATRED

The New Testament recorded bitter disagreement between some in the Jewish community and early Christians. The opposition seems to have come primarily from the Sadducees and certain groups of Pharisees. The struggle was a real one, over significant beliefs, but the disciples and apostles continued to seek to persuade Jewish people to follow Jesus (Romans 12), just as Jesus Himself had done.

It was long after New Testament times when Christians began to blame all Jews for rejecting and crucifying Jesus. The destruction of Jerusalem and the Temple, a fate that caused Jesus to weep (Luke 19:41–44), was triumphantly held up as God's revelation of the curse against His *former* people. Church fathers like Augustine and Justin Martyr taught that the Jews were now eternally cursed by God. Soon regular sermons were preached on the Christian holy days of Good Friday and Easter, blaming the Jews for Jesus' death. Little was said about the Roman soldiers who actually crucified Him. The fact that Jesus went willingly to His death and that He went because of the sins of those who now condemned the Jews was mentioned even less. Constantine, the first Christian emperor, passed many anti-Jewish laws. Popes like Gregory VII forbade interaction between Jews and Christians, and barred Jews from holding office. Jews were the enemies of God. Forced conversions and baptisms became increasingly common.

In spite of this oppression, the Jewish communities survived and flourished. That only increased the resentment and abuse the Jewish people received. Local violence flared occasionally, and entire communities were wiped out over the rumor that Jews were guilty of blood libel for stealing the "Host" from the Mass and profaning it to renew Jesus' suffering. Jews were also accused of killing Christian children so their blood could be used to make unleavened bread for Passover. Such charges, insane to us, were widely believed, though not a single example has ever been shown to have actually happened. But it didn't matter. Thousands of innocent Jewish people died at the hands of their "Christian" neighbors.

The Crusades simply expanded what had regularly occurred on a smaller scale. Now Muslims were included as well. But the bloodshed did not end with the Crusades. Jewish property was routinely seized for hundreds of years. The Inquisition, from the 1100s through the 1500s, brutally destroyed entire communities of Jews and tortured thousands of innocent people. In 1298, over 100,000 Jews were killed in Germany alone. Two thousand were burned in Strasbourg. Thousands were forced to convert in Spain. Three hundred thousand Jews were expelled from Spain the year Columbus discovered America. Martin Luther wrote "Against Jews and Their Lies," a strident treatise condemning Jews forever to the flames of hell. The persecution continued in Russia, Poland, Hungary, and the Ukraine. Still the Jewish communities flourished.

Then came the Holocaust, the child of the beast.

CONCLUSION

There were certainly godly Crusaders. And good things did come from some of the Crusades. But the greatest legacy was the reputation the Crusaders earned for Christianity. To non-Christians, Europe was a Christian monolith. To them, what Europeans did was what Christianity stood for. That's the way whole civilizations judged the Crusades. Only recently have formal steps been taken to renounce this part of our history. The Roman Catholic Church's Second Vatican Council affirmed the Jewish roots of Christianity and repudiated collective Jewish guilt for Jesus' death. The Lutheran Church in the United States recently voted to repudiate the teachings of Martin Luther that are anti-Semitic. Many individual Christians have awakened to the devastating effects the Crusades have had on non-Christians' views of Jesus and His teachings. Many are rediscovering the Jewish roots of Christianity.

Unfortunately, many of us are still ignorant of how far removed the soldiers of the cross were from the methods and teachings of Jesus. The One who said, "Love your enemies, love one another, and put away your sword," became the One in whose name unspeakable violence was committed.

Because Christians hold crusades and sing from Crusader hymnals, many people still believe we support Crusader ideals. We must correct this misinterpretation. If we are to become true followers of Jesus, we must commit ourselves totally to following Him and His ways, renouncing the ideals and methods of the "soldiers of the cross."

LIVING WATER

For the Teacher

This lesson is different from the previous ones. It is more meditative and reflective, encouraging students to understand some of the "pictures" the Bible writers used to describe life, God and our relationship to Him, difficult experiences, and our tendency to draw upon our own strength. These concepts can raise difficult issues for people. Be sensitive to your students' needs. The lesson will enable you and your students to find comfort and encouragement by understanding the cultural background of biblical images used to describe God.

Your Objectives for This Lesson

At the completion of this section, you will want your students:

To Know/Understand

1. The location of En Gedi in the Judea Wilderness.
2. The meaning of living water imagery in the Bible.
3. How Jesus applied living water to Himself and its relationship to the feast of Sukkot.
4. The meaning of the feast of Sukkot.
5. A mental picture of the wilderness and oasis of En Gedi.
6. The use of cisterns in Jewish culture.
7. How the story of David's flight from Saul fits the context of En Gedi.

To Do

1. Plan to establish an "En Gedi," a regular time to be refreshed with living water.
2. Discover God as "shade" and "honey."
3. Identify the broken cisterns of their lives, recognizing the need for living water.
4. Plan specific ways to become living water to others.

How to Plan for This Lesson

Because of the volume of material in this lesson, you may need to divide it into several class sessions. To help you determine how to do that, the lesson has been broken into several segments. Note that the time needed may vary considerably depending on the leader, the size of the class, and the interest level of the class.

If you wish to cover the entire lesson in one session, you should complete Unit One, a discussion of major points in the video. It does not go into great depth. You may go into greater depth, or enhance your background knowledge as class leader, by selecting parts or all of the remaining material.

How to Prepare for This Lesson

Materials Needed

Student copies of the maps: "The Kingdom of Herod the Great"
                                                 "The Judea Wilderness"

Overhead transparencies: "The Kingdom of Herod the Great"
                                               "The Judea Wilderness"

Student copies of the handout: "The Joy of Living Water: Jesus and the Feast of Sukkot"

*Video: **Living Water***

Overhead projector, screen, VCR

1. Make copies of the maps and handout listed above for your students. (If possible, they should receive and read the handout before the lesson.)

2. Prepare the overhead transparencies listed above. (You'll find them at the back of the book.)

3. Determine which **Steps** and which **Digging Deeper** sections, if any, you wish to use in your class session(s). NOTE: You can use these sections in any order you wish (e.g., you might want to use **Digging Deeper III,** but not **Digging Deeper I** or **Digging Deeper II**).

4. Review the geography of the lands of the Bible from the "Introduction."

5. Prepare your classroom ahead of time, setting up and testing an overhead projector and screen (for the overhead transparencies) and a VCR. If you plan to hand out biblical references for your students to look up and read aloud, prepare 3x5 cards (one reference per card) to distribute before class.

Lesson Plan
UNIT ONE: Video Review

1. Introductory Comments

This lesson will explore Jesus' claim to be "living water" (John 7:38). To fully understand that metaphor, students should be familiar with the desert background of living water and the contrast between living water and other water. This will help them apply the beautiful biblical imagery to specific situations in their own lives.

In the Bible, life is often compared to a wilderness—it can be hot, dry, and barren. But biblical writers reveal that God is like an oasis in the wilderness that offers shade and flowing streams of water, making the most arid desert bloom.

2. Map Study: The Judea Wilderness and the Oasis of En Gedi

HINT: *Begin this map study session by reviewing the geography of the overall region and working down to the area the lesson is dealing with—the Judea Wilderness and En Gedi.*

Using the overhead transparency titled "The Kingdom of Herod the Great," point out the following areas and have your students locate them on their maps.

> Bethlehem
> Jerusalem
> Galilee
> Sea of Galilee
> Negev
> Judea

Using the overhead transparency titled "The Judea Wilderness," point out the following areas and have your students locate them on their maps.

> Dead Sea
> Jericho
> Judea Mountains
> Judea Wilderness
> Jerusalem
> Masada
> Qumran
> En Gedi
> Bethlehem

3. Show the Video *Living Water* (24 minutes)

4. Guided Discussion: Water in the Wilderness

a. To help your students understand the metaphor of God as living water in the wilderness, have them read the following passages and answer the questions listed below.

- Psalm 63:1
- Deuteronomy 11:11–15
- Jeremiah 17:5–6

1. What is the wilderness like?

2. In each passage, life is compared to a desert. What in your own experience could be described as a desert? Why is that a good description?

- Psalm 78:15
- Isaiah 41:17–18
- Isaiah 49:10

1. In each passage, what does God provide?

2. God's provision always overcomes the difficulties of the desert. How can God's provision in your life be described as water or relief like it is in these passages? Why is this such a good description?

- Psalm 63:1, 42:1

1. Have you ever been thirsty for God? Be specific. How does one develop a thirst for God?

- Isaiah 32:2

1. What happens to the one who drinks God's living water?

2. Have you ever been living water for someone else?

b. Using the desert metaphor to describe the struggles of life, and living water as God's provision, we might say that life is like a desert—the only way to survive the harsh conditions of the desert is to refresh and restore oneself with the shade and flowing water found in an oasis such as En Gedi.

1. How can you find an En Gedi? Where is your living water? Give some examples. (For example: where you meet God and satisfy your thirst) Can you survive spiritually without significant time with God?

c. Cisterns are pits dug into the ground, plastered, and filled with rainwater. The water, though better than nothing, is usually dirty and stagnant. Cisterns need constant care because they often leak, leaving one without water.

- Jeremiah 2:13, 14:3

1. What is God like?

2. What did His people prefer?

3. Why is this picture so foolish (i.e., leaving fresh, flowing water for dirty, bad-tasting cistern water)?

4. If En Gedi and its gushing springs of water is God, then God provides for our needs in the wilderness of life. If cistern water is what we create, then when we take our water from cisterns we've made, we're relying on our own strength to survive and not God's.

   Relate a time when you tried to accomplish something on your own strength (cistern water) without God (living water). (For example: parenting, dating, career choice, athletics, marriage) What happened? How did things change when you came to "En Gedi"?

d. Jesus, too, is described as living water in the Bible.

- John 4:13–14, 7:37–38

1. How does the water image describe Jesus?

2. How do you know the "water" He provides is living (gives life, stays fresh and alive, never fails)?

3. What does the person who has Jesus' living water become for others?

e. Prayer: Spend a few moments in prayer, asking God (1) to show you how barren the desert is; (2) to be your shade and your living water (your En Gedi); and (3) to help you recognize the times you drink from your own cistern (those times when you try to make it without Him).

UNIT TWO: "If Anyone Is Thirsty . . ."

1. Introductory Comments

The topography of Israel is quite varied. The mountains of Jerusalem are fertile, with sufficient rainfall for grapes and olives to grow. Galilee is nearly tropical in some places. The Valley of Jezreel is a "breadbasket" with its rich soil for raising grain.

Israel also has significant wilderness areas that played important roles in biblical times. (See, for example, Lesson Nine in Set 2 of this curriculum series, and Lessons Twelve and Thirteen in this set.) In this section, we're going to study the Judea Wilderness, particularly focusing on the spring of En Gedi, living water in the midst of barrenness.

This study involves much self-reflection because of the Bible's metaphoric use of a desert to describe our daily lives and living water to describe God's provision. To grasp the significance of these images for our own lives, we need to understand the geography and topography of the Judea Wilderness.

2. Map Study: The Judea Wilderness

HINT: *Begin this map study session by reviewing the geography of the overall region and working down to the area the lesson is dealing with—the Judea Wilderness.*

Using the overhead transparency titled "The Kingdom of Herod the Great," point out the following areas and have your students locate them on their maps.

> Bethlehem
> Jerusalem
> Galilee
> Sea of Galilee
> Negev
> Judea

Using the overhead transparency titled "The Judea Wilderness," point out the following areas and have your students locate them on their maps.

> Dead Sea
> Jericho
> Judea Mountains
> Judea Wilderness
> Jerusalem
> Masada

Qumran
En Gedi
Bethlehem

3. Show the Video *Living Water* (24 minutes)

4. Guided Discussion: David in the Wilderness

NOTE: Part of this section is repeated from Lesson Twelve, Unit Two, Guided Discussion 4.

David was one of the great heroes of the Old Testament. Not only was he the one through whose line the Messiah would come and the one whose throne the Messiah would hold (Luke 1:32), but he also became the example of one whose relationship with God was to be imitated. In fact, Samuel the prophet said of David: "The LORD has sought out a man after his own heart" (1 Samuel 13:14). David's faith in God, his willingness to submit to His will, and his sorrow when he sinned have become the model for modern-day believers. Though a study of David's life would be instructive, it is beyond the scope of this book. Instead, we're going to concentrate on one particularly important lesson that David learned in the Judea Wilderness. It illustrates why David is a model for us.

a.   Have your students read the following passages and answer the questions.

- 1 Samuel 15:10–11. Why did God reject Saul as king? Compare the reason God selected David (1 Samuel 13:13–14). What can we learn as we try to be the people God has called us to be?

- 1 Samuel 17:48–49. David became a hero. What was his motivation (1 Samuel 17:46–47)? Why is this series titled *That the World May Know?* (Note also 1 Kings 18:36–37; Isaiah 37:18–20.) What is God's lesson through David for us?

- 1 Samuel 18:6–8. David became famous, and Saul grew jealous. Why? What in the spiritual makeup of each man made this reaction predictable?

- 1 Samuel 18:10–11, 19:9–10. David was hated by Saul, who spent the rest of his life trying to kill David. What would David's state of mind have been during that time? Read Psalm 62:4–6, believed to have been written at this time. Following God always brings opposition (John 15:20). It did for David and it will for any follower of Jesus. How have you experienced this?

- 1 Samuel 23:14,25. David hid from Saul in the wilderness. Note that the Desert of Ziph is the part of the Judea Wilderness west of En Gedi, and the Wilderness of Maon is the part of the Judea Wilderness west of Masada. This wilderness is barren, arid, rugged, and crisscrossed with wadis that can flood at a moment's notice, sweeping away everything in sight. Steep mountains are separated by deep, narrow canyons. The wild deer (ibex) move from rock to rock in the barren wasteland.

   Have you ever experienced such "barrenness" in your life? Ask several students to relate their experiences without describing whether or how God brought relief.

5. Guided Discussion: God as Living Water

During this time of exile in the wilderness, David described God as being his Rock (Psalm 19:14) and his Fortress (Psalm 18:2). In another psalm, David found comfort in thinking of God as shade (Psalm 121:5). These metaphors are powerful to those who have experienced life as wandering in a danger-filled wilderness. When we see God as David did—as a rock (strong, sheltering, secure), a fortress (protecting), and shade (providing enough relief so the heat can be tolerated)—our wilderness times will be softened by the encouragement and comfort God provides.

But there is another wilderness "picture" of great comfort to followers of Jesus. He is also water. It is that image we're going to explore further.

Have your students read each set of passages and answer the questions.

- Psalm 63:1 (note the title); Deuteronomy 11:11–15; Jeremiah 17:5–6 (note the reference to "salt land"—this term usually refers to the Dead Sea area, which means this passage is set in the same desert as En Gedi); Psalm 107:4–5; Isaiah 49:10.

  1. What was the desert like?

  2. Each passage describes life as a desert. What description of the desert do you get from each passage? What circumstances of life have you experienced that are like the deserts described above? (Give students time to discuss their experiences.)

- Psalm 78:15,20; Psalm 105:41; Psalm 107:4–9; Isaiah 41:17–18, 44:3–4, 49:10, 35:6–7; Jeremiah 17:7–8; Psalm 1:3; Isaiah 58:11, Deuteronomy 8:15.

  1. What did (does) God provide in the desert? What is God like?

  2. Each passage describes God's blessing during the "desert" times of life as an abundance of water. When have you experienced the water from God while in the desert? (NOTE: Refer students back to the experiences they shared from the previous question.) Did God provide water? What was it? Was it unexpected (from a rock)? Did it satisfy?

  3. How does the experience of water in the past help us face the "desert" of today or tomorrow?

  4. Reread Psalm 63:1. Have you ever felt this thirsty? Isn't God (as water) wonderful? No matter how severe our desert is, God will provide. This doesn't lessen the difficulty of the desert experience; however, finding God's provision in the wilderness should strengthen us and give us the courage to keep going.

- Isaiah 32:2; Matthew 10:42; Mark 9:41; John 7:38. This theme is much less frequent than God as water, but it is clearly present.

  1. What happens to those who follow God?

  2. What must we become to others?

  3. Think of someone who was cool water for you when you "were thirsty in a barren land." Tell the class.

  4. Think of a time when you were cool water to a parched person. What was his or her reaction? (If they feel comfortable, students should relate their examples to the class.)

  5. Conclusion: Have your students respond to the following questions:

     - To be water for someone else, what needs to happen to us?

     - How do we become filled with the living water God provides?

     - How is life like the wilderness of Judea where En Gedi is?

     - How is God like the oasis of En Gedi?

     - Why did David need to come to En Gedi to get water?

     - Why do we need to come to En Gedi?

     - Where/what is your En Gedi? (Your En Gedi is the place and time you find to meet with God to satisfy your thirst—devotions, Bible study, worship, prayer, retreat, and meditation.)

     - What happens to us if we have no En Gedi? Would we have cool water to give to others?

Review with your students some of the other analogies the audience in the video drew from En Gedi.

- The desert should make us long for En Gedi. How does this relate to God?

- Our culture is like a desert. How?

- Some people don't get into the desert (the tough times in life, our own or others) to appreciate En Gedi. Is this true? Explain.

- Even the attractive things of our culture become a desert without En Gedi (God). How can good things be like a desert?

- Others are used by God to be an En Gedi for us. Who is En Gedi for you? Have you thanked them? Thanked God?

- The Dead Sea looks refreshing, but its bitter saltwater does not satisfy. Our culture is like that. What looks like it would satisfy but really doesn't? Can you give an example from your own experience?

- It is tempting to stay at En Gedi, but God calls us to live in a difficult world (the wilderness) so that we can be His witnesses. Although we must leave En Gedi and go back to the wilderness, we should return regularly to be refreshed.

6. Discussion: Broken Cisterns

The rainfall in Israel varies greatly, from over 20 inches per year in the mountains to under two near the Dead Sea. The rainy season runs from November through March. Since fresh springs like En Gedi are rare, preserving rainwater was important to the people of Israel. It often meant the difference between life and death. Most cities and towns and even houses had cisterns, pits dug into the rock where the rainwater could be trapped. These plastered pits often collected the rain from the roof or from the area around the cistern. This water, though fresh, was not clean, clear, and cold like the spring of En Gedi. But it was the best the people had.

These cisterns are mentioned in the Bible. Joseph (Genesis 37:20–28) and Jeremiah (Jeremiah 38:6–13) were imprisoned in cisterns. Proverbs 5:15 described marital fidelity as "drinking from your own cistern." Prosperity meant you had your own cistern (2 Kings 18:31). People hid in cisterns (1 Samuel 13:6) and used them as tombs (Jeremiah 41:7,9); kings built them (2 Chronicles 26:10). There were laws given about them (Leviticus 11:36), and God's judgment to withhold rain meant dry cisterns (Jeremiah 14:1–6). The Israelites were familiar with them. They were necessary for life.

Building cisterns required an enormous amount of effort. First, a person had to dig a pit out of solid rock and plaster the walls. The ground around the cistern had to be sloped so that the water would drain into it. And despite a person's best efforts, the water trapped in the cistern wasn't always clean. (Even today travelers sometimes come across cisterns with dead animals floating in them.) The plaster tended to fall off and then the water would leak. A spring of living water like En Gedi was obviously far better than water trapped in a homemade cistern. Living water was always fresh and never leaked out or dried up. The Bible used this strong contrast often to symbolize God and our relationship with Him.

- God is living water (Psalm 107:9; Jeremiah 17:13) and provides water (Isaiah 35:6–7, 58:11; John 4:13–14, 7:37–38).

- Cisterns are created by people and can run dry (Jeremiah 14:1–6).

- Read Jeremiah 2:13. In the passage, God described the foolishness of idol worship. What two foolish acts are mentioned? Why are they completely stupid? What are they "pictures" of? (Not honoring God is like leaving a cold, fresh spring like En Gedi. Honoring idols is like trying to drink from a cistern where the plaster has fallen off and the water has leaked out.) How do you think people reacted to Jeremiah's "picture"? Why is being unfaithful to God and serving other gods like that? How do we leave "the spring of living water" for "broken cisterns" today?

- In the video, this analogy was extended to indicate that the spring of En Gedi is a picture of God as living water. Trusting Him for life means taking the time to come to En Gedi to be refreshed from the wilderness of life. Cisterns represent, in one sense, our own efforts and strength. Trying to do without God is like leaving the gushing spring of En Gedi for the broken cisterns we carved ourselves and drinking the dirty water they contain. How do you trust your own strength and efforts? What does God offer instead? Ask your students to think for a few moments of an area in their lives where they need to seek God's living water and learn to depend on Him.

Prayer: Spend some time together in prayer. Ask God to help you give up your dirty cisterns and drink from His living water. Plan time to be with Him (your En Gedi).

OPTIONAL — Digging Deeper I: Cisterns and Springs (20–45 minutes)

(This section requires the use of the optional full-color overhead-transparency packet. For information on ordering it, see p. 243.)

HINT: *For those who have the optional full-color overhead-transparency packet for Set 1 of this curriculum series, Overhead Transparency 22 is of En Gedi. Its description is on page 39 of the Leader's Guide for Set 1.*

Overhead Transparency 46. Oasis of En Gedi. This photograph demonstrates the complete contrast between the wilderness surrounding the oasis and the stream of water that literally comes out of a rock, though actually several hundred yards beyond the waterfall. En Gedi is a major oasis along the eastern edge of the Judea Wilderness. The Dead Sea is less than a mile from where this photo was taken. It rarely rains here. The water flows inside the rock from miles away in the Judea Mountains, where it does rain. In this area, several springs emerge from the rock. This stream comes from one appropriately called the David Spring. The sudden appearance of water brings life out of the barrenness of the desert.

Since En Gedi belonged to the tribe of Judah, it was the place David hid from Saul (1 Samuel 23:19,24). It is helpful to understand that experience in its setting. For some time, David had hidden from Saul in the wilderness (on the left). It was hot, dry, and barren. Then David and his soldiers discovered the lushness of the oasis. One can almost picture their reaction as they entered the shade and the thick growth (on the right). Suddenly, they came to this natural amphitheater, and found the waterfall. In that context, David wrote Psalm 42 and Psalm 63.

Have a student read aloud Psalm 42:2 and 63:1 as the class looks at this photograph. Then ask the students the following questions:

- What was David's and his men's reaction to this oasis?

- What does it tell you about how David pictured his relationship with God?

Overhead Transparency 47. Scenes from En Gedi. These pictures show several typical scenes from En Gedi that inspired biblical images.

Upper Left: Water from the Rock. This small stream literally runs out of the rock. Miles away, rainfall seeps in the cracks in the rock until eventually it emerges like this. Many Bible passages speak of water gushing from the rock (Deuteronomy 8:15; Exodus 17:6; Psalm 105:41). The miracle is not that the water comes out of the rock—that is commonplace in this land. The miracle is that it came where and when God commanded. The rock shown here is a picture of God because the Bible described the rock from which the water came as God Himself (Deuteronomy 32:4,31; Psalm 78:35; 1 Corinthians 10:3–4). This photograph provides a beautiful metaphor of the Christian life: God is the Rock. I am thirsty. Living Water comes from the Rock.

Upper Right: Living Water Brings Life. The result of living water is clearly seen. The barren wilderness on the right contrasts sharply with the lush growth on the left produced by the water. Many Bible passages describe God's care for His own as providing water (Isaiah 35:6, 41:18, 49:10, 55:1; Psalm 65:9; John 7:38), revealing our need to be rooted in "streams of water" (Isaiah 49:10; Jeremiah 17:5–8; Psalm 65:9; John 7:38) and our call to become living water for others (Isaiah 32:2; John 7:37–38).

Lower Left: Pools in the Desert. The desert around En Gedi is hot, barren, and dry. God's promise to His people was to turn the desert into "pools of water" (Psalm 107:35; Isaiah 43:19). Even the barrenness is made fruitful by the living water from God. The water and shade seen in this photograph provide relief and the ability to handle the extreme desert heat. This, too, is a picture of God's care. He is the cool shade that protects the weary from the sun's heat; He is the water that soothes the parched throat of the thirsty (Psalm 63:1,7; Isaiah 32:2).

Lower Right: Ibex. En Gedi is the home of desert goats known as ibex. These heavy-horned males and graceful does (Proverbs 5:19) graze on the sparse grasses in the surrounding desert. The only available water for miles around is the spring of En Gedi. This photograph doesn't exactly depict the "deer that pants for water" (Psalm 42:1), but it is clearly the image the psalmist used to describe his need for God. These beautiful animals will come to drink even when there are people nearby because they are so thirsty. It is the same with us believers. We are so spiritually thirsty that we seek God as an ibex pants after water.

Overhead Transparency 48. A Broken Cistern. **HINT:** *Overhead Transparency 26 ("Cistern of Masada"), in Lesson Twelve, and Overhead Transparency 30 ("An Essene Cistern"), in Lesson Thirteen, would apply here also. Their descriptions are found on pages 43 and 65, respectively.* The people of the Bible used cisterns regularly for their water supply. Rainfall was limited, coming only five months of the year, from November through March. People would dig pits into the rock, sometimes entirely underground (as in the cistern at the Old Testament city of Arad) or in the ground and covered with a roof (as in the cistern at the New Testament city of Chorazin). The walls of the cistern were plastered (as seen here) to prevent the water from seeping out. An area would be prepared to collect the water (e.g., a rooftop, a courtyard, or even the street), and the water would be channeled into the cistern. It was fresh water, but not particularly clean. The cistern shown here has decayed and partially collapsed, so it no longer can hold water.

While displaying this overhead transparency, have someone read Jeremiah 2:13, 14:3. Compare Overhead Transparency 46 ("Oasis of En Gedi") with this one. Ask students to explain what Jeremiah meant. Would they leave a flowing spring for a dry cistern? That's what it is like to serve or find meaning in something or someone other than God.

7. Guided Discussion: Living Water

Students should read the handout "The Joy of Living Water: Jesus and the Feast of Sukkot" before beginning this discussion.

a. Living water is fresh, flowing water. It cannot be drawn or carried. In a sense, it is life-giving and alive. The Hebrew word for this kind of water is poetic: *mayim chayyim* (pronounced "my-eem chy-eem," with the *chy* guttural). The spring of En Gedi is this living water.

b. Read Psalm 107:9; Isaiah 35:6–7, 58:11; Jeremiah 2:13, 17:13; Zechariah 14:8.

- What do these passages teach about God as living water?

- How is God living water for you?

c. Read John 4:13–14, 7:37–38.

- What do you know about Jesus, your living water? What qualities does He have?

- What did living water have to do with the "last and greatest day of the feast"? (John 7:37)

- How does this help you understand Jesus?

- Whom does John say the living water symbolizes? (John 7:39)

d. Read John 4:13–14, 7:38.

- What is true of this living water within a person?

- How does that affect others?

- Do you have this stream within you?

Prayer: Spend a few moments in prayer. Encourage the students to ask God to become "living water" within them. Help them understand that the Spirit of God becomes a never-ending source of flowing water (like En Gedi) that provides living water for others as well.

OPTIONAL — Digging Deeper II: En Gedi *(10–25 minutes)*

This poem was written and set to music by Ben Lappinga, a 17-year-old high school student, while he was visiting the oasis of En Gedi. (The words and the music can be heard in the video *Living Water.*) It combines many of the images that have been the basis for this curriculum series, *That the World May Know.* Have someone read the poem aloud and then, as a class, reflect on the questions below.

En Gedi

Life is not so easy,
As a Christian standing stone.
It's a barren wilderness,
You can't make it on your own.

For work to be a good thing
You must face the dusty heat.
But you're called to find some rest,
Gaining strength to not be beat.

Do not dig a cistern,
Letting pleasures get ahead.
For the water you need clean,
Will be stale and dry instead.

But the waters of En Gedi,
Are fresh and flow with life.
So find the Lord in prayer,
Quench your thirst, and end your strife.

Chorus:
Oh, En Gedi, taking refuge in the Lord,
En Gedi, letting Jesus' words reward.
Drinking living water,
Resting in the shade.
Finding all the comfort,
To never be afraid.
En Gedi, a quiet peace with God.

- What is a Christian "standing stone"?

- Why is life like the dusty heat?

- What is a "cistern" in the metaphor of water?

- Why is En Gedi like taking refuge in the Lord?

- What is living water?

OPTIONAL — Digging Deeper III: Pictures in the Wilderness *(45–80 minutes)*

There are several other wilderness images that can illustrate Bible truths. Ask for volunteers to read each of the following passages.

Heat and Shade

1. Read Psalm 32:4; Psalm 121:6; Isaiah 25:4–5, 49:10, 58:11; Genesis 21:14–16; 1 Kings 19:3–4; Jonah 4:5–8.

   - One way to understand these passages is to see that life is often like being in the brutal heat of the sun. Anyone who has been exposed too long to the fierce desert sun understands. You feel dried out, weak, and overheated. You feel unable to carry on. Sometimes life's circumstances are like that, too. Ask the class to share experiences that could be described as being in the hot, desert sun. (NOTE: Be prepared. Some people may share traumatic experiences from their lives.) Did you reach a point at which you felt that the heat of the circumstances was unbearable?

2. Read Psalm 17:8, 36:7, 63:7, 80:10, 91:1, 121:5; Isaiah 4:6, 32:2, 49:2, 51:16.

   - God can be described as the "shade" or "shadow" that provides relief. The deserts of the Middle East have very *dry* heat. This means that when it is hot, even a small amount of shade, a slight breeze, and some water make the heat bearable. Again, ask the class to relate experiences in which God provided shade. What form did the shade take? Did it make the heat bearable?

3. Ask your students to respond to the following questions:

- Life is like the heat of the desert sun, and God is like shade. Does God promise to *take away* the heat? (This is an important part of this image in the Bible. We often want God to take away the brutal heat of life's tough circumstances. God can and does do that sometimes. Usually, however, He asks us to continue to face the heat of loneliness, grief, sickness, broken relationships, and all the other struggles we have. But He does promise to provide us with *enough* shade to make the heat bearable, though no less hot.)

- Ask if any of your group has had the experience of God providing just enough shade so they could live one day at a time with the heat. For those who are willing, let them relate their experiences briefly to the class.

Rocks and Honey

1. Read Psalm 27:2, 56:13, 91:12; Proverbs 3:23; Isaiah 8:14, 40:30; Jeremiah 31:9.

Israel is a rocky country. Usually, the word "stone" in biblical passages represents something strong and secure. But there is another image. Walking the narrow, steep paths on hillsides in this rocky country, people often stumble over countless stones underfoot. Here God promises a smooth path. One Jewish application of this concept is that living is like walking on a path. The stones in the path represent the obstacles and stumbling blocks of life.

Ask your students to relate some of the "pebbles" on their life's path (e.g., car failure, loss of a wallet or purse, a child with a bad habit). Ask them if they have ever had "boulders" in their walk (e.g., loss of a job, illness, problem in a relationship). Ask them if anyone ever had a "boulder" so big that it seemed impossible to walk around it.

Point out that sometimes God promises a smooth path (Jeremiah 31:9), and other times He does not.

2. Read Exodus 3:8; Deuteronomy 8:8; Psalm 19:10, 34:8, 119:103.

Honey was the only naturally sweet substance ancient peoples had. Sometimes bees made their hives in the rocks of the wilderness or in the mountains. Honey was a much sought after treat. The Bible describes God's blessings as honey. In that sense, to experience God was to "taste" Him.

Read Psalm 81:16; Deuteronomy 32:13. Ask your students to respond to the following questions.

- Where does the honey come from? How does this fit the culture?

- Have you ever experienced "honey" (i.e., God's unexpected, undeserved, richest blessings)?

- If we use the image of rocks as things we kick, stumble over, and agonizingly try to get around in our walks in life, then where is the honey? In a sense, God promised His blessings in the toughest times—like honey in a rock. It may not make the rocks smaller or less painful, but somehow the honey makes them bearable. That means when we face the rocks (the tough times), we should look around for honey (God's provision).

    Ask the class if anyone ever had honey in a rock in this sense. Did it make the rock less painful? Did it allow the person to deal better with the pain?

Prayer: Spend a few moments in prayer. Ask God to give us His honey, particularly to anyone whose "rock" is especially painful right now. Ask God to give us the wisdom to remember past honey experiences so the next rock we encounter won't be so formidable.

A Final Thought: A Jewish rabbi once said, "If you pray for honey, God may send it in the rocks."

Conclusion

Life can be a wilderness. The heat of difficult circumstances; the barrenness of failure, loss, and hurt; the thirst of unsatisfied needs are like being lost in the desert. But God is shade and thirst-quenching water; He is the rock from which streams of water flow to make the desert blossom. Unfortunately, our tendency is to rely on ourselves instead of God, so we turn away from the refreshing streams He offers us and dig our own broken cisterns that soon fill with dirty, stagnant water.

Use the images we've discussed in this lesson to challenge your students to seek a relationship with God, have regular times of refreshment in devotions and study, and identify those parts of their lives where they are depending on their own strength. After restoring themselves in En Gedi, they will be much better equipped to face their wildernesses.

THE JOY OF LIVING WATER: JESUS AND THE FEAST OF SUKKOT

With joy you will draw water from the wells of salvation.
(Isaiah 12:3)

Water was of great importance to the people of the Bible. They lived in a dry country, completely dependent on the seasonal rains. Fresh water was not available everywhere and the task of digging wells and cisterns was a difficult one. Such an important resource as fresh water would naturally be a picture or symbol of spiritual reality as well. God frequently made use of common cultural phenomena to teach the truths of faith. He was Shepherd, Potter, and King. The people were sheep, clay, and subjects. Water became symbolic as well.

LIVING WATER

There were different types of water found in the land of Israel. Cistern water was rainwater trapped in pits dug into rock and plastered to prevent leakage. Most homes and public buildings had them. The water was often dirty, having flowed from roofs or streets into the cistern. This source of water was not dependable because one season it might not rain or the plaster might leak and the water seep away.

Running water, especially springwater, was different. It stayed fresh and clean. And most springs were dependable, providing water year round. This constant fresh source of water was called "living water," probably portraying its life-giving qualities as well as its constant freshness. God provides (and is described as) living water (Psalm 107:9; Isaiah 35:6–7, 58:11; Jeremiah 2:13; Zechariah 14:8; John 4:13–14, 7:37–38). Living water was cleansing (Leviticus 15:1–3). The ritual bath of Jesus' day, the *mikveh*—used before coming into the presence of God at the Temple or to the synagogue worship service—contained flowing water, or living water. John the Baptist's choice of the Jordan River for his symbolic cleansing likely was based on the need for fresh, moving water to symbolize cleansing. Jesus described Himself as living water (John 4:13–14, 7:37–38), and the people of His day understood the meaning. Only God could provide living water. It would not fail to satisfy any thirst. But it was the connection between living water and the feast of Sukkot that gave Jesus' image of living water the clearest meaning. He chose that feast day to reveal that He was living water.

THE FEAST OF SUKKOT

In the Old Testament, God instituted a religious calendar for the Israelites to follow. The seventh day, the seventh year, and the end of seven "seven years" were significant to Him. Within each year, there were seven specified feasts (Leviticus 23). In the spring, three feasts were celebrated together: Passover, Unleavened Bread, and Firstfruits. These feasts remembered, respectively, Israel's deliverance from Egypt, God's gift of the Promised Land, and the spring harvest. Fifty days after Passover came Shavuot, sometimes called Pentecost, which celebrated the end of the grain harvest and the anniversary of the giving of the Torah on Mount Sinai. In the fall were the holy days of Rosh Hashanah, or the feast of Trumpets, and Yom Kippur, the day of atonement when Israel went before the Lord and asked forgiveness to escape His judgment. Immediately after these two feast days came the most joyous one of all, the only feast God commanded the people to "rejoice before him" (Leviticus 23:40)—the feast of Sukkot, or Tabernacles as it would come to be known. And rejoice they did.

The week-long celebration began after the fall harvest (figs, pomegranates, dates, and grapes) had been gathered and the olives hung heavy on the trees. Now was the time to be glad. Following God's command the people built booths of olive, palm, and myrtle branches (Nehemiah 8:15). The booths provided shade, but there needed to be enough space in the branches so the people could see the sky, reminding them of their years in the wilderness. These booths, or *sukkot* (pl. *sukkah*) gave the feast its name.

For seven days, the people ate, lived, and slept in these booths. Since this was one of the three feasts in which everyone was commanded to come to Jerusalem (Passover and Shavuot are the others), thousands of people crowded the streets of the city, and there were *sukkot* everywhere. The children loved it, and so did the adults. It was a time to praise God for the past gifts of freedom, land, and bountiful harvests.

The Pharisees had adopted another custom based on God's commands in Leviticus 23:40. They took the branches of the three trees—olive, palm, and myrtle—and tied them together. Holding this cluster of branches (called *lulav*; pl. *lulavim*) in one hand and a citron (the fruit they decided was mentioned in Leviticus 23:40) in the other, they carried them to the Temple for each of the seven days of the festival (as religious Jews still do today). Here the people, and even the youngest children, would wave their *lulavim* joyously, as they danced, sang, and chanted the *Hallel* (Psalms 113–118) in a time of great celebration rivaling any holiday the world has ever known. A procession of priests—who made the festive sacrifices (literally hundreds of animals were offered) and carried water and wine to be poured into the silver funnels on the altar as drink offerings—would lead the men and boys around the altar in the priests' court in front of the Temple. Whenever they came to the Hosanna (Psalm 118:25), they waved their *lulavim* toward the altar as they sang, "O Lord, save us! O Lord, grant us success!" After several hours of intense rejoicing before the Lord, the people returned to their booths to rest, eat, and prepare for the next day's celebration.

SUKKOT IN HISTORY

The commands in Leviticus 23 leave little doubt as to the importance of this great celebration to God. But three historical events added even more to the joy the people felt on this great fall festival. The first, described in 2 Chronicles 5–7, was the dedication of the First Temple of Solomon (see 2 Chronicles 5:3, 7:9), which took place during Sukkot. For seven days, the nation of Israel celebrated and rejoiced because God had chosen to live among them. The ark, the resting place of God's glorious presence, was moved into the Temple, God's earthly home, in a spectacular display of His glory (2 Chronicles 5:13–14). After the people said an impassioned prayer for God's presence (2 Chronicles 6), God sent fire from heaven to consume the sacrifices, a stunning display of His power and love (2 Chronicles 7:1–3). On the day the Temple was dedicated, Solomon and the people offered more than 140,000 sacrifices, a measure of their joy. Afterward, everyone went home filled with happiness (2 Chronicles 7:10). The people of Jesus' day, though Solomon's Temple had been destroyed and the ark had disappeared, remembered their joy and celebrated God's presence in the Temple of Herod, still in the same location. Their jubilation was no less than in Solomon's time.

The second event was the celebration of Sukkot following the reconstruction of Solomon's Temple (destroyed by the Babylonians) by the exiles after their return from Babylon. Though this building was not as glorious as the first, the people's devotion to their God was stronger than ever. When the Torah was read and the feast of Sukkot described, Nehemiah, the high priest, commanded that it be celebrated again (Nehemiah 8:13–18), and the people's joy was "very great" (Nehemiah 8:17). As the people of Jesus' time remembered this ancient celebration, their joy grew greater, for God had not forgotten them.

The third event is not mentioned directly in the Bible. Between the Old and New Testaments, the Jews were severely oppressed by the Hellenistic Greeks from Syria. Antiochus, the king of the Syrians, was determined to Hellenize the Jews, so he outlawed the Sabbath, circumcision, and the study of Torah. Sacrifices were ordered to the pagan king, even in the Temple itself. The great altar of the Temple was defiled by the offering of pigs on it. The entrails of these unclean animals were dragged around the Temple courts, defiling them as well. A statue of the king was placed in the Temple. It was a time of great anguish for the Jewish people.

But God sent deliverance. An old priest, Mattathias, began a revolt by refusing to make the royal sacrifice in a small town near Jerusalem. His son, known as Judah Maccabee, led a group of freedom fighters against the far stronger Greek army. Trusting God, these rebels miraculously defeated the army of Antiochus and reclaimed the city of Jerusalem. Reaching the Temple, Judah ordered a complete cleansing and rededication of the building, and the altar was rebuilt.

The menorah, or eternal light, in the Holy of Holies had been extinguished while Jerusalem was under Syrian control. Though only a small supply of sacred oil remained, Judah ordered the lamp lit. Miraculously, it burned for eight days, the entire time of the rededication of the Temple, when new oil was purified. The celebration of this great deliverance of God became known as the Feast of Dedication, or Hanukkah (which Jesus also celebrated—see John 10:22–23). It was celebrated after Sukkot that year.

But Judah and the religious leaders were concerned. Sukkot was the celebration of God's goodness and the time to pray for His future blessings, especially for the fall rains. Judah ordered Sukkot to be held even though the time was past (2 Maccabees 10:5–8). So the Sukkot celebration took on even greater happiness as it recalled God's miraculous deliverance and preservation of His people and His Temple for a third time. Several Sukkot and Hanukkah customs became intertwined. The palm branch became the symbol of political as well as religious freedom. The chant of Hosanna (or "O Lord, save us") now was understood to mean not only the salvation of deliverance from Egypt, the provision of rain for next year's harvest, and the forgiveness requested by the sacrifices, but it also was a prayer for political freedom. (This connection, along with the waving of palm branches, was to have interesting application in the ministry of Jesus—see Luke 19:28–44.)

Four great menorahs (over 75 feet high), placed in the women's court in remembrance of the miraculous unending supply of oil on Hanukkah, were also lit on Sukkot, commemorating God's deliverance of His people from the Syrians. (The bowls on top of the branched candles held more than 10 gallons of oil. The wicks were made from the worn-out breeches of the priests.) The light of the candles could be seen in every house in Jerusalem. Tradition records that the people, upon seeing the light, sang these words: "Our ancestors turned their backs on the Temple of the Lord, but our eyes are on the Lord." Truly the feast of Sukkot was one of great celebration. A rabbi once said, "Whoever has not seen Sukkot has not witnessed real joy."

SUKKOT AND LIVING WATER

There was another special element to the celebration of Sukkot, and it involved living water. Sukkot took place at the end of the dry season. The rains needed to begin immediately to ensure a harvest the following year. Thus the celebration of God's harvest was coupled with fervent prayer for next year's rains. Some believe this custom came from Solomon's prayer at the Sukkot dedication of the Temple (2 Chronicles 6). He prayed that God would forgive the sins of the people when they prayed toward the Temple and that He would not withhold the rains (2 Chronicles 6:26–27). The people knew that no rain meant no life. So the priests added a ceremony that included a prayer for rain. They may have based this ceremony on Isaiah 12:3: "With joy you will draw water from the wells of salvation."

This part of the ceremony involved a procession of priests, accompanied by flutes, marching from the Temple to the Pool of Siloam, which was fed by the Spring of Gihon. One of the priests filled a golden pitcher (more than a quart) with water, and the procession returned to the Temple. They arrived just after the sacrifices were laid on the altar. The priest carrying the pitcher entered the priests' court through the Water Gate and, to the blast of the shofar, approached the altar. He made one circle around the altar as the crowd sang the *Hallel*. Then the priest climbed the ramp and stood near the top of the altar. Here there were two silver funnels leading into the stone altar for the daily drink offerings. As the crowd grew silent, the priest solemnly poured the water into one of the funnels. Again the people, accompanied by the Levitical choir, began to chant the *Hallel*. The sound was deafening because of the thousands of pilgrims jammed into the Temple courts. In this way, they asked God for life-giving rain. The living water they used apparently acknowledged it was God who brought rain and life. The chant of the Hosanna—"O Lord, save us!"—now meant "Save us by sending rain as well."

It seems hardly possible, but the celebration became even more intense as the week drew to a close. When the seventh day of the feast arrived, the courts of the Temple were packed with worshipers. Chants of praise were heard throughout the city, and thousands of *lulavim* waved in the air. The priestly procession went to the living water of the Pool of Siloam. As the massive crowd waited expectantly, the sacrifices were offered, and the priests chanted, "O Lord, save us! O Lord, grant us success!" (Psalm 118:25).

The procession returned and entered the Court of the Gentiles, then went through the Water Gate into the priests' court. As hundreds of priests chanted the Hosanna ("Deliver us! Save us!") and thousands of people jammed into the Temple courts, the procession circled the altar seven times (remembering the walls of Jericho, which fell after seven circuits because of God's great power). Then there were three blasts on the trumpets, and the crowd grew still as the priest poured the living water into the funnel. Now the chanting became even more intense: "Save us, hosanna! Help us, hosanna!" and the next verse: "Blessed is he who comes in the name of the LORD" (Psalm 118:26). The waving of the *lulavim* reached a frenzy as branches were beaten against the ground until the leaves fell off.

Gradually, the people fell silent as they returned, exhausted, to dismantle their booths before journeying home. God had blessed them. They had celebrated joyously His presence, thanking Him for His gift of land and the bountiful harvest. They had begged for His continued blessing of the rains and had pleaded for political freedom as well. They were now prepared to face another year.

JESUS' TEACHING

In the context of Sukkot, the water ceremony, and the menorah blazing with light, Jesus dramatically presented the message of His new kingdom. It was during the last week of His life on earth. He had gone to Jerusalem for Sukkot (John 7:10) and had spent time teaching the great crowds who thronged the Temple (John 7:14). On the "last and greatest day of the Feast" (John 7:37), in the midst of the water ceremony, the chanted prayers, and the plea through the offering of living water, Jesus stood and said, "If anyone is thirsty, let him come to me and drink. Whoever believes in me, as the Scripture has said, streams of living water will flow from within him" (John 7:37–38).

Did He say this during the silence that fell as the priest poured the water? Was His shout heard above the chants of "Save us"? Or was it as the crowd began to leave that Jesus explained His ministry in the symbol of living water, streams that flow from within those who believe? Did Jewish tradition support His teaching that living water represented God's Spirit (John 7:39)? It is not stated in the Bible. But the setting Jesus chose to give this lesson, and the similarity of His meaning to Jewish tradition, meant that His shouted promise in the Temple must have had stunning impact. "Let him come to *Me!*"

John's gospel also recorded another teaching during the time of Sukkot. Though it is not placed on the exact days of the feast, it is during Jesus' visit to Jerusalem for Sukkot. In the context of a joyous feast, ended each day with the blazing candles in the Temple courts, Jesus said, "I am the light of the world" (John 8:12). The crowd, having just seen how the Temple candles had lit up the city, must have been strongly affected by Jesus' words, the mastery of His teaching, and the Old Testament background. Jesus is "living water," as taught during the water ceremony, and He is the "light of the world," in the context of the great Temple lights.

CONCLUSION

The importance of the Jewish background to Jesus' work cannot be exaggerated. It gave Him the context He needed to make His teachings relevant, powerful, and practical. The feast of Sukkot has additional lessons. It was (and is) a feast of great joy. Jesus experienced that emotional celebration of God's goodness. In many ways, the Christians of today have exchanged the ability to celebrate before the Lord for the shallow "happiness" of the secular world or for the always somber mentality of worship. There were solemn times in Temple worship, reminding the Jewish people to be sober, holy, and serious about their faith. But they also had Sukkot. It reminded them that God wants His people (including us) to celebrate before Him (Leviticus 23:40). How many modern-day Christians truly celebrate with this kind of joy before the Lord?

A second lesson can only be suggested here. The seven Jewish feasts also became the outline for Jesus' ministry. He died on Passover, was buried on the feast of Unleavened Bread, and was raised on the feast of Firstfruits. He sent the Holy Spirit on Shavuot (Pentecost). Rosh Hashanah (the trumpet call to judgment) and Yom Kippur (judgment day) in some sense will be fulfilled upon Jesus' return, though He has already fulfilled some elements of these two feasts.

And what comes after the final judgment? Heaven! The new Promised Land! Sukkot is the feast that celebrated the Promised Land, God's deliverance, living water, and God's blessing. Sukkot is a feast that will be fully realized in heaven. There will be living water (Revelation 7:17), the eternal presence of God (Revelation 21:22), and the light (Revelation 22:5).

Sukkot taught the Jewish people to be joyful, in anticipation of heaven. Take the most joyful celebration that ever existed and imagine it lasting forever. That is heaven. No wonder some Jewish Christians (and some Gentile ones, too) celebrate Sukkot.

GLOSSARY

Aeolia Capitolina: Hadrian, the Roman emperor, destroyed Jerusalem after defeating the Jews during the Second Jewish Revolt (A.D. 132–135). He renamed it Aelia Capitolina (correct spelling) and erected a temple (over the ruins of the Jewish Temple) to the Roman god Jupiter.

Antonia: Herod the Great rebuilt the Hasmonaean fortress (Bira) in Jerusalem next to the Temple Mount and renamed it the Antonia after Mark Antony. Roman troops were stationed here.

Babylon, Babylonians: Hebrew, *Babel.* Capital city of Mesopotamia, located on the Euphrates River and neighbor to Assyria. Considered at the time of the prophet Jeremiah to be the greatest and most beautiful city of the Near East. An enormous political and economic power that held great influence over the Israelites. The Babylonians took the children of Israel into exile in 586 B.C. for 70 years. The return from this exile established a people to whom Jesus would be born, and a kingdom in the land of Israel.

Bar Kochba Revolt: Another name for the Second Jewish Revolt against Rome (A.D. 132–135). The leader of the revolt was a man named Bar Kochba.

Belial: Hebrew meaning "useless." Came to be applied to the devil by the Essenes and the early Christians (2 Corinthians 6).

Bethsaida: One of the three main towns of Jesus' ministry in Galilee. This small, prosperous fishing village on the north shore of the Sea of Galilee was renamed Julias and rebuilt by Philip the Tetrarch. Home of apostles Peter, Philip, and Andrew. Near this village, Jesus performed the miracle of feeding 5,000 people. Its location was uncertain until recently when archaeologists excavated the ruins.

Beth Shean: City at the eastern entrance to the Jezreel Valley. The Philistines hung Saul's and Jonathan's bodies from its walls.

Caesarea: Port city and provincial capital of the Roman province of Judea. Herod built a spectacular man-made harbor with two breakwaters to link the country with world commerce

Caesarea Philippi: Large Hellenistic city rebuilt and renamed by Philip the Tetrarch. Located on Mount Hermon in the upper Jordan Valley near the spring of Panias, one of three headwaters of the Jordan River, and site of a great pagan temple dedicated to Pan, the Roman fertility god.

Canaan, Canaanite: Old Testament name for the Promised Land, meaning "land of purple," probably referring to the color of dye produced by shellfish along Canaan's coast. *Canaanite* refers to one who lived in Canaan; a synonym for merchant or trader; the people in Israel before the Israelites arrived.

Chorazin (OT Korazin): City just north of the Sea of Galilee where Jesus performed many miracles. Jesus condemned the city for its unbelief.

colonnades: Rows of columns spaced evenly apart that support arches or a roof. First-century Roman streets often had colonnades on both sides.

Copper Scroll: One of the Dead Sea Scrolls, etched on copper, claiming to identify a great treasure that had been hidden before the Temple was destroyed.

crèche: Nativity scene

Dead Sea: An inland lake in the Great Rift Valley known as the Salt Sea; 50 miles long and 10 miles wide, the salt content is five times more concentrated than the ocean and is uninhabitable by marine life. The Essene community lived in the wilderness along the Dead Sea.

Dead Sea Scrolls: Commentaries or instruction manuals for the Essene community discovered in 1947 by the Dead Sea in caves near the ruins of Khirbet Qumran. They provide valuable insights into the beliefs of one religious community from the time of Jesus; contain many references showing common themes, language, and beliefs with the teachings of Jesus, John the Baptist, and the early church. Help verify the most accurate texts of the Old Testament. Though these scrolls are 1,000 years older than other Hebrew manuscripts, there are few differences, and they indicate the miracle of God's protection of His Word throughout history.

Decapolis: Ten Hellenistic cities established at the time of Alexander the Great east of the Sea of Galilee and north of the Perea. Later, the Roman emperor Pompey organized the cities into a league named the Decapolis, largely populated by Roman army troops. In one ancient Jewish belief, the area was populated by pagans Joshua had driven out of the Promised Land (Joshua 3) and became "off limits" to Jews who followed God's law. In the New Testament, it refers to some cities where Jesus ministered to Gentiles and demonstrated his willingness to bring His message to everyone who needed to hear His words. The 10 cities included Pella, Damascus, Philadelphia, Canatha, Dium, Scythopolis (Beth Shean), Hippus, Gadara, Raphana, and Gerasa.

Egypt, Egyptian(s): Land and civilization south and west of Israel that flourished along the banks of the Nile River. During the time of Moses, home to enslaved Jews. Part of the Roman Empire during the first century. Throughout the Bible, Egypt was economically dependent on the eastern civilizations of Mesopotamia (Babylon, Assyria, and Persia). Trade routes connecting Egypt to these empires ran through mountain passes of Israel. By placing His people between the Egyptians and the eastern empires, God guaranteed that the whole known world would hear His message.

En Gedi: Means "place of the spring goat." A canyon and surrounding hills filled with springs that enabled a lush oasis to flourish on the Dead Sea's barren, western shore. Here David hid from Saul and possibly wrote several psalms.

Essene(s): A highly organized religious group that renounced the priestly establishment and saw themselves as God's soldiers. They strengthened their bodies, minds, and spirits for the battle they believed would usher in the new age. The Dead Sea Scrolls found at Qumran may have been their library. Some believe that John the Baptist belonged to this group, because his message was similar to that contained in the Dead Sea Scrolls. Some of the beliefs and practices of the Essenes resembled those of Jesus and the early church.

fresco: Design created by painting water colors onto wet plaster.

frieze: A design or series of low-relief sculptures forming an ornamental, horizontal band around a room or between the architrave and cornice of a building.

Gamla: Aramaic, meaning "camel," because from a distance this ridge in the Golan Heights (Gaulanitis) looks like a camel's hump. Located north and east of the Sea of Galilee. Home to nationalistic Pharisees (Zealots) who sought deliverance from Roman oppression and probably were responsible for the frequent questions to Jesus regarding the nature of His kingship and an ongoing desire to appoint Him king. After a brutal battle, the city fell to Vespasian in A.D. 67. Josephus recorded that 9,000 people died rather than surrender to the Romans.

Gennesaret. *See Sea of Galilee*

Great Rift Valley: Valley east of Israel where the Sea of Galilee and the Dead Sea are located. Also known as the Jordan Valley.

Hallel: A selection comprising Psalms 113–118 and 135–136 chanted during Jewish feasts.

Hasmonaean: Dynasty of Jewish kings belonging to the family also known as the Maccabees.

hazzan: Synagogue leader or administrator who cared for the facility and how it was used.

Hebron: Means "league." Ancient city of Judah at the southern edge of the Hebron Mountains, north of the Negev and approximately 19 miles south of Jerusalem. Abraham lived here and purchased a tomb in this area where he, his wife Sarah, Isaac, Rebecca, Jacob, and Leah were buried. David's capital for the first seven years of his reign. Herod built a large enclosure around the cave of Machpelah, where Abraham was buried.

Hellenism: Name for the culture and worldview of the Greeks. It was antithetically opposed to the God-centered worldview of the Jews. Hellenism makes the human being the ultimate in reality. The human mind is the basis for truth, the human body is the ultimate in wisdom, and human pleasure is the ultimate goal in life. It is the ancestor of modern humanism.

Herod the Great: Decreed king of Judea by the Romans in 40 B.C. Poorly accepted by the Jews because of his questionable heritage as a descendent of Esau and a native of Idumaea (Edom). Most infamous for trying to kill the infant Jesus by ordering the slaughter of all male babies under two years old in Bethlehem. Remembered for the brutality of his reign.

Herodian: Anything pertaining to Herod the Great and the Herodian period; or the political party that dominated Herod Antipas's territory and politically and economically supported Roman overlords.

Herodion: Fortress built by Herod the Great (c.a. 20 B.C.) near Bethlehem. It was a fortified palace and is reported to be the place of Herod's burial.

hippodrome: Greek, *hippus* ("horse") and *dramas* ("course"). Referred to a horse racing course or circus. Herod built hippodromes in Caesarea, Jericho, and Jerusalem, where horse races, chariot races, and Olympic-style games were held as part of his attempt to Hellenize Israel.

Idumaea: Another name for the city of Edom, meaning "red." Located south of the Dead Sea and west of Arabah; home of Herod the Great. Some early followers of Jesus came from Idumaea (Mark 3:8).

insula (pl. insulae): A family household arrangement common in Capernaum and Chorazin, where many rooms—residences for various family members—were built around a central courtyard.

Jericho: Oasis next to a spring in the Great Rift Valley north of the Dead Sea. First city captured by the Israelites after wandering in the desert for 40 years.

Jerusalem: Located in the Judea Mountains west of the Dead Sea on the rim of the Great Rift Valley at the edge of the Judea Wilderness. King David captured the mountain spur and the existing town, Jebus, become "David's City," the Israelites' religious and political center. David purchased a threshing floor, the traditional site where Abraham prepared to sacrifice his son Isaac to God, as the future site of God's Temple that Solomon eventually built (2 Chronicles 3:1). God sent Jesus to Jerusalem to complete His messianic work by being executed, buried, and raised on the same mountain of Abraham's attempted sacrifice and where sacrifices in the Temple were made. This created a physical link between events of Jewish history and followers of Jesus. In the Bible, "heavenly Jerusalem" symbolized God's heavenly kingdom that will come at the end of time.

Jezreel Valley: Means "valley of Megiddo." A fertile, agricultural valley whose strategic location led to frequent battles for control over the world trade route between the west and Mesopotamia/Babylon. Used by biblical writers as the symbolic setting of the final triumph of God's power over evil, Armageddon. Nazareth is nearby.

Jordan River: Hebrew, *Yarden* meaning "the descender." Headwaters fed by snow melt on Mount Hermon and underground springs; flows into the Dead Sea; where John the Baptist baptized Jesus.

Josephus: Jewish historian named Josephas Flavius, author of four major extra-biblical texts of Jewish life and culture. Born to a priestly family about the time of Jesus' death, he died approximately A.D. 100; he was a Galilean commander in the First Jewish Revolt. Trapped in the doomed city of Jotapata, Josephus convinced other survivors to commit suicide, arranging that he would be the last one alive. He surrendered to the Roman commander Vespasian and prophesied that Vespasian would become emperor. Vespasian made Josephus a scribe and a member of his own family; he became a Roman citizen. He wrote extensively about the First Jewish Revolt and Jewish history, and confirmed that New Testament descriptions of life and culture were accurate.

Judea: Region of Israel, named for the tribe of Judah, where Jerusalem was located. Ruled by Herod the Great and later given to his son Archelaus; then directly under Roman authority. The Judean Temple leadership resisted Jesus' message and ministry.

Judea Wilderness: Eastern slopes of the Judea Mountains form a 10-mile wide, 30-mile long hot, dry wilderness frequently used as a refuge for those in hiding or seeking a spiritual retreat, including the Essenes at Qumran, John the Baptist, David, and Jesus. Site of Masada, the last battle in the First Jewish Revolt.

legion: A military designation. Composed of spear men, archers, tacticians/strategists, calvary, and reserves. Some of the best Roman legions, including the tenth, were stationed in Israel during the first century. *Legion* also was used to describe a host of demons or an army of angels.

Maccabee: Family of high priest Mattathias and his son Judah, who revolted against oppressive Antiochus, king of Syria, a Seleucid Greek; Judah cleansed the Temple after defilement by the Syrians. The Jews remained free, ruled by the Maccabees (family name: Hasmonaean) until 63 B.C. The Maccabee symbol of a palm branch became a national symbol of freedom. Hanukkah (or the Feast of Dedication) celebrated Judah Maccabee's cleansing of the Temple.

Manual of Discipline: One of the writings of the Essenes found among the Dead Sea Scrolls; it describes the rules of the community.

Masada: A fortress expanded by Herod the Great to include a palace; on a mountain plateau on the Dead Sea's shore near Idumaea. David wrote, "The Lord is my rock and my fortress" (Psalm 18:2), a possible reference to this flat mountain plateau. Along the 1,000-foot mountaintop, Herod built a wall with 37 towers to defend against attackers and carved a three-level palace into the mountain face. Fearing Mark Antony would give his kingdom to Cleopatra of Egypt, Herod fortified Masada as an escape. Last place held by rebels in the First Jewish Revolt; they committed suicide rather than surrender. A symbol for the Jewish people, of their determination to remain free.

messianic banquet: One way to describe the great banquet (also called the wedding feast of the Lamb) that will occur when the Messiah comes.

mikveh **(pl. *mikvoth*)**: A ceremonial bath where a person immerses to become ritually clean according to Jewish law. A *mikveh* must be at least four and a half feet deep and hold no less than 195 gallons of water. Most water was piped in from cisterns filled by aqueducts that were connected to rivers or streams, necessary to provide "living water" (clean, cold running water) to ensure purity. Water often was stored next to the *mikveh* in a special reservoir (*otzar*). Worshipers

immersed before entering the Temple Mount. Background to Christian baptism; probable that a *mikveh* was used for baptisms on the Christian fulfillment of Pentecost.

Mount Arbel: Mountain ridge 1,000 feet above the Sea of Galilee. Site of a brutal battle in 38 B.C. between Galilean Jews and Herod the Great for control of Galilee.

Nabatean: Arabs who lived south and east of Israel and significantly impacted New Testament events. A highly advanced civilization that developed the ability to farm wilderness areas. Controlled the spice trade and trade routes that crossed Israel from Arabia.

Negev: Means "dry" or "parched." Desert on the southern edge of Israel, south of the Judea Mountains. The Israelites wandered here during their 40 years in the wilderness. Home of Jacob, father of the 12 tribes, and many desert nomads and spice traders. Elijah ran from Queen Jezebel into the Negev.

Palestine: Name given to the Promised Land after the Second Jewish Revolt (A.D. 132–135). It derives from the word *Philistia* and was used by the Romans to denigrate the Jews.

peristyle garden: Cultivated garden inside a colonnaded area. Herod the Great built several peristyle gardens, including Jericho and the Herodion.

Pharisees: Means "separated ones." Descended from the Hasidim ("pious ones"); considered obedience to Torah to be the heart of a godly life. Separated from sinful ways and people in their desire to be faithful. Believed strongly in God's judgment and a resurrection where men would be rewarded or punished according to their deeds. Constituted the largest Jewish sect during Jesus' lifetime; exerted great control over society through synagogues.

Pool of Siloam: Located near where the Tyropoeon Valley joins the Kidron; supplied drinking water for a large portion of Jerusalem. Water for the pool came from the Spring of Gihon through Hezekiah's tunnel. Jesus sent a blind man He had healed here to wash the mud off his eyes.

procurator: Roman military governor. Pontius Pilate was procurator of Judea.

Ptolemies: Descendants of Ptolemy I (one of the generals of Alexander the Great) who ruled over Egypt from 323 B.C. until 198 B.C. Israel was under their control during this time. Generally, they were benevolent rulers, though they sought to spread the influence of Hellenism among the Jews.

Qumran: A small community near the northern end of the Dead Sea, inhabited from 130 B.C. to A.D. 70, probably by Essenes. The Dead Sea Scrolls were found near this settlement.

rabbinic Judaism: Jewish religious practice after the Temple was destroyed (A.D. 70) that centered around the Torah and its interpretation by the rabbis.

Sadducees: Means "righteous ones." Wealthy Jewish aristocracy, claiming descent and authority from the high priest Zadok. Oversaw Temple; theology based on the first five books of the Bible; did not believe that God interfered in human lives or in any afterlife. Notoriously corrupt; disliked by the common people; helped to preserve their own political power and wealth by collaborating with the Romans. As the majority of the

70-man religious council (Sanhedrin), they wielded great authority over the nation's everyday affairs. Had the most to lose by Jesus' ministry, as He challenged Temple authority. Many scholars believe the Sadducees were responsible for plotting to kill Jesus—having Him arrested, interrogated, and then released to the Romans.

Sanhedrin: Means "council." Jewish supreme court; highest religious council, composed of 70 members and the high priest. The number 70 traditionally was based on Moses' appointment of 70 elders (Numbers 11:16) to administer Israel's affairs. Used by the Romans to administer daily affairs. Predominantly Sadducees, the religious faction most threatened by Jesus' ministry, who plotted against, interrogated, and released Him to the Romans.

scriptorium: Name given to a room in the Qumran community in which many scholars believe the Essenes wrote some of the Dead Sea Scrolls.

Scythopolis (Beth Shean): One of the oldest Decapolis cities. Originally, Beth Shean, renamed Scythopolis, or "City of Scythians," following Alexander the Great's conquest. Reputation for abundant water and fertile land. Located on the road Galileans walked in the Great Rift Valley to Jerusalem.

Sea of Galilee: Freshwater lake filled by the Jordan River, located in the Great Rift Valley and site of first-century commercial fishing industry; significant for a trade route on its northern shore. Jesus spent the majority of His ministry here, including the miracle of walking on water.

Sepphoris: Greek for Hebrew *zippor*, meaning "bird," because the town perched like a bird on a mountaintop in Lower Galilee. Hellenistic city built as Herod Antipas's regional capital; a major urban center of Hellenistic culture and power, with 20,000 inhabitants. Built three and a half miles from Nazareth during Jesus' childhood and youth; likely that He and His father, Joseph, worked here as a *tektons* (builders).

Septuagint: Means "70." Greek translation of the Old Testament made during the rule of the Ptolemies over the Jews. Frequently quoted by the authors of the New Testament.

Shavuot: Means "weeks"; also known as Pentecost or the Feast of Weeks. It's celebrated 50 days after the Sabbath following Passover.

shofar: Elaborate trumpet made from a ram's horn. Linked to the ram caught in a thicket and sacrificed by Abraham in place of Isaac. Used to intimidate enemies, call people to assembly, and announce prayer time, the start and end of Sabbath, and holy days, like Rosh Hashanah, Yom Kippur, Succoth, and Passover. Believed that this trumpet will signal the final judgment at the end of time.

sicarri: An extremist sect of the Zealots heavily involved in the First Jewish Revolt. They were named after their short, curved dagger *(sica)*, which they used to assassinate Romans and Jewish collaborators.

sons of light: Name the Essenes (writers of the Dead Sea Scrolls) gave themselves as followers of God. Their enemies (Romans and the apostate priesthood in Jerusalem), in their opinion, were the sons of darkness. The New Testament uses this language also (1 Thessalonians 5:5).

Syria: Nation or area north and east of Israel. Old Testament: a bitter enemy of Israel. New Testament: large province (including Israel) under Roman control. At the time of Jesus, a large Jewish community lived in its capital, Damascus.

Tabernacles (Festival, sanctuary, Succoth): The seventh yearly feast (Leviticus 23) when all males were required to come to Jerusalem. The people celebrated Israel's wandering in the desert by living in temporary shelters. Included a water ceremony as part of prayer for rain.

tel: Mound of debris composed of layers of ruins of cities. Locations for cities were limited in Israel by access to water, an economic occupation, and a defensible location. Over time, a city grew, was conquered and destroyed by enemies, to be rebuilt by other people over the old city's ruins.

Temple Mount: The ridge on which Jerusalem's Temple was built, and/or the platform on which the Temple and its courts stood. King Herod's platform was supported by massive walls, the tallest standing 160 feet, and measured more than 1,500 feet long, north to south, and more than 900 feet wide, east to west. It accommodated 200,000 pilgrims.

tetrarch: A Roman political office; meant one-fourth of a kingdom. When Herod died, his three sons and others received parts of his kingdom; two sons become tetrarchs, one an ethnarch.

Tiberias: Capital built by Herod Antipas on the Sea of Galilee's western shore; named for Tiberius Caesar. Believed to be built over a cemetery and considered unclean by religious Jews. After A.D. 70, it became a center of Jewish religious thought.

Torah: Hebrew, "a teaching"; the first five books of the Bible, God's covenant with Israel, given to Moses. Primarily a teaching about God and His people; a guide to live by rather than a collection of laws. When Jesus said He came to fulfill Torah, He meant how to live by the teachings and demonstrate the meaning of Torah.

triclinium: A reception or banquet hall or dining room. The tables were placed in a U-shape and surrounded by couches, where diners reclined as they ate.

Via Maris: Latin, "way of the sea." Possibly the name of the international trade route between the Mesopotamian empire (east) and Egypt (west), or a small portion of one near the Sea of Galilee. Matthew: Jesus settled near Capernaum by "the way of the sea," meaning the Via Maris, and as such He conducted His ministry in an area that was public because of the main road that ran through it.

wadi: Mountain canyons that carry water only when it rains; dry riverbeds with occasional flash floods. Wadi Kelt was a significant pass into and through the Judea Mountains between Jericho and Jerusalem.

Yahweh: Israel's God, means "I am" or "I am what I am," indicating that God is completely self-determined, dependent on no one for His being or power. The most sacred and holy name of God; other references to the divine as God, Lord, or Almighty are titles. Jewish people of Jesus' time avoided saying this name for fear of using it in vain. To refer to God they used *Adonai* (Greek, "Lord" or "Master").

Zin Wilderness: Name of part of the Negev wilderness just west of the Great Rift Valley. Named after the riverbed in the area: Zin.

APPENDIX

The Roman Empire

Persia

Caesarea
Jerusalem

Israel
Palestine
Judea

Arabian
Desert

Nile River

Egypt

Mediterranean Sea

Greece

Rome

Italy

Topography of Israel: New Testament

Sea of Galilee

Mediterranean Sea

Dead Sea

Via Maris: Way of the Sea

Coastal Plain

Shephelah

Central Mountain Range

Judea Wilderness

RIFT VALLEY

Jerusalem

Jericho

Qumran

En Gedi

GREAT

Negev

Moab Mountains

The Kingdom of Herod the Great

Decapolis

Herod Philip ‎1

Herod Antipas ‎2

Archelaus ‎3

Sea of Galilee

Caesarea Philippi ‎1

Gaulanitis ‎1
Gamla

Galilee ‎2

Decapolis

Caesarea
Samaria ‎3

Perea
Jericho ‎3

Judea ‎3

Qumran

Judea Wilderness ‎3

En Gedi

Masada

Idumaea ‎3

Jerusalem
Bethlehem
Herodion

Negev

Nabatea

Mediterranean Sea

Dead Sea

CHRONOLOGY
OF BIBLE TIMES

BC

586 BC	Babylonian Captivity of Judah
538 BC	Return to Israel
332 BC	Alexander the Great conquers Palestine
330–198 BC	Rule of Hellenistic Ptolemies over Jews
198–167 BC	Oppression under Hellenistic Seleucids
167 BC	Maccabee revolt
167–63 BC	Hasmonaean (Maccabee) kingdom
63 BC	Roman conquest of Judea
37 BC	Herod's reign begins
4 BC	Herod's death
4 BC–AD 6	Archelaus rules Samaria, Judea, and Idumaea
4 BC–AD 39	Herod Antipas rules Galilee and Perea
ca 6 BC	Jesus' birth
ca AD 27–30	Jesus' ministry
ca AD 30	Jesus is crucified
AD 66–73	First Jewish Revolt against Rome
AD 70	Roman destruction of Jerusalem during First Jewish Revolt; the Temple is destroyed
AD 73	Masada falls
AD 131–135	Bar Kochba Revolt (Second Jewish Revolt)

AD

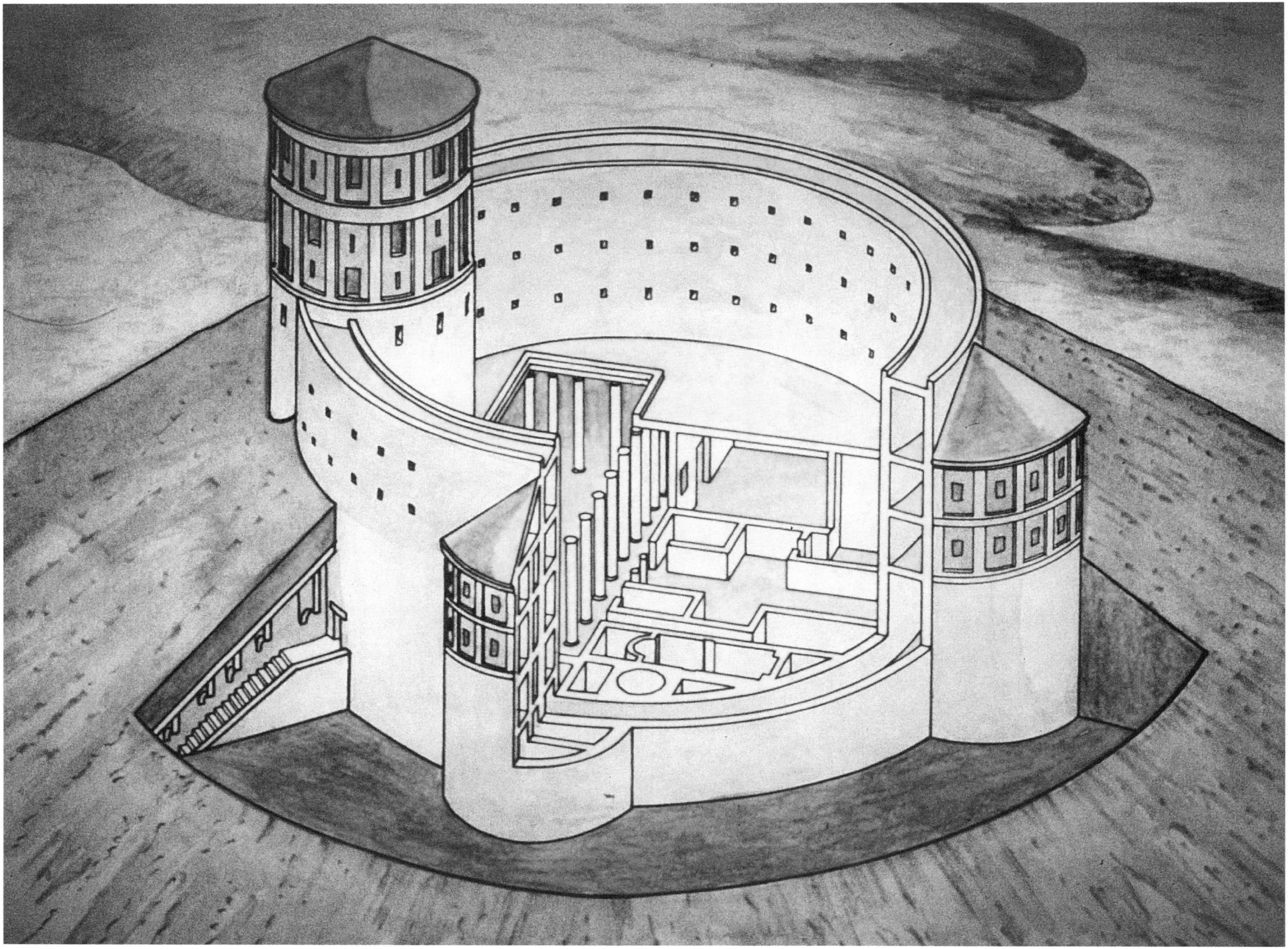

The Judea Wilderness

Jordan River

Jericho

Qumran

Dead Sea

En Gedi

Masada

Jerusalem

Bethlehem

Judea Mountains

Judea Wilderness

1. The Mountain 2. Northern Palace 3. Western Palace 4. Roman Bathhouse 5. Cistern 6. Storehouses

Northern Palace

1. Aqueduct and Reservoir System 2. Defense Tower 3. Scriptorium 4. Main Assembly Hall and Refectory 5. Potters' Workshop 6. Possible *Mikveh* 7. Cemetery

RELIGIOUS MOVEMENTS OF JESUS' TIME

	PHARISEES	SADDUCEES	ESSENES	ZEALOTS
Origins	• Descended from Hasidim freedom fighters of the Maccabee era	• Descended from Solomon's high priest, Zadok • Became a faction in approximately 200 B.C.	• Resisted the Maccabees' claim to the high priest-hood in approximately A.D. 170.	• A movement formed against a Roman census in A.D. 6 and led by Judas the Galilean
Membership	• Were middle-class merchants numbering about 6,000	• Were priests who were wealthy, aristocratic, and often Hellenistic	• Were possibly dissident Sadducees or Pharisees who preferred isolation in the wilderness to participation in Temple services led by corrupt priests	• Were extreme Pharisees and religious Jews living primarily in Galilee
Beliefs	• Believed in the entire Old Testament as law • Accepted the oral interpretations of the Old Testament as binding • Believed the study of the Torah (law) was the highest act of worship • Believed that keeping the law was God's desire • Believed in bodily resurrection and life after death	• Believed in only the Torah as God's law • Rejected oral traditions • Believed the Temple was the only path to God • Did not believe in bodily resurrection	• Believed in withdrawal from corruption • Believed true priests were descended only from Zadok • Believed in rigid adherence to the Torah • Believed they had been chosen to prepare for the imminent arrival of the kingdom of God	• Theology resembled that of the Pharisees—however, only God could rule • Slavery was the worst evil • Taxes were due only to God
Practices	• Supported the synagogue for the study, interpretation, and teaching of the Torah • Believed in strict, detailed obedience to the oral and written law • Accepted Rome as a necessary evil so long as they could practice obedience to their beliefs	• Ran the Temple and all the ceremonies • Dominated the Sanhedrin, the religious ruling council • Lived a Hellenistic lifestyle • Received Roman support	• Worked at copying and studying the Torah • Lived in isolated communities • Shared property and communal meals • Practiced ritual cleansing • Rejected Hellenism	• Practiced terrorism against the hated Romans • Refused to pay taxes • Adhered carefully to the Torah and oral interpretations

Galilee

Set 3–Overhead Transparency 10. Galilee

CHORAZIN כורזין

RECONSTRUCTION שחזור הכפר

OF THE VILLAGE

© L. RITMEYER

0   50 m

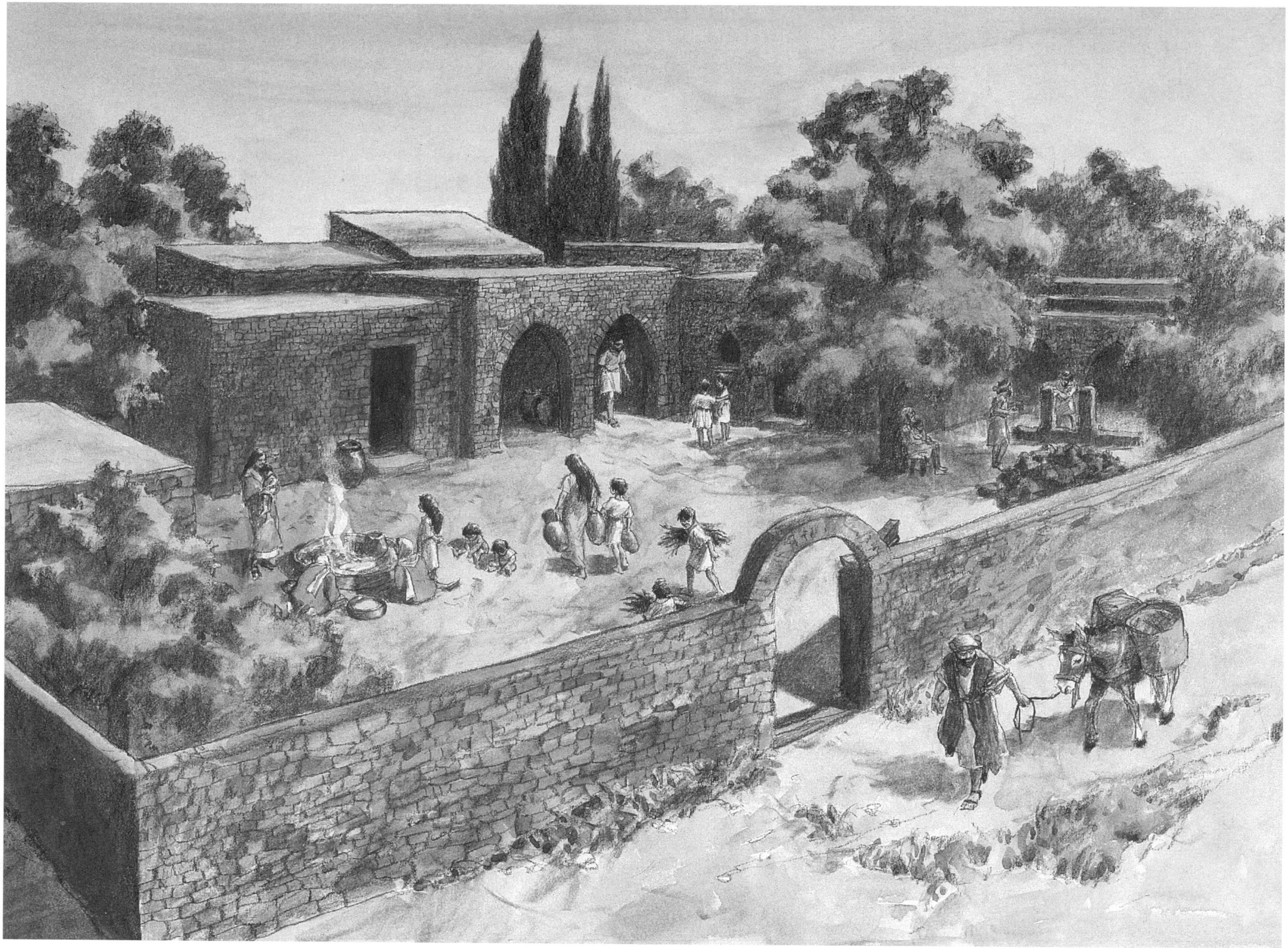

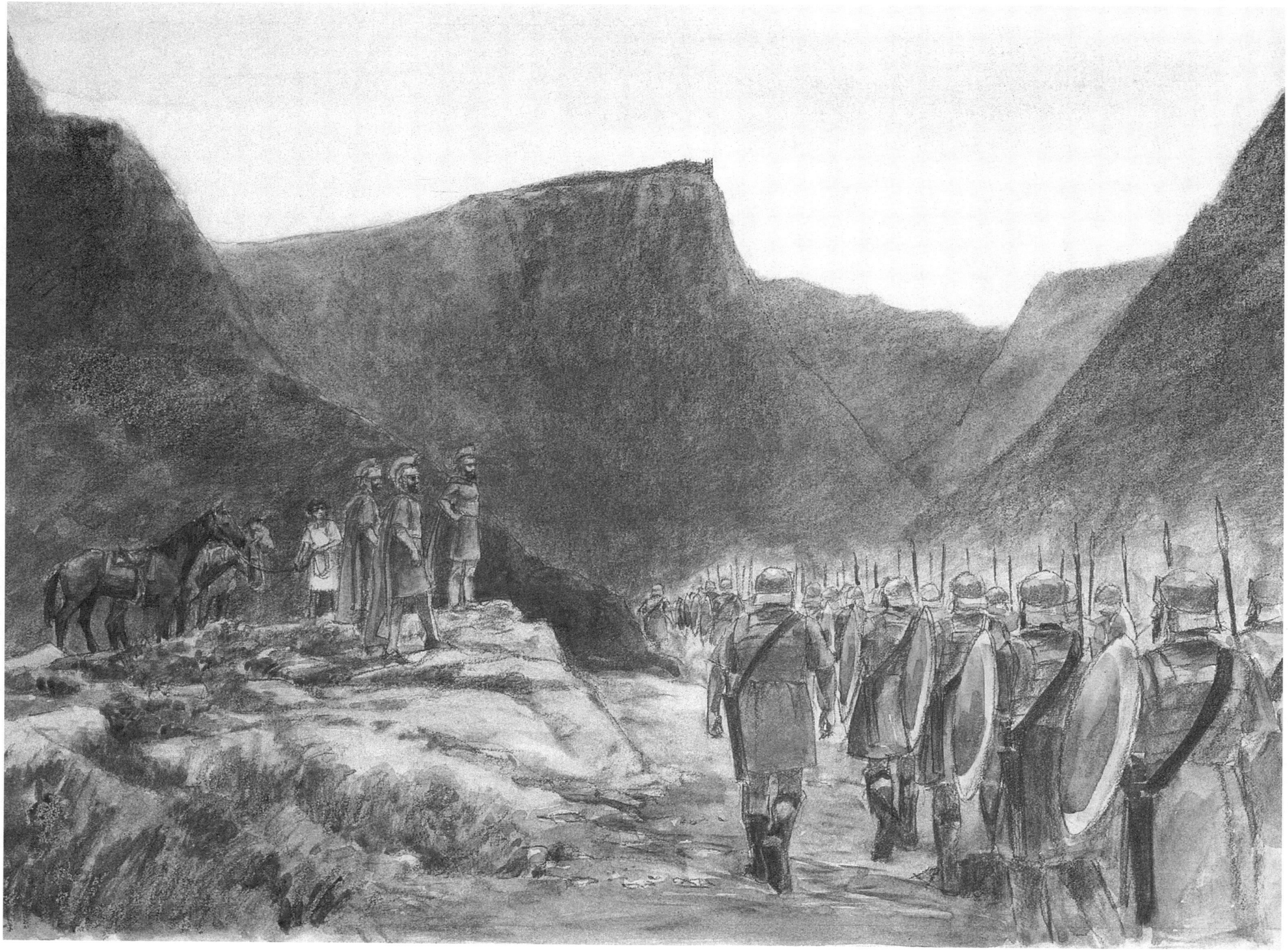

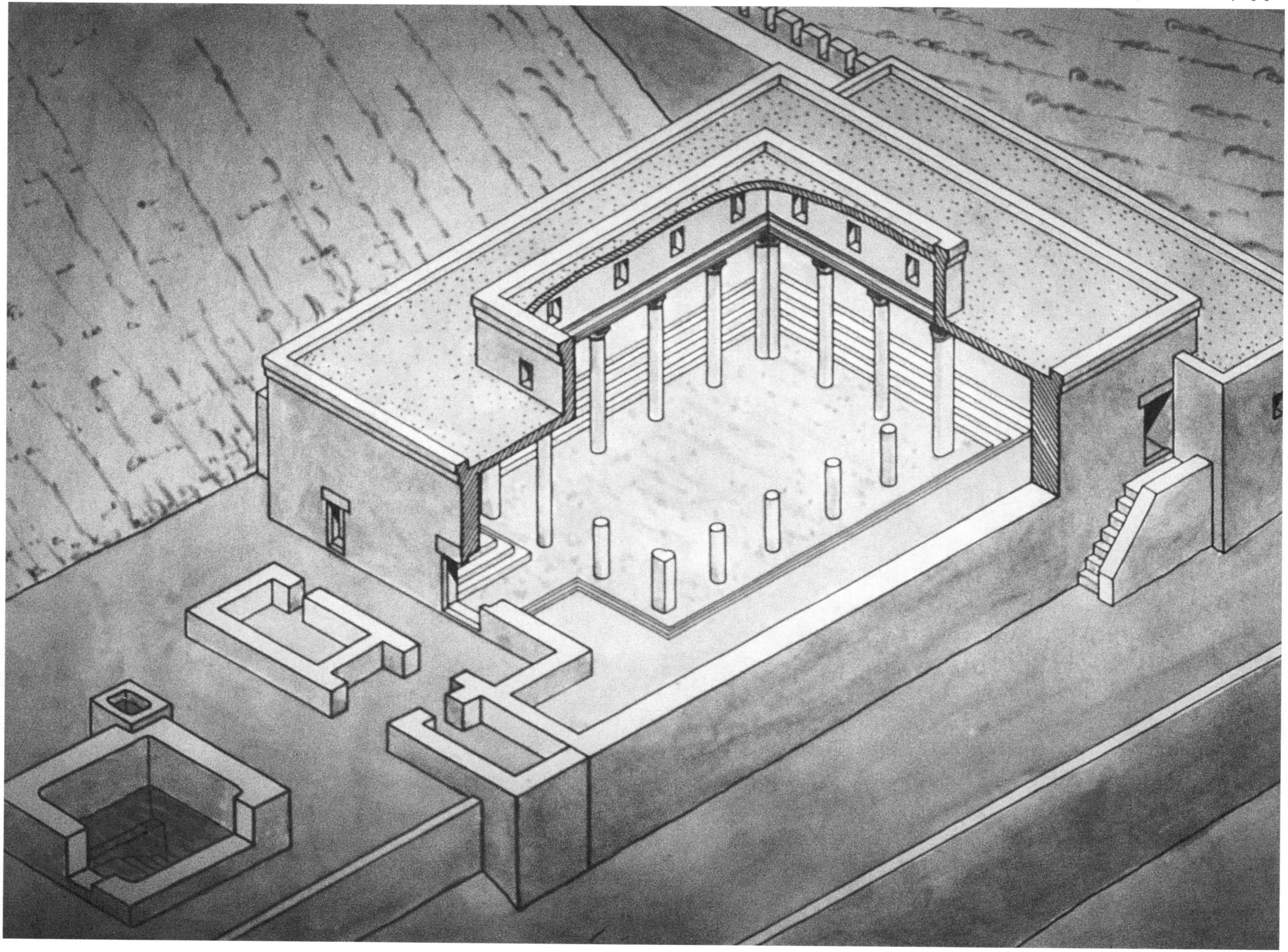

THE ZEALOT MOVEMENT

HASIDIM

Called the "Pious Ones," they resisted Hellenism by being totally devoted to Torah.
They fought with Judah and the Maccabees against the Syrian Greeks (Seleucids) in 167 B.C.

The Hasmonaeans, the Maccabees' descendants, became as Hellenistic as the Seleucid Greeks.

Hasidim became two movements.

PHARISEES

- Resist Hellenism and the pagan worldview
- Totally devoted to Torah

ZEALOTS

- Resist Hellenism and the pagan worldview
- Totally devoted to Torah
- Were terrorists

ZEALOTS

Hezekiah

- Resisted Rome and Herod (47 B.C.)
- Was executed by Herod

Judah of Gamla

- Attacked Sepphoris in 4 B.C. to gain control
  of its arsenal
- Founded Zealot party with Zadok the Pharisee in
  A.D. 6, at the time of the census
- Was probably killed by Herod Antipas (see Acts 5:37)
- Beliefs: 1. God alone may rule Israel
           2. Pay taxes to no one but God
           3. Slavery is worse than death

Sons of Judah

Jacob
- Crucified for terrorism
  in A.D. 48

Simeon
- Crucified for terrorism
  in A.D. 48

Yair

Grandsons of Judah

Eleazar Ben Yair
- Son of Yair
- Commander of Masada
- Committed suicide in A.D. 73

Menahem
- Leader of a revolt in Jerusalem
- Killed by opponents in A.D. 66

THE HEROD FAMILY TREE

Antipater (Idumaean)

HEROD THE GREAT

- Died in 4 B.C.
- Effective administrator, cruel, supported by Rome
- Visited by wise men, killed Bethlehem babies
- Greatest builder the ancient Near East ever knew
- Had 10 wives, three of whom were:

Cleopatra	Miriam	Malthace

PHILIP

- Effective, popular king
- Ruled north and east of Galilee
- Built Caesarea Philippi

(Luke 3:1)

ANTIPAS

- Effective king
- Ruled Galilee and Perea
- Killed John the Baptist
- Built Tiberias and Sepphoris
- Tried Jesus before crucifixion

(Luke 3:19; Luke 23:7–12; Luke 9:7–9; Matthew 14:1–12; Luke 13:32)

ARCHELAUS

- Poor ruler, deposed by Romans
- Ruled Judea
- Mary and Joseph settle in Nazareth to avoid him

(Matthew 2:22)

HEROD AGRIPPA I

(Grandson of Herod the Great)

- King of Judea
- Killed James, put Peter in prison
- Struck down by an angel

(Acts 12:1–24)

AGRIPPA II

- King of Judea
- Paul defends his faith before him

(Acts 25:13–26:32)

DRUSILLA

(Sisters of Agrippa II)

- Married Felix, the Roman governor

(Acts 24:24)

BERENICE

- With her brother at Paul's defense

(Acts 25:13)

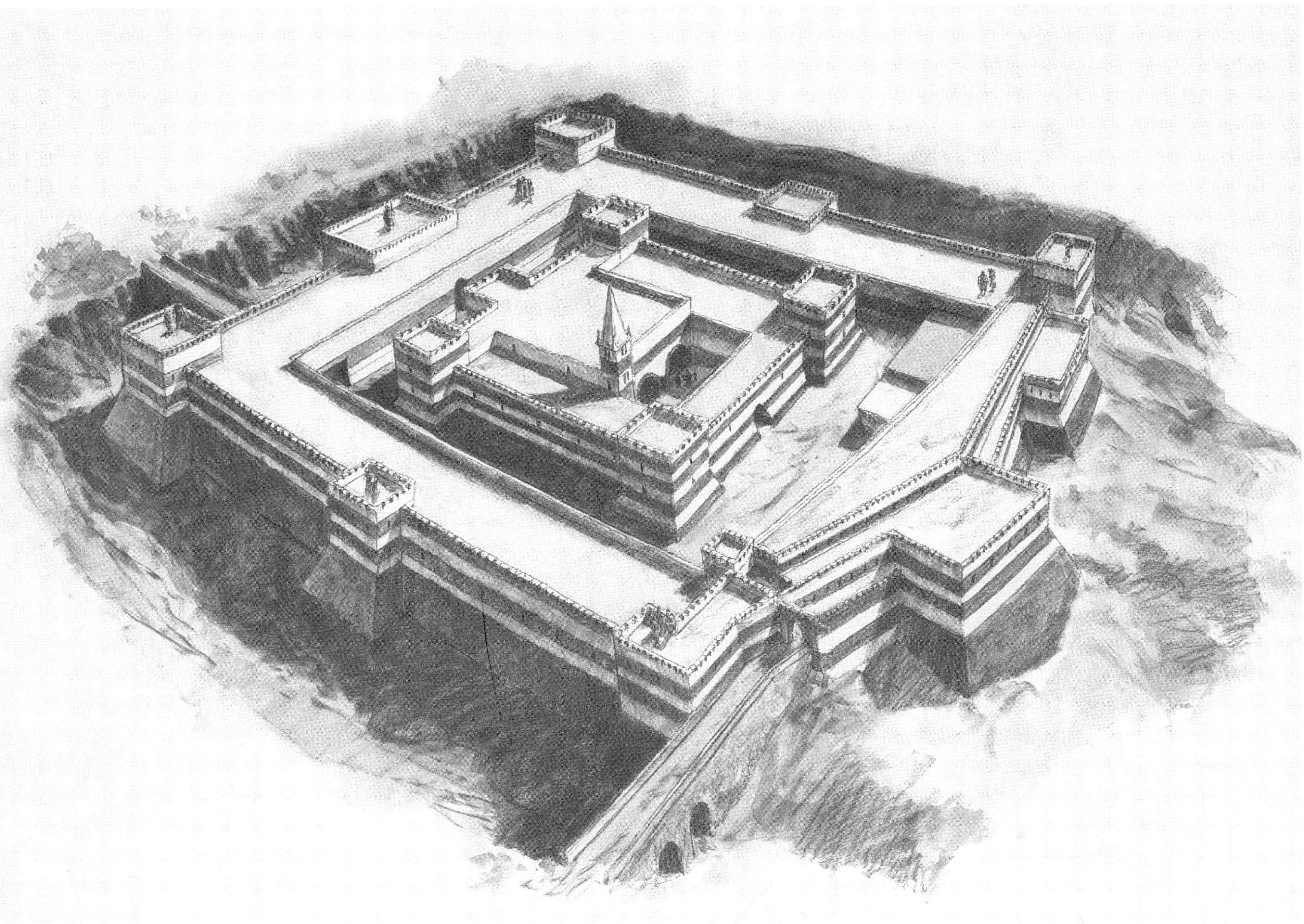

Ray Vander Laan is an ordained minister in the Christian Reformed Church and has taught the Bible in Christian schools for 18 years. He has degrees from Dordt College and Westminster Seminary and is completing doctoral work at Trinity College. Ray Vander Laan has immersed himself in the cultural context of the Bible throughout his career. Deeply committed to the inspiration of the Scriptures, he applies God's Word specifically to modern culture and life situations. The series **That the World May Know** ™ is based on study tours that Ray Vander Laan leads regularly in Israel.

To order the optional full-color overhead-transparency packet for Set 3, Faith Lessons 11–18, write to Focus on the Family, Educational Resources Department, P.O. Box 15379, Colorado Springs, CO 80935-5379, or call 1-800-932-9123.

That the World May Know ™ would make a great gift for family and friends. Sets 1, 2, and 3 are available at a Christian bookstore near you.

NOTES